Prais

'Demonstrates powerfully w
testing took place, the emo
the Australian psyche, just as do Gallipoli, Bodyline and Singapore. The cost in terms of damage to health, the environment and public trust in government will remain with us for generations to come.'

Weekend Australian

'An original and compelling account that succeeds in exposing the subterfuge and myopia of both British and Australian governments.'

Saturday Paper

'Well done to Frank Walker for his excellent examination of a dark chapter in Australian history.'

Australian Defence Magazine

'Sparks a rage in the reader that human beings could be treated with such contempt, such cold-blooded, Nazi-like calculated evilness by a nation that, at the time, was regarded as our best friend and ally. It's simply horrifying. Walker's book is a well written unmasking of a dirty secret that remains a black stain on our history.'

Law Society Journal

'The story reaches out and grabs you by the throat.'

Dr Clare Wright, author of *The Forgotten Rebels of Eureka*

'An extraordinary story – there are things here that would make your hair stand on end.'

Philip Clark, ABC Radio Canberra

'This book will make you angry, and the details of the botched clean-up will make you nervous about the Abbott government's plans to make Australia the world's dumping ground for nuclear waste.'

The Morning Bulletin

'Shocking revelations'

Margaret Throsby, ABC Classic FM

'This book should be on the school syllabus.'

Andrew O'Keefe, *Weekend Sunrise*

'Riveting and confronting'

Ian Freckelton QC, *Journal of Law and Medicine*

Praise for *The Tiger Man of Vietnam*

'One of those great untold stories . . . Walker tells it with verve and excitement and with meticulous attention to detail.'

Sydney Morning Herald

'Walker's finely researched book goes beyond the biographical account of an Australian war hero.'

Sun-Herald

'It's been suggested Petersen was the model for the character of Colonel Kurtz in the film *Apocalypse Now*. But this remarkable true story is much richer and more compelling than anything Hollywood could conjure.'

West Australian

Praise for *Ghost Platoon*

'Walker, and others like him, are doing their country a great service by bringing both the good and bad deeds of Aussie diggers out of the shadows and into the light.'

Sunday Age

'His findings are a shocking indictment of the long term effect of war.'

Sunday Examiner

FRANK WALKER

MARALINGA

THE CHILLING EXPOSÉ OF
OUR SECRET NUCLEAR SHAME
AND BETRAYAL OF OUR TROOPS AND COUNTRY

First published in Australia and New Zealand in 2014
by Hachette Australia
(an imprint of Hachette Australia Pty Limited)
Level 17, 207 Kent Street, Sydney NSW 2000
www.hachette.com.au

This edition published in 2016

10 9 8 7 6

National Library of Australia
Cataloguing-in-Publication data:

Walker, Frank, author.

Maralinga: the chilling exposé of our secret nuclear shame and betrayal of our troops and country/Frank Walker.

978 0 7336 3593 9

Nuclear weapons testing victims – South Australia – Maralinga.
Radiation injuries – Government policy – Australia.
Veterans – Diseases – Australia.
Veterans – Medical care – Australia.
Nuclear weapons – Testing – Health aspects – South Australia – Maralinga.
Atomic bomb – South Australia – Maralinga – Testing.
Radioactive fallout – South Australia – Maralinga.
Nuclear weapons – Great Britain – Testing.
Maralinga (S. Aust.) – History.

363.1799099423

Cover design and maps by Christabella Designs
Cover photograph courtesy of Newspix
Internal photos by Frank Walker unless otherwise credited
Text design by Bookhouse, Sydney
Typeset in 12/15.7 pt Simoncini Garamond Std by Bookhouse, Sydney
Printed and bound in Great Britain by Clays Ltd, Elcograf S.p.A.

CONTENTS

Location of Key Places and Test Sites

Direction of Fallout

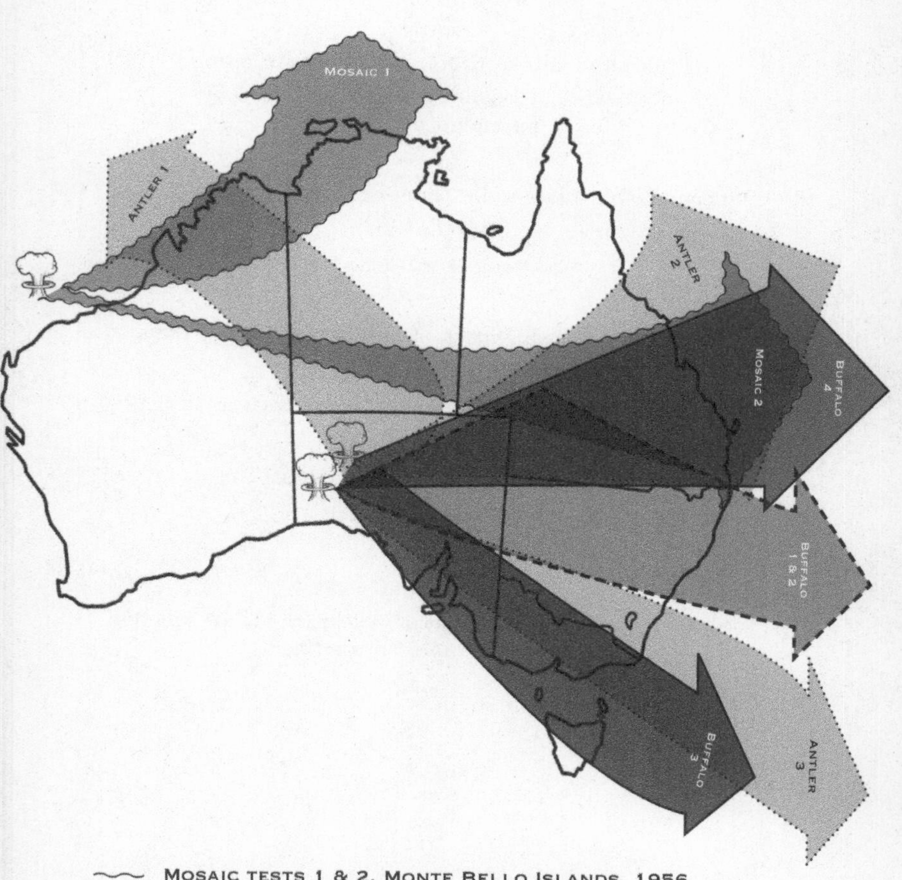

Mosaic tests 1 & 2, Monte Bello Islands, 1956
Buffalo tests 1 & 2, Maralinga, Sept/Oct 1956
Buffalo tests 3 & 4, Maralinga, October 1956
Antler tests 1, 2 & 3, Maralinga, Sept/Oct 1957

Note: There were no monitoring stations for the first three tests at Monte Bello and Emu Field

'I think the only word to describe it is beautiful.'

Professor Ernest Titterton, on seeing the biggest atom bomb ever exploded in Australia

'No conceivable injury to life, limb or property could emerge from the test.'

Prime Minister Robert Menzies, 1953

'Soldiers everywhere. Guns. We all cry, cry, cryin'. Men, women, children, all afraid.'

Alice Cox, Aboriginal elder, describing being forced off their land for the atomic tests

'What did the bastards do to us?'

Nuclear veteran Jeff Liddiatt

'A pity, but we can't help it.'

British Prime Minister Anthony Eden's reaction when warned in 1955 of health risks to soldiers and sailors in nuclear tests

PROLOGUE

Bring me the bones of Australian babies,
the more the better[1]

Harwell, England, 24 May 1957

The nuclear scientist who fired the world's first atomic bomb, Ernest Titterton, peered around at the scientists and officials seated in the boardroom of the UK Atomic Energy Research Establishment.

It was a bright spring morning in 1957 and they were all there to hear Titterton deliver an edict on where they should go next. They had already exploded nine atomic bombs in Australia and taken thousands of measurements at the blast sites at the Monte Bello Islands off Western Australia, as well as Emu Field and Maralinga in central Australia.

The next stage in the British atomic experiment was to determine the long-term effects of the bomb on the whole of Australia and its people.

Official records of the meeting, stored deep in the British National Archives, reveal the extent to which the scientists and officials were prepared to go.[2]

File number DEFE 16/808 exposes in chilling scientific language that the agenda of the British on that bright sunny spring day was to turn the whole of Australia into one giant nuclear laboratory. They wanted to use the Australian population as human guinea pigs for decades to come.

First, the scientists agreed that in order to find out the amount of fallout the nine atomic bombs had already caused on Australia they needed to collect samples of soil from pasture regions near the five mainland cities – Perth, Sydney, Brisbane, Melbourne and Adelaide.

Second, they would test vegetation and thirdly, they wanted samples of dairy cows' milk. The reason was simple – radioactivity spread through the air from atomic tests falls on soil, grass grows in soil, cows eat grass, cows produce milk and, finally, humans – particularly children – drink the milk.

After some technical discussion of sample sizes, the scientists determined they needed two samples of milk every year. The aim was to see how much Strontium-90 was getting into milk. Strontium-90 is a radioactive isotope produced by nuclear fission with a half-life of 29 years. It is ingested and absorbed into bones and is the best marker for radioactive fallout from nuclear tests. It can cause cancer and is the most dangerous component of fallout.

'Animal samples,' said Titterton. 'We have to have bones from animals to see if Strontium-90 is getting into domestic animals.'[3]

After some discussion of the mechanics of the sampling, the scientists decided to take samples from twelve sheep stations 200 to 300 miles (482 to 804 kilometres) along the path the radioactive clouds would be expected to drift in the prevailing winds.

Not satisfied with that, they decided to increase the sampling all the way to the east coast to see what happened when radioactive clouds reached the most populated areas of Australia.

Titterton looked around at his fellow scientists. So far so good. No objections to where this was going. No questions about the morality of what they were doing to the people of Australia. Never one to be squeamish or subtle, he spelled out the next step. 'We have to find out if Strontium-90 is entering the food chain and getting into humans.'

The biggest consumers of milk are babies, infants and young children. Milk was handed out free at Australian schools. If the scientists got bones from babies and Aussie kids, they'd quickly and efficiently know how much fallout was getting into the food chain. Babies and kids would be best for the test as their bones were still growing and Strontium-90 collects in the bones.

None of the scientists questioned what they were about to embark on. The group nodded to each other. This was science. They were all professionals. The group agreed they needed to take the bones of dead Australian babies to test for Strontium-90. How many bones wasn't up for discussion. It was simple. The more bones from dead babies the better. There were no questions. It was all written down.

'As many samples as possible are to be obtained,' the official minutes of the meeting recorded.[4] The minutes noted, as though this might be a problem, that the number of dead babies would probably be small.

The scientists didn't discuss the morality of taking baby bones from grieving Australian families. They didn't think it necessary to ask Australians whether they could rob graves for bones.

But they did determine exactly what sort of bones they wanted. It was coldly clinical.

'The bones should be femurs. The required weight is 20–50 grams wet bone, subsequently ashed to provide samples of weight not less than two grams. The date of birth, age at death and locality of origin are to be reported.'[5]

The bones would be crushed into a powder and sent to the UK for analysis along with the soil, animal samples and vegetation.

Professor Titterton said he would make arrangements for the Australian Safety Committee to collect all the samples and dispatch them to the UK. Titterton would make it happen. He was supposed to be representing the interests of Australians on the Atomic Safety Committee. In reality he was running the experiments and the atomic tests solely for Britain.

The scientists' concern that the number of dead baby bones they could get would be low proved to be unfounded. They underestimated the enthusiasm of pathologists, morticians and autopsy attendants for a quick buck.

Workers were more than happy to extract thigh bones from baby corpses in a cash-in-hand deal with the collectors for the atomic scientists. Distraught parents were not to be asked for permission. They weren't to be told what was happening to their lost loved ones. It was to be done in a clandestine operation that would last for decades.

Over the next twenty-one years a staggering 22,000 corpses of babies, infants, children, teenagers and younger adults were pilfered for bones and tested for Strontium-90. It was the longest experiment of its kind in the world. The data gleaned by the body snatchers went not to Australia, but to nuclear authorities in the UK and the US. It was used to further both the nuclear industry and the development of nuclear weapons.

This is the story of how the people of Australia were unknowingly used as guinea pigs in bizarre nuclear tests. It is the story of the betrayal of a nation and its people by its political leaders. It is the continuing disgrace of thousands of servicemen being lied to and treated like dirt by successive governments. It began with the worst act of betrayal against Australians by their Prime Minister, Robert Menzies.

1

OF COURSE YOU CAN EXPLODE YOUR ATOM BOMBS IN AUSTRALIA

Robert Menzies couldn't say yes quickly enough when Britain asked if they could explode their atom bombs in Australia. The Australian prime minister received the polite and rather casual request on a Saturday. He said yes on Monday.

Menzies enthusiastically offered his young nation to be used in any manner the mother country might desire.

He didn't waste time asking his own cabinet colleagues before he agreed to the request.

He didn't ask the British if there was any possibility of harm to Australians or the Australian environment.

He didn't ask Australian scientists whether there was any possible health risk to the population from exploding atom bombs on Australian soil.

He even offered up Australian servicemen to help the British scientists in their atomic bomb experiments – no questions asked about the dangers they might face.

Menzies hoped Britain might let a few atomic crumbs fall from their table, perhaps so that Australia might be able to develop its own atomic industry.

But when the British said no to that, and cut Australia out of any scientific know-how that would come from atom bombs exploded in Australia, Menzies rolled over and said that was fine too. Sorry for asking.

This lap-dog behaviour was true to form. Despite his iconic hero status among conservatives, Menzies was never a fighter for Australia's interests.

When the First World War broke out, Menzies was a twenty-year-old law student at Melbourne University. He was a lieutenant in the university army reserve regiment and an enthusiastic supporter of the war. He strongly supported conscription. Naturally, being destined for greatness, he felt this didn't apply to him.

He spent the entire war safely studying in Melbourne, winning university prizes while his student comrades volunteered and left to fight and die in the war. He passed his masters degree and became a barrister in 1918, aged twenty-four, when there were many vacancies in chambers due to the heavy war toll.

Menzies moved into politics and became a fawning and obsequious Anglophile, spending his life tugging his forelock to the British. He described himself as 'British to the bootstraps' and is said to have even entertained the notion, while he was in London in 1941, of serving in the British war cabinet, maybe even succeeding Churchill as British prime minister.[1]

Menzies never explained why he didn't join up in the First World War. Two of his brothers did. Maybe his family thought two were enough. Staying home during the war later came to dog him. But, of course, he was alive when many weren't.

Young Menzies had a rapid rise in politics. He entered the Victorian parliament in 1928 and federal parliament in 1934, quickly being given the post of attorney-general. Many in politics openly despised the rising conservative star.

A conservative rival, Prime Minister Earle Page, had served as an army medical officer in the First World War. Page made a vitriolic attack on Menzies in parliament for not serving in the war, virtually accusing him of cowardice.[2]

Labor stalwart MP Eddie Ward quipped Menzies 'had a brilliant military career cut short by the outbreak of war'.[3]

Menzies, however, was no shirker when it came to sending others off to war. During his sixteen-year prime ministership after the Second World War, he sent Australian soldiers to the Malayan Emergency, the Korean War and the Vietnam War.

But it was in his first term as prime minister in 1939 that Menzies was most unflinchingly loyal to the mother country.

Within an hour of Britain's Prime Minister Neville Chamberlain declaring war on Germany on 3 September 1939, Prime Minister Menzies went on radio to announce solemnly, 'Great Britain has declared war upon her [Germany] and that, as a result, Australia is also at war.'[4]

It was automatic. There was no question. No hesitation.

In reality Australia was always going to follow Britain into declaring war. Opposition Labor leader John Curtin supported the declaration. But in Menzies' choice of words he made it clear Australia was cemented to Britain, and that made it automatic Australia would willingly follow Britain wherever it went.

In January 1941 Menzies made the perilous wartime journey to London and stayed for four months. Ostensibly his purpose was to persuade Churchill to commit more forces to the defence of Singapore, and therefore Australia.

It was a critical period in the war. Japan was advancing through China and an attack on Singapore seemed inevitable. Australians were battling in Tobruk. British cities were bombed daily. Germans were advancing towards Greece.

Menzies' time in London, however, was a disaster. Churchill steamrolled him. Instead of obtaining more British military support in the Far East to stop the Japanese advance, Menzies ended up agreeing to commit Australian forces to join Churchill's plan to defend Greece against the advancing Germans. Churchill patronisingly assured Menzies that Australia was the 'Number One Dominion' and Menzies lapped it up.[5] He was in thrall to Churchill and he disregarded concerns by his political colleagues back home that Australian forces were being committed to a European war when they were needed back home to face Japan.

When the Germans hit Greece they vastly outnumbered the Australian, New Zealand and British forces, and simply rolled over them. In a brief, savage campaign, the Allies retreated to Crete. Hundreds of Australians were killed and thousands taken prisoner.

Parallels with the failed attack on Gallipoli in the First World War were obvious. Churchill was the mastermind behind that disaster too. Menzies' long stay in London, wining, dining and preening under Churchill's flattery, had resulted in total failure for Australia's interests. Not to mention dead diggers left in Greece and Crete.

Menzies seemed oblivious to the reality. He'd even sent a message to his ministers back in Australia that he should stay on in London. Aghast, they quickly knocked back that idea. He'd done enough damage. Australia's High Commissioner in London, Stanley Bruce, a Gallipoli veteran and former prime minister, wrote to a friend that Menzies had left the impression 'he would not mind coming back here and leading the Conservative Party himself'.[6]

On the way home, Menzies stopped to talk with Canada's Prime Minister Mackenzie King, who wrote: 'I sensed the feeling that he would rather be on the War Cabinet in London than Prime Minister of Australia.'[7]

On arrival in Canberra, Menzies was shocked how much support he'd lost. He gave public speeches praising Churchill even though it was clear the British Bulldog's war strategy had once again needlessly sacrificed Australian troops. Three months later, when Menzies proposed he go back to London, his colleagues revolted. Menzies was forced to resign as prime minister and in October 1941 Labor's John Curtin won the election. Six weeks later, Japan attacked Pearl Harbor. Menzies spent the war years in Opposition, founding the Liberal Party in 1944.

When the Second World War was over, tension ratcheted up to face another menace. The Reds were on the march. The Soviets installed puppet communist governments in Poland, the Baltic States, Romania, Bulgaria and Czechoslovakia. The US backed anti-communist regimes around the world and started erecting a string of atomic missiles pointed at the Soviet Union.

The Cold War got even hotter. In 1948 the Soviets blocked overland access to West Berlin, leading to an eleven-month airlift of food and fuel. Menzies was once again in London, and he was impressed by the anti-communist mood that gripped Britain.

In 1949 the Soviet Union declared its occupied eastern part of Germany to be an independent communist nation. Mao Tse Tung won the communist war against the US-backed nationalists, and China went Red. Finally, on 29 August of that tumultuous year, the Soviet Union exploded its first atomic bomb. The Red Bomb exploded in Kazakhstan with the force of twenty-four kilotons – far bigger than the sixteen-kiloton bomb the Americans had dropped on Hiroshima and bigger than the 21-kiloton bomb dropped on Nagasaki.

News that the Soviets had the bomb stunned the US. Experts had calculated the Soviets wouldn't be able to build their own atomic bomb until 1953 at the earliest.

The Cold War was reaching fever pitch. Menzies, a staunch anti-communist, won the December 1949 election promising to ban the Communist Party, a referendum he later lost.

The British government was alarmed that even though British scientists had been key in helping the US develop the wartime bomb, there was still no atom bomb with a Union Jack on it. Britain was part of the newly formed NATO European mutual defence pact with the US, but Britain had been frozen out of access to American nuclear technology. The US didn't trust the British to keep American atomic secrets. They had good reason.

Klaus Fuchs was a German-born scientist who fled to England before the war and later worked on the Manhattan Project. After the war, Fuchs was exposed as a Soviet spy who had passed atomic secrets to the Kremlin. On top of that, several senior British intelligence officers had been revealed as double agents for the Soviets. In 1946 the US passed the McMahon Act, barring non-Americans from working on US atomic programs. Britain was frozen out of the ongoing US nuclear weapons testing program and could not use the testing ground in Nevada for its own testing.

Britain searched for somewhere else to blow up its own atomic bombs. They looked at Canada and remote islands in the Pacific and Indian Oceans. But they liked Australia best. It was remote, friendly and extremely compliant.

They were well aware of Menzies' long history of tugging the forelock to the Queen and kowtowing to the mother country. The British government never doubted Menzies would agree to a request to explode British atomic bombs on Australian soil.

The paperwork behind the momentous deal is surprisingly sparse. Britain had already picked out the Monte Bello Islands off the coast of Western Australia as a suitable site to explode its first atomic bomb. It was 160 kilometres from the nearest town, a one-pub coastal settlement called Onslow. Nobody lived on the islands, and they were easy to control.

On Saturday 16 September 1950 the British High Commission in Canberra passed a 'top secret and personal message' from British Prime Minister Clement Attlee to Menzies. For such a monumental issue it was remarkable for being so casual.

> During recent months we have been considering the arrangements which will be necessary for testing our own atomic weapon when it is ready. Among the most important of the

various decisions which must be taken is the choice of a suitable testing range.

We asked the United States authorities earlier in the year whether they would let us use their own testing site at Eniwetok but so far we have had no firm reply and it is not clear when one may be expected.

Meanwhile it is clearly advisable if only as a precaution to consider possible alternative sites in British Commonwealth territory and to carry out a reconnaissance in the selected area. This would not of course necessarily involve a firm decision to hold the test there.

One possible site which has been suggested by our experts is the Monte Bello Islands off the north-west coast of Australia.

I am telegraphing to you now to ask first whether the Australian government would be prepared in principle to agree that the first United Kingdom atomic weapon should be tested in Australian territory and secondly, if so, whether they would agree to our experts making a detailed reconnaissance of the Monte Bello Islands so that a firm decision can be taken on their suitability.

It will clearly take some little time for the survey to be organized and for its results to be studied and if reconnaissance is to be really useful and effective we should like it to be put in hand at once.

If you agree that the survey may be made we can then work out with your authorities the detailed arrangements for it; these would include special arrangements for safeguarding secrecy.

Royal Commission Report[8]

It's not known whether Menzies was handed the cable straight away or if it sat on his desk over the weekend. We do know Attlee got a positive reply on the Monday. There is no evidence Menzies even bothered to consult his political colleagues, scientists or military leaders before he embraced the British proposal to use Australia as a nuclear testing ground.

Three days later, on 20 September 1950, Menzies gave a national radio broadcast declaring only the atom bomb was keeping the world from a global war. 'The atom bomb, horrible as it was, was not an instrument of war but of peace,' Menzies thundered. 'Do you think this communist enemy would hesitate to overrun western civilization if the United States did not have the atomic bomb? Don't let's pretend about the bomb. It's real.'[9]

Menzies knew just how real the atom bomb was about to become for Australia. He was softening up Australians to accept the atom bomb when the British would inevitably explode it on its former colony.

Seven months later, Attlee sent another top secret personal message to Menzies.

He said British experts had studied Monte Bello with the help of Australian authorities and found it would be possible to conduct an atomic weapons trial on the remote islands. Attlee said, for climate reasons, October was the only suitable month for an atomic test at the islands. Winds would take the radioactive cloud out to sea.

Attlee said the US had once again rejected their approach to test weapons at a US testing range.

> If therefore your government would agree, we should like to go ahead now with preparations for a test in the Monte Bello Islands in October 1952, which is the earliest date by which a prototype of our weapon will be ready.[10]

Attlee said there was one last aspect of the test he should mention.

> The effect of exploding an atomic weapon in the Monte Bello Islands will be to contaminate with radioactivity the north-east group and this contamination may spread to others of the islands. The area is not likely to be entirely free from contamination for about three years and we would hope for continuing Australian help in investigating the decay of

> contamination. During this time the area will be unsafe for human occupation or even visits by e.g. pearl fishermen who, we understand, at present go there from time to time and suitable measures will need to be taken to keep them away.[11]

How the British came to pick three years as the period the test site would be contaminated is a mystery. Scientists at the time already knew radioactive contamination could last for decades, even centuries.

Menzies replied he couldn't give a final decision until after the Australian election in May 1951. This delay had nothing to do with wanting to make sure he had a mandate from the people for such an agreement. It was because he didn't want news of an imminent British atomic test on Australian soil getting to the public before the election. It stayed secret. There was a swing to Labor, but Menzies scraped back in.

As soon as he was re-elected Menzies gave the green light to Britain. The British made it clear they would be in charge of the operation. Britain would control the conditions and explosion of the bomb. The UK military hoped to learn the effects of various types of atomic explosions on 'equipment, stores and men with and without various types of protection'.[12] They would be in charge of safety and deciding the amount of radiation servicemen would be exposed to.

Not that they had worked out how much was safe. That was what the tests were all about. Australian troops and the whole of the Australian population were about to become the experiment's guinea pigs.

It wasn't until almost a year later that the Australian and British government jointly announced to the public there would be an atomic test held in Australia.

On 18 February 1952 Menzies released this brief statement:

> In the course of this year the United Kingdom government intends to test an atomic weapon produced in the United

> Kingdom. In close co-operation with the government of the Commonwealth of Australia, the test will take place at a site in Australia. It will be conducted in conditions which will ensure that there will be no danger whatever from radioactivity to the health of the people or animals in the Commonwealth.[13]

There was no shock, no questioning, no debate. If anything, the reaction was one of excitement. The press speculated the test would be held at Woomera rocket-testing range in the north of South Australia. Monte Bello was still a tightly kept secret. Menzies set up the legislative framework for the tests in the Defence (Special Undertakings) Bill introduced to parliament in June 1952. It barred Australian citizens from entry to huge zones of their country for the atomic tests. The law sailed through parliament with little opposition. It was a valuable bit of legislation for government secrecy and is still used today to bar public entry to US satellite-signalling stations at Pine Gap near Alice Springs.

Menzies never really bothered to explain to the Australian people why he gave such enthusiastic support to the British atomic tests and how the bomb blasts would be good for the country. He assumed all Australians would be behind the mother country testing its atom bombs on Australian soil.

It wasn't until May 1955, after the British had already exploded one bomb at Monte Bello and two at Emu Field in central South Australia, that the pompous Minister of Supply, Howard Beale, the minister handling the nuclear test deal, publicly explained why Australia should welcome the tests:

> It is a challenge to Australian men to show that the pioneering spirit of their forefathers who developed our country is still the driving force of achievement. The whole project is a striking example of the inter-commonwealth cooperation on the grand scale. England has the bomb and the know-how; we have the open spaces, much technical skill and great willingness

> to help the motherland. Between us we shall help to build the defences of the free world and make historic advances in harnessing the forces of nature.[14]

The picture painted by Menzies and Beale that Australia was in an equal partnership with Britain in the tests was totally misleading. Britain controlled everything – from the scientific knowledge to having overall military authority of the tests and the testing ground. Australians were there simply to provide the labour, the bodies needed to get the tests done, the land to explode atom bombs on, and, as it was later revealed in secret documents, to function as lab rats for the British scientists.

•

If you were looking for the face of evil you wouldn't give British scientist William Penney a second glance. He came across to the public as a humble, gentlemanly boffin who'd rather be pottering around in his garden than building atom bombs. Penney insisted to all he met that he be called Bill rather than Professor, Doctor or Sir William – or even Lord Penney as he became after his work was done. He was much respected and liked by those who encountered him. He certainly wasn't part of the English upper class who were usually the ones given senior government posts.

Penney was born in Gibraltar, son of an army warrant officer. At school he was recognised as a maths genius and won scholarships to Cambridge University. By age twenty-seven, he was an assistant professor of mathematics. During the Second World War Penney made his name as an expert on the shockwave effect of explosives, invaluable in the use of mines for protecting harbours. He was a key figure in the top secret Manhattan Project.

Two days after the bomb exploded over Hiroshima, Penney was invited to be the British scientific observer on board the US bomber as it dropped the second, more powerful, atom bomb over Nagasaki. Penney later went in on foot to both Hiroshima and Nagasaki to see the bombs' effects first hand. While walking through the destruction, and as other scientists were diligently taking measurements and photographs, Penney noticed petrol tins in the rubble around the city were crushed and dented to different extents depending on how far they were from the centre of the blast. He filled bags with the battered tins and took them back to his lab in England.

The Americans asked Penney to be part of their first post-war atomic test at Bikini Atoll in the Pacific in 1946. Penney endeared himself to the American military men by joining in, filling hundreds of army petrol tins with water and placing them at set distances from the blast point. To the troops Penney looked like the original nutty professor. But when the Americans' complicated instruments recording the shock wave failed to work properly, it was Penney's damaged tins that showed how far the shock wave reached, revealing the power of the bomb.

Penney believed dropping the atom bomb not only ended the war with Japan and avoided thousands more being killed if the Allies had to continue the fight, but also that Allied possession of the atom bomb would keep the peace with the growing power of the Soviet Union. After the Soviets stunned the West with their first atomic explosion in 1949, the British military forecast the West would need 600 atomic bombs by 1957 to effectively target the Soviet Union – 400 of these bombs would come from the US, 200 would have to come from Britain.[15]

There was no rationale behind these figures. Some key British generals said the target of building 600 atom bombs within eight years was little more than a 'Dutch auction'.[16] Although these projections were top secret, there was no public opposition in the early 1950s to developing more and more atom bombs. On the contrary, most public discussion hailed the coming of the atomic age as one filled with scientific and economic promise. Atom bombs were seen as providing security against the new communist evil.

Australia's leading nuclear expert at this time was Mark Oliphant. Adelaide-born Oliphant was one of the first physicists in the world to show that an atom bomb was feasible, and he was part of the team working on the Manhattan Project. But Oliphant was disturbed by the direction the research was going. While he agreed the Allies had to develop the bomb before the Nazis, he feared the use of nuclear power against humans. He preferred to distance himself from the core scientific team working on the bomb. Oliphant worked on enriching uranium with a team at Berkeley in California. When the bombs were dropped on Hiroshima and Nagasaki, Oliphant said he was proud as a scientist that the bombs had worked – but added he was 'absolutely appalled at what it had done to human beings'.[17]

After the war Oliphant was appointed Director of the Research School of Physical Sciences and Engineering at the new Australian National University in Canberra. When secret moves began for the British to use Australia as a nuclear testing ground, Oliphant was clearly the best placed Australian to be in charge of protecting Australia's scientific interests, particularly ensuring Australia's safety.

But Oliphant was on the outer for what he had said about the bombs dropped on Japan. The Americans didn't trust him. He wasn't in the pro-bomb club. In 1951 the US blocked his visa to attend a nuclear physics conference in Chicago. He supported developing nuclear power, but only for peaceful purposes. He wasn't a security risk, but he was too outspoken for the pro-bomb governments in the US, Britain and Australia. He spoke openly of the fear that if there were another major war, nuclear weapons would be used and they would obliterate the human race.

So when it came time to pick the men for the key posts of running the British nuclear tests in Australia, Oliphant was deliberately excluded. Penney was to be the scientist in charge of the whole project. Menzies certainly wasn't pressing to have an Australian at the top of the command structure. His interest in the running of the atomic bomb projects was minimal. Cabinet papers show he devoted more time to organising the young Queen Elizabeth's first visit to Australia than he spent on the atomic tests.

But the British – or at least Penney – knew they needed to have the right scientist to head Australia's side of things. Someone had to be in charge of health and safety measures. They needed a scientist who would tick off the explosions and say everything was OK, a scientist who believed in atom bombs, a scientist who wouldn't raise difficult questions, a scientist who could keep his mouth shut.

Why pick an Australian when a perfectly good British-born scientist could do the job? Britain already had their man in mind: Ernest Titterton.

Titterton was a British physicist who had been a crucial part of the wartime Manhattan Project in the US to build the first atomic bomb. It was his finger that pressed the button on 16 July 1945 for the world's first atomic test at Alamogordo in New Mexico. He was a senior and valued member of the atom bomb team and his work on the triggering mechanism allowed the bombs to be exploded at a height causing the most destruction on Hiroshima and Nagasaki.

Titterton was so crucial to developing the American atomic weapon program that he was one of only two non-Americans permitted to work on post-war US atomic tests. The other was William Penney, who had determined the height at which the bomb should detonate to have the most destructive result. Both scientists would be essential to the British atomic tests in Australia.

Titterton was a successful early salesman for nuclear power. He became a popular English boffin among the Americans, giving lectures on nuclear physics in layman's language to the ships' crews as they waited for good weather to explode atom bombs at Bikini Atoll in the Pacific. He even repaired a ship's movie projector when it broke down mid-movie. Titterton was given the honour of calling the countdown to the Bikini bomb and it was his British accent Americans heard before the blast. He was utterly convinced of the need for nuclear weapons, and spoke whenever he could of the benefits nuclear power would provide for humanity.

In 1947 Titterton took up a senior research post at the newly formed Atomic Energy Research Establishment (AERE) at Harwell, a former RAF base about twenty-one kilometres south of Oxford. He continued working on the top secret government project to develop Britain's own atomic weapons. The project was led by William Penney.

In 1950 Oliphant offered Titterton the inaugural chair of nuclear physics at the Australian National University. Titterton accepted, but he had some work to finish first. Before Titterton left for Australia, the British approached Menzies, who was once again visiting London. They asked whether Titterton could be made available for the British atomic test program. Menzies immediately agreed without even asking Oliphant.

The extent to which Titterton was Britain's man at the tests rather than Australia's was to be a hot point of contention at the Royal Commission into British Nuclear Tests in Australia that began, after much pressure from nuclear veterans, and the public, in 1984. Had he been planted by the British from the start? Had his safety role with the test program already been stitched up before he moved to Canberra?

Royal Commission researchers found a letter Titterton had written in 1953 in which he wrote that before he left for Australia in 1951, Penney had already asked him to act as technical director for the Monte Bello tests. This clashed with Titterton's insistence to the Royal Commission that the first he knew of the Monte Bello tests was in early 1952, when Menzies' office asked him to work with the British at the test. When Royal Commission lawyers asked about the discrepancy, Titterton sniffingly replied he couldn't be expected to remember every detail.[18]

Titterton's official task at Monte Bello was to help with telemetry, the science of remote measuring. But Titterton and the two other scientists representing Australia at the Monte Bello test were denied access to core data from the nuclear tests. One of these scientists, Alan Butement, was born in New Zealand and grew up in England. His work in radio waves was crucial in developing radar and wartime defences. He moved to Australia in 1947 and became the government's chief scientist. The other scientific representative for Australia was Leslie Martin, physics professor at Melbourne University, the only born-and-bred Australian. All three were denied access to the bomb itself. They were allowed to be present only as observers. Titterton, however, was given more access as he was there at the personal invitation of Penney. The British had plans for more tests in Australia, and Titterton was crucial for those plans to go ahead.

The wellbeing of Australians in the British nuclear tests was in the hands of a British scientist who had moved to Australia only a year before the first test at Monte Bello, a man who was an ardent believer in the need for nuclear weapons and whose biggest concern was that something might happen to stop them.

2

'THE SIGHT BEFORE OUR EYES WAS TERRIFYING'

The British Royal Navy frigate HMS *Plym* performed admirable service during the Second World War. For two long years under Lieutenant Commander Alan Foxall she battled freezing winds, stormy waters and German submarine and dive-bomber attacks of the dangerous Arctic convoys. The convoys were essential for keeping supplies going to the beleaguered Soviet forces on the Eastern Front.

But like many warships, as soon as the war was over the plucky *Plym* was superfluous to the needs of the navy. Still a fairly new ship, commissioned in 1943, she seemed destined for an undignified end in the scrapyards. In 1952 *Plym* was selected for a far more violent death.

Britain's defence chiefs were keen on knowing what would happen if the Soviets managed to smuggle an atom bomb inside a ship and sail it into a British port, or even up the Thames into the heart of London. If the scientists were going to explode an atom bomb, defence chiefs deemed it worthwhile to test it in the hold of one of their own warships to see what sort of damage would be done.

While the Australian government kept a tight lid on the mission, on 15 May 1952, the Australian press reported Number 10 Downing Street had revealed the Monte Bello Islands off Western Australia would be the site for Britain's first atomic test.

'Australian government and fighting services are closely cooperating,' reported the *Queensland Times*. 'The operation will be commanded by Rear Admiral A. Torlesse and will be under the scientific direction of Dr. W. Penney of the Ministry of Supply.'[1]

But the details of when and how the bomb would be exploded were a tight secret from both the public and the crews of the ships involved. Every attempt was made to throw off enemy agents. The British secret service MI5 leaked to Australian newspapers that leading nuclear scientists, including Penney, would be visiting Western Australia in November. The spooks even booked seats on planes in the scientists' names. The subterfuge was part of Operation Spoofer, a plan to deceive journalists and foreign agents that the test would be in November rather than October. Journalist Basil Atkinson thought he had the scoop back in September but smelled a rat – the top secret information had come a bit too easily from a UK Ministry of Supply official and he didn't file the story.[2]

HMS *Plym* quietly slipped out of the UK with a minimal crew accompanied by the flagship of the expedition, aircraft carrier HMS *Campania*. Two other British Navy ships involved in the operation – tank carriers HMS *Narvik* and HMS *Zeebrugge* – had left for Australia months earlier.

Deep in the *Plym*'s hold was the closely guarded secret – the frame of the atom bomb. Crew members who managed to sneak a peek described it as looking like a big washing machine. Hardly spectacular. The vital radioactive core, the deadly chamber that made it explode with incredible force, would be delivered separately via RAF airplane. While *Plym* was still on her way to Australia, the preparation was already well under way at the Monte Bello Islands, 1300 kilometres north of Perth.

The secret wasn't kept too well as the day got closer. *The West Australian* newspaper reported on its front page 'Atomic Fleet Sails from Fremantle' with a photo of HMS *Narvik* leaving for a secret destination 'believed to be the Monte Bello Islands'.[3] The paper reported the mission was cloaked in secrecy and officials refused to comment, but the bush telegraph had been working overtime as locals watched naval activity build up.

British and Australian military had been busy on the Monte Bello Islands for months, setting up buildings and structures for the test. The Monte Bello Islands are a 20-kilometre-long string of flat, rocky islands that have been visited by pearlers and native fishers for hundreds of years. A five-kilometre-wide lagoon is protected between the largest island, Hermite, and the rocky Trimouille Island. The navy laid electric cables on the bed of the lagoon while the army laid shore links and connected the cables to generators and measurement instruments brought in by scientists. Concrete platforms and steel towers were built to house the cameras and monitoring equipment on the atolls some distance from the lagoon where the bomb would be exploded.

For soldiers and sailors carrying out the work, most of it was a mystery. Tight security meant they had no idea what the scientists were hoping to learn from the explosion. Selected key officers were given lectures on what they were to do after the explosion and how they were to assist scientists retrieve the instruments. They practised with protective clothing and were shocked at how difficult it was to move and work in the thick overalls, helmet, gloves, boots and respirator in the stifling heat. Helicopter pilots practised flying in to ground zero to hover over the explosion site to collect water samples.

At Onslow on the West Australian coast, 140 kilometres from the Monte Bello Islands, locals were excited by the sudden influx of big city folk. The pub and spare rooms in homesteads were booked out for weeks ahead as journalists from all over Australia and the UK based themselves in the town waiting for the imminent explosion. Nobody knew exactly when it would happen, and they had to be ready at any time.

It was a long wait. The *Canberra Times* reported on its front page that the annual Onslow Cup horse race left the town deserted as everyone gathered at the town's dirt race track. The odds-on favourite Bungarra cleaned up the pack, and townsfolk drank the local pub dry celebrating.[4] They were running a sweepstake on when it would be A-Day – Atom Bomb Day. By the end of September, local wisdom was the bomb was imminent as planes stopped flying over and the navy ships had all left Onslow's harbour.

There was quite a flotilla of ships being deployed for Operation Hurricane, the name given to the first atomic test. Australia supplied twelve navy ships: the aircraft carrier HMAS *Sydney*; destroyer HMAS *Tobruk*; frigates *Shoalhaven*, *Murchison*, *Culgoa*, *Hawkesbury* and *Macquarie*; the small survey vessel HMAS *Warreen*; boom defence vessels *Koala* and *Limicola*; and two motorised lighters.

Britain had five Royal Navy ships: aircraft carrier and flagship HMS *Campania*, medical ship HMS *Tracker*, the sacrificial bomb ship *Plym*, and landing ships HMS *Zeebrugge* and HMS *Narvik*.

•

On board HMAS *Hawkesbury* making its way to the Monte Bello Islands off the north coast of Australia was 23-year-old seaman Kelvin Gough. The ship's mission was to patrol against inquisitive Soviet submarines. Gough joined the navy in 1950 as he was 'young and foolish and wanted to see the world'.[5] His father had fought in Tobruk and his grandfather in Flanders. Gough hoped to fight in Korea. Instead he was about to witness the most destructive force ever devised.

'We picked up an echo on the sonar. It was a long way off but the skipper thought it was a Soviet submarine following us so he ordered we drop a couple of depth charges to warn them off. It must have worked because the mysterious echo disappeared.'

The *Hawkesbury* picked up a group of scientists in Singapore and took them down to Monte Bello. 'We dropped off the boffins and sailed on to the mainland coast. I was part of several groups put ashore to chase away any Aborigines who were there. I was with a patrol on the beach when we saw some Aborigines on a hill in the distance. We fired our guns into the air to scare them away. I don't know if it worked, but the officer with us later spoke to some Aborigines we saw on the coast. He told them to get far away as there was a big bang coming.'

•

Meanwhile, as HMS *Plym* approached the Monte Bello Islands, the captain addressed the crew. He finally confirmed the rumours that had been swirling around the ship ever since it left London and people had seen that strange structure in its hold. The captain told his crew their ship would be the sacrificial lamb in the atomic test, and the device stored in their hull was, as they suspected, the atom bomb.

The *Plym* arrived at Monte Bello on 8 August and dropped anchor in the still, blue lagoon. The main engines were rung off for the last time. The ship fell silent but it was a busy time as scientists poured all over the vessel, connecting wires and ensuring all was ready.

The bomb's radioactive core, a sphere of plutonium sealed inside a container, was flown from England in a special flying boat. The flight took three days and W.J. Moyce, the scientist given charge of the lethal device, had strict orders that if the aircraft got into trouble, he was to strap the container to his chest and parachute out of the plane. The core was packed into a cork box that would float. If the cork box came into contact with sea water a bag of dye would leak out to help searching planes find it, presumably along with the lucky Mr Moyce. The trip was uneventful and the sea plane landed at Monte Bello in mid September and the core was transferred to HMS *Plym*. The ship's crew were now sitting on top of an atom bomb.

By 1 September 1952 there were only twenty-five people left on board the *Plym*: three officers, fifteen crew and seven scientists. The ship's captain even had to run the ship's boat himself, ferrying people back and forth. On Saturday 20 September the *Plym* went through a pre-dawn dress rehearsal, evacuating the remaining ship's crew to a nearby Royal Navy ship and waiting for the countdown. Dr Penney came aboard and made the final inspection.

On 30 September the 'stand by' period began, and the amount of people on board was reduced to a dozen. Only one ship was left in the lagoon near the *Plym* to take those men to safety before the explosion.

The day of the test depended on the weather. The winds at the beginning of October were expected to go north-west, away from the Australian mainland. That would take the radioactive cloud towards Indonesia, but that wasn't mentioned as a concern in the official records.

There was a growing disharmony between the military men and the scientists, and quite a deal of resentment. Navy men didn't like the arrogant manner the scientists went about their business on board their ship. Scientists largely treated the sailors and soldiers offhandedly. As one *Plym* sailor later wrote: 'Tension began to heighten as more boffins descended to make final adjustments and cold bloodedly asked which bits of our ship they could take away as souvenirs.'[6]

On the early morning of 2 October, the crew were told there would be a one-day delay as the wind was not in the right direction. The navy men left on the *Plym* groaned as the ship's cook had gone with the last contingent and the half-dozen men left on board had to eat a dinner prepared from cans by a 'keen amateur'. They even washed up all the dishes as it was tempting fate to leave unwashed dishes for a second cancellation. Before dawn early next morning the wind was just right, and the men made their final checks.

Royal Navy mechanic Henry Carter told the Royal Commission 32 years later that he was one of the last to leave.[7] His job was to take the remaining two scientists off the ship to safety, but to return them if there was a malfunction and the bomb didn't go off. They climbed into a small rowing boat and rowed to shore. They left the rowing boat and climbed into a waiting motor boat with five other people. They manoeuvred around the islands until they reached a spot they'd picked out earlier – an overhang of rock on the far side of one of the islands. They pulled a tarpaulin over the boat and lay down waiting for the blast. They were just three kilometres away from *Plym* and the atom bomb.

At precisely 8 am on 3 October, on board HMS *Campania*, Penney gave the order to fire the bomb. With him were Rear Admiral Arthur David Torlesse, the commander of the military side of the mission, and three scientists representing Australia present only as observers: Ernest Titterton, Leslie Martin and Alan Butement. The Royal Commission later determined no Australian ship was closer than twenty nautical miles to the explosion, a safe distance. Some sailors are still convinced they were far closer than that.

Three metres below the water level in the hold of HMS *Plym*, the command sent an electronic signal to spark high-powered explosives packed around the plutonium core. In one hundred thousandth of a second, the shock wave from the explosion compressed the core, kicking off the fission reaction. The force split the nucleus of the plutonium atom, sending neutrons crashing into other plutonium atoms in a rapidly expanding chain reaction. Each split atom – the fission – released a huge amount of energy that exploded with immense force: the power of an atom bomb.

The prime aim of the designer of the bomb is to create a weapon that will not be blown apart until it has produced the size of explosion required. To do this, what is called a critical mass of material is needed – in the case of plutonium-239, about four kilograms. The radius of this plutonium sphere is only about five centimetres. This is surrounded by a shell of material like beryllium that reflects the neutrons back into the sphere.

In the first few thousandths of a second after the explosion starts, there is a burst of ultraviolet radiation from the fireball as it rises. This is followed by a second burst of radiation called thermal radiation, which lasts just a few seconds in a blinding intense light. It is the second burst of thermal radiation that creates the heat. People caught within two kilometres of a nuclear weapon exploding at ground level with a yield of sixteen kilotons (the size of the Hiroshima bomb) will suffer third-degree burns. If that bomb is exploded at higher altitude – say 300 metres like the Hiroshima bomb – the blast will kill every living thing within five square kilometres. The ionising radiation released will rise with the mushroom cloud and drift with the wind.

The blast down in the hold of the *Plym* instantly disintegrated the ship. The twenty-five kiloton explosion blasted a crater thirty metres wide and seven metres deep in the seabed under the ship. The crater was lined with black mud – magnetic iron oxide – all that was left of the ship. Debris, smoke and radiation was blasted 4000 metres into the sky. Curiously, the boiling cloud from *Plym* didn't form the mushroom shape known from previous atomic bomb blasts. Many photos had been published of the thirty-three atomic weapons tests exploded since the end of the Second World War and the public knew what to expect. Instead the 4000-metre-high tower of boiling cloud blown skywards by the test formed a Z shape. The winds first took it west over the Indian Ocean. When the cloud reached higher altitudes it encountered a wind taking it east towards the mainland. The experts shouldn't have been surprised. Any local could have told them the prevailing winds over Australia headed west to east. The wind shift was to have serious consequences.

•

Lying in the boat covered by only a tarpaulin just three kilometres from the explosion, sailor Henry Carter was terrified. Thirty years later he described what happened to the Royal Commission into the British tests: 'The signal came over the radio to prepare for countdown and a black heavy canvas tarpaulin was pulled over the boat so we were now in darkness. We all then draped jungle green towels over our heads and I pressed the palms of my hands into my eye sockets. I was dressed in shorts and a pair of shoes. At zero there was a blinding electric blue light of an intensity I had not seen before or since. I pressed my hands harder to my eyes, then I realised I could see the bones of my hands. It seemed that this light was passing through the tarpaulin and towel for about ten to twelve seconds and there seemed to be two surges and two detonations with a continued rumbling and boiling sensation. My body seemed first to be compressed, and then billowing like a balloon.'[8]

•

None of this reached the public at the time. Instead they received carefully vetted propaganda. A Royal Navy officer on board HMS *Narvik* wrote anonymously for the public his own eyewitness account of the explosion. Undoubtedly the report went through military censors and didn't appear in the press until almost a year later – just before the next round of atomic tests took place. The press called him Lieutenant X.

Lt. X reported that as the countdown began, all the ships were battened down, doors and hatches closed and heavy steel deadlights clamped down over all ports. Every available crewman was on deck, ordered to face away from the blast. The voice counted down the minutes, then seconds to the blast, five, four, three, two, one, zero.

> In that instant despite a blazing tropical sun intensified by reflection from the water all around a blinding light bathed the ships and the ocean from horizon to horizon. The calm voice from control chanted on with the count . . . one, two, three, four . . . eight, nine, ten. The captain's voice came from the bridge, 'You may look now.'
>
> The sight that met our eyes as we turned was vastly more terrifying than can be appreciated from the photographs. The great grey-black mass just flowering at the top like a tremendous cauliflower appeared even at this distance to be towering over us. Within the minute the blast wave hit us, a sharp pressure wave of air that really hurt the ear drums followed almost at once by the reflected wave.
>
> We watched awestruck as the cloud continued to rise at great speed, until the high winds overcame its own velocity and whipped it away, first north-westerly and higher to the north-east to form a fantastic Z shape . . . A mist spreading outward from the base of the explosion was noticeable as recondensing water and some sediment fell back from the cloud into the surrounding waters and within a minute or two thick black smoke rising from the islands showed that widespread fires had been ignited in the spinifex and bush.
>
> There was hardly any feeling of anti-climax, hardly any feeling at all to be quite honest. We were all rather stunned at this, our first sight of the terrifying weapon in action.[9]

•

The explosion was front page news across Australia. The coming of the atom bomb to Australian soil was greeted with pride by the press.

Despite being barred from the atomic test zone, journalists had been keeping a tense 24-hour watch for five long weeks from the top of the closest mountain on the mainland, about 100 kilometres from the Monte Bello Islands. Even from that distance they reported a 'brief lightning-like flash' followed by a huge expanding cloud that took about three minutes to reach 12,000 feet and about a mile wide.[10] They didn't feel the ground shake, but four and a quarter minutes after the flash they felt a heavy air-pressure pulse and heard a clap of thunder followed by a prolonged rumble like the sound of a train going through a tunnel. 'The air and ground shocks were sufficiently intense to cause slight pain in the ears,' one reporter wrote.[11]

Another said:

> The immediate flash resembled the top quarter of a setting sun. A dense and magnificently turbulent cloud almost immediately shot up to a height of 2000 feet. At first deep pink it quickly changed to mauve in the centre with pink towards the outside and brilliantly white turbulent edges. Within two minutes the cloud, which was still like a giant cauliflower, was 10,000 feet high. A small pure-white milling ball rested on top.[12]

Press photographers who'd kept a 'round-the-clock watch for more than two weeks at their cameras recorded a series of pictures as the boiling atom cloud shot into the sky. Film went straight to a portable darkroom on the mountaintop and was processed within minutes. A driver then rushed the prints to the nearest airstrip twenty-seven minutes' drive away where a plane was waiting to rush them straight to Perth, 1300 kilometres away. From Perth they were flashed around the country and to Britain.

•

The blast took six minutes to reach Onslow. Crockery shook on tables, windows rattled and doors swung on their hinges. People ran from their homes to the beach to see the growing atomic cloud shooting skywards on the horizon. Reporters ran to the post office to file their stories by phone. One press photographer heard the noise while having breakfast at the Beadon Hotel, and literally leaped through an open window to run to the beach with his camera. Nobby Clarke was harnessing a horse to a cart when the rumble hit. The horse shied and bolted across a paddock with Mr Clarke in hot pursuit. Schoolmaster Rex Bandy took his class down to the beach to explain the science behind what had happened as they watched the atom cloud in the distance. Matron H.W. Rencoule at the local hospital said all the doors on the verandah were suddenly slammed shut by the blast. With the town looking to celebrate and journalists keen on ending their long vigil, the shocking news came that there were only three crates of beer left in the only pub in town.[13]

On Monte Bello the dangerous work was about to begin. This was the treatment of Australian and British military men the governments would insist remain top secret. The men had been told everything they experienced at Monte Bello was subject to the Official Secrets Act and they could never talk about it. What happened after the explosion stayed secret for decades.

•

On board HMAS *Hawkesbury* Kelvin Gough reckoned they were the closest Australian ship to the explosion.[14]

'They said we were thirty kilometres away but we were much closer – about twenty kilometres. A minute before the bomb went off we all stood on the deck with our backs to the explosion. We saw a huge flash and when we were told to turn around I saw this massive explosion rising into the air. Different coloured smoke and dust from the island was boiling up into the sky. It was supposed to drift out to sea, but after a while it drifted back towards the mainland.

'Five hours after the blast we moved close to the islands along with the British navy ships. Everything was flattened, absolutely levelled. No birds, nothing. Dead fish and sharks everywhere in the water. We were told not to eat the fish. After a bit we went on to the islands and bits and pieces of metal from the British ship *Plym* were lying everywhere. We picked them up and put them into drums. We had no protective gear. This went on for about two days.'

The *Hawkesbury* returned to Sydney after the test where Gough said the ship was stripped of its gear and all their clothes taken. 'No one was allowed on board. They collected radiation monitor cards which were on us but we were never tested for radiation or ran a Geiger counter over us.'

Gough left the navy in 1956 with a clean bill of health. He'd developed a bad cough that stayed with him forever. Two years later government health officials asked him to undergo tests in Sydney.

'They ran some sort of reading device over me but they didn't tell me what it was. Other navy and army people later told me the same thing happened to them. I never heard what the results were and that was it for me.' Kelvin Gough never had children.

•

On board HMAS *Murchison* seaman John Quinn swears he was almost blown off the ship by the force of the atomic blast. 'I'd seen action in the Korean War and I knew what it was like to be shot at. We were grounded on a mud bank and the communists shot at us from land. I was in the engine room when a shell came in through the side of the ship and dropped down at my feet. It was a dud. I later gave it to the Australian War Museum in Canberra. Well, at Monte Bello our radar operator told me we were about eight nautical miles [fifteen kilometres] from the blast even though the official limit was ten miles [18.5 kilometres]. I was on the upper deck at the funnel to see the explosion with a couple of young national servicemen. We turned our backs and the flash blinded us for a bit and then the ship suddenly rocked from the force of the blast and if it wasn't for the railing which we grabbed we would have gone over the side.'[15]

Twelve years later Quinn was told he had blood cancer. His records show his blood was clear before he was at Monte Bello. 'My doctor said I could have got it from radiation exposure at Monte Bello, but there is no way of knowing for sure.'

It wasn't HMAS *Murchison*'s first encounter with an atom bomb. Six months after the atom bomb was dropped on Hiroshima, the Australian frigate was the first ship of any nation to enter Hiroshima harbour. Noel Jensen-Holme was a young sailor on board *Murchison* when the ship dropped anchor on 25 February 1946 'amongst the horrific sight of ships sunken or listing at anchor, gutted by the atomic firestorm.'[16] Jensen-Holme said forty of the crew were allowed four hours ashore to wander around the devastated city. The ship left port the next day. 'Over the next month every person on board *Murchison* suffered with a series of unusual medical complaints from minor to quite serious stomach ailments including diarrhea, headaches, eye problems, unusual body aches and pains and even nervous problems that could be termed depression.'

He said it made no difference whether a person had been ashore or not. They all fell sick to varying degrees. The medical problems were put down to food poisoning. The ship's crew received no medical advice about possible contamination from the Hiroshima bomb. The sickness passed in time, but no record was kept on the fate of the crew. The lack of records became a common theme around radiation exposure.

•

The day after the atom bomb exploded at Monte Bello, the closest big city newspaper, *The West Australian*, said in a long, glowing editorial that the bomb proved Britain had the skill to produce its own atomic weapons and will 'yield the initiative to none' providing a reliable shield for the Commonwealth.

'The reaction to the Monte Bello operation must be one of profound satisfaction at an immense potential strengthening of the British Commonwealth with a strong sense of pride in British achievement.'[17]

Other commentators proclaimed exploding an atom bomb on Australian territory would help protect Australia. The *Sydney Morning Herald* said, 'Australia may well be proud to have been associated with Britain in a great enterprise for it not only emphasises the close and understanding cooperation between these two Commonwealth partners, it also has an immensely important practical bearing on the security of this country.'[18]

•

Days after the test, Penney acknowledged the terrifying power of the bomb, but insisted it was a power that would keep the peace. He gave this personal account of what he saw in a recording that was broadcast after he got back to England:

'The sight before our eyes was terrifying. A great greyish-black cloud being hurled thousands of feet into the air and increasing in size with astonishing rapidity. A great sandstorm suddenly sprang up over the islands . . . Mr Churchill has said that the results of our atomic weapon program should be beneficial to public safety. As a scientist I should like most strongly to agree with this view. The energy and enthusiasm which have gone into the making of this new weapon stemmed essentially from the sober hope that it would bring us nearer the day when world war is universally seen to be unthinkable.'[19]

It was a justification Penney and the scientists would maintain for decades to come. Churchill was thrilled by the success of the operation and immediately announced Penney, aged just forty-three, would be recognised with a knighthood.

•

Ernest Titterton prepared an article for the newspapers as the official Australian representative at the British atomic tests. Under the heading 'Some "Good Guesses" on Future of Atomic Energy', Titterton wrote that those who scrawl 'Ban The Bomb' on walls in cities of the world either misunderstand the reality or are 'propagandists who have an ulterior motive'. He continued:

> It is not atomic bombs which we have to ban but war itself. All wars are horrible and wasteful of lives and material, whatever weapons are employed. Far from deprecating the capability of the Western Allies to manufacture atomic weapons it is a matter of satisfaction that it is these nations, with the lover for freedom and democracy and the high value they place on human lives, which have in their custody the majority of these weapons of mass destruction. Indeed as Mr Winston Churchill has said it is probable that possession of the atomic bomb was the reason why Western Europe was not overrun by the Communists at the time of the Berlin Blockade. In this sense our possession of atomic weapons may have prevented war.[20]

Titterton went on to speculate that atomic energy would power spaceships, treat cancer and provide electricity for huge cities.

•

A few days after the blast, British army engineer Thomas Wilson was sent ashore with a squad to retrieve food and other exposed material to test for radioactivity.[21] They were given overalls, a hat and gas mask. 'We had to remove the mask time and again,' he told the Royal Commission in 1985. 'The heat was so bad it was very hard to breathe and we could not see because the condensation impaired our vision. We got covered in sand and grit thrown up by the wheels of the Land Rover.'

•

Able Seaman Maurice Westwood told his story to the Royal Commission thirty years later when all veterans of the tests were assured the Official Secrets Act no longer applied. He was on HMAS *Koala*, which, despite its name, had nothing cute or cuddly about it. *Koala* was a tough little vessel designed for laying booms around harbours and conducting salvage operations. She had the right winching equipment and was sent to Monte Bello to carry out a crucial role in the lagoon in the heart of the blast zone. For days prior to the blast the *Koala* ferried equipment around the islands. On the morning of 3 October she was far from the blast zone, but on the very same day was ordered back into the lagoon.

Westwood told the Royal Commission: 'We had to raise a barge that had sunk in the lagoon after the explosion. This was about two miles from the blast zone. We had no protective gear, just dressed in normal shorts and sandals. The diver who went down to attach cables came up and was sent to a nearby laboratory ship to check for radiation exposure. He went through the room that had a Geiger counter and really set it off.'[22]

Westwood said the crew crawled all over the barge as they were winching it up and hauling it on board. They were later sent over to the laboratory ship and tested with a Geiger counter.

'First they sent us through fully clothed and the Geiger counter went off. So they told us to strip off and go through without clothes and it still set the machine off.'

The sailors were ordered to shower and wash thoroughly until they no longer set off the counter. The clothes were thrown into a barrel of wet cement that was later dumped at sea.

The barge was raised and put on the forecastle of HMAS *Koala*, where it stayed until they offloaded it at Fremantle. The crew also raised several buoys in the lagoon. Westwood said many of the crew brushed against the barge as they moved around the ship to do their work. The barge wasn't checked for radioactivity while it was on board the *Koala*. The ship's captain, Lieutenant

Commander Anthony Taudevin, later committed suicide. His widow, Sheila, told the 1984 Royal Commission: 'He expressed to me the thought that he felt that his ship and his company were being put in a very tricky situation. He told me he felt very unhappy about it.'[23]

•

Nineteen-year-old Lewis Rice had been in the navy for just six months when an officer called for volunteers for the upcoming atomic tests.

Rice's hand shot up. 'I thought it would be fantastic. It would be exciting to see an atom bomb go off. We knew nothing about radiation. It was supposed to be secret but it wasn't much of a secret as it had been mentioned in the newspapers.'[24]

Rice was posted to HMAS *Macquarie*, a frigate built at the end of the Second World War, recommissioned especially for the atomic tests. The ship was assigned to patrol waters 160 kilometres from the Monte Bello Islands.

'We were told we were looking for Taiwanese fishing boats, but we knew that was nonsense as we were really looking for Russian submarines which might try and take samples to see what kind of atomic bomb it was.

'We were 100 to 200 miles [160 to 320 kilometres] from the blast on October 3 and I didn't see the explosion or the mushroom cloud. But after the blast we steamed straight towards Monte Bello. I think we moved into the lagoon just a few hours after the blast.

'There were dead fish in the water everywhere. We scooped them up, and cooked them up for a feast. No one told us not to. A day and half later the captain told us he had got a signal from Melbourne saying not to eat the fish. That sure came a bit late as we'd all eaten fish from the lagoon.'

Rice was part of the *Macquarie* crew sent ashore to assist the British scientists.

'There were a few buildings that had been put up for the blast made from different materials to see which sort of building would stand up best in the explosion.'

Rice wandered around the island and saw divers going down to the wreck of the British frigate HMS *Plym.*

'I had a quick chat with one of them and they said everything down there was red. The ship had just disappeared. All they could find was a bit of anchor chain.'

HMAS *Macquarie* left Monte Bello after a few days, ending Rice's part in the atomic tests. Eight years later he married and his wife had a baby girl. She died after just one day.

'The hospital asked if they could have the body for scientific tests. We said yes as we thought maybe the research might help others and some good might come of her death. They never told us what the body was used for, but I heard many years later they had been taking baby bodies for years and testing them for Strontium-90 for radiation exposure. I don't know if she was one of those.

'But I do know a lot of my shipmates from HMAS *Macquarie* died from cancer. I don't know if it was from exposure at Monte Bello.'

•

On the aircraft carrier HMAS *Sydney*, hundreds of sailors gathered on the flight deck to witness the explosion. *Sydney* was well away from the blast but many sailors later reported they believed the radioactive cloud had passed over the huge ship.

Howard 'Dick' Bird served in Korea before the *Sydney* was deployed to Monte Bello. 'I saw the huge cloud go up after the explosion and it changed direction. I believe it went over the top of us – they sure had us washing the decks down thoroughly afterwards.'[25]

Two years later Bird married and in 1955 had a son. Another son was born two years later. 'He had no backside and his innards were perforated. He died when he was six weeks old. We got no explanation. I didn't connect it with me being at the atomic tests at the time. We later had a daughter born with physical and mental problems and our first son later developed back problems. I wasn't too good either but that was probably the grog. We lost a grandchild at birth and a granddaughter had many operations for medical problems. Our daughter's doctor thought the family's tragedies might stem from my exposure at Monte Bello, but we don't know.'

•

Carl Godwin, aged eighteen, was on the flight deck of the *Sydney* dressed in shorts, sandals and shirt, excitedly waiting to see the atomic bomb go off.

'We didn't have to watch it but it was something no one wanted to miss,' he said.[26] They turned their backs until a few seconds after the explosion then spun around.

In the distance Godwin could see the mushroom cloud climbing into the sky. A few minutes later the blast force reached the huge ship. 'It shook the ship like a leaf. There was a big vibration. I'd never experienced anything like it.'

Godwin's thoughts went to the pictures he'd seen of the atomic bomb dropped on Hiroshima and Nagasaki. 'Those poor bastards under that massive bomb, it must have been terrifying.'

HMAS *Sydney* left the area and Godwin eventually married. In 1963 – eleven years after witnessing the atom bomb – he had a baby son.

'He started dying when he was just six months old. He never walked or crawled. All he could do was smile. They called it petit mal or absence seizure. He died when he was twelve. We never knew what was wrong with him. Then our next son had a strangled hernia. I thought something terrible had been visited upon our family. Why were we hit with these problems? Was it the bomb? I don't know.'

•

What men like Godwin, Bird and Rice were never told was that British scientists had no real idea what effect the nuclear bomb would have on the men involved in the tests or on the whole of Australia.

A top secret document prepared in London just a few months before Operation Hurricane admitted: 'We have no information about the spread of fission products when an atomic bomb is detonated on the surface of the ground or on the surface of the sea. It is in fact one of the objects of the experiment to fill some extent this gap in our knowledge.'[27] In the document British scientists predicted about ten per cent of the fission products from the explosion could be deposited on the Australian mainland, thirty per cent would rise in sea spray and fall back into the water, and sixty per cent would be blown up into the cloud. It would spread over such a wide area that the radioactive contamination would be 'negligible'. In case fallout did spread across northern Australia, arrangements were made to test radioactivity as far away as Cairns. Civilian planes flying from Sydney to Noumea and Fiji would have dust-collecting filters attached to pick up signs of the radioactive cloud. RAAF pilots would fly into contaminated clouds over Broome and Townsville as 'British scientists would not fly on these sorties'.

Another document prepared by Rear Admiral Torlesse before the Monte Bello test wanted two safety standards – a general one and a special 'once only' standard set for 'volunteers'. The admiral in charge of the operation cynically noted that, while all government 'servants' are entitled to compensation for injury on duty, health problems arising from Operation Hurricane would be (1) long delayed and (2) an illness unconnected with the operation might have caused the same symptom. In other words, the military bureaucracy had its excuses ready long before the bomb went off.

The confidential admiralty document shows the military mandarins feared safety standards would be set too high and defeat the purpose of the exercise. 'Some degree of risk must be run by some people if we are to achieve the full purpose of the trial.'[28]

It's clear that from the very start the British regarded exploding atomic bombs in Australia as a chance to use troops, sailors and airmen as guinea pigs in their experiments, and Australia was to be regarded as one big laboratory.

3

'FLYING INTO THE GATES OF HELL'

Long before the Monte Bello test in October 1952, the British were already planning to expand the tests to the Australian mainland. In September 1952 Menzies secretly approved Penney making a top secret visit to a site about 650 kilometres north-west of the restricted weapon-testing area of Woomera in central Australia. The flat, dry plain was called Emu Field. Penney gave it the thumbs up. But the British government felt they should do something to avoid any opposition that might develop among Australians. An internal British government Foreign Office memo before the Monte Bello test reveals their motives:

> The Commonwealth Government are likely to be nervous about allowing the use of a site in the heart of the continent for atomic weapons tests, and may have to face criticism from their own people. It is obviously desirable that one of their own scientists should be able to advise them from first hand knowledge, and it seems right to use the Monte Bello test as an opportunity for indoctrinating such a scientist. The best way to prevent the Australians from feeling that we are 'attempting to use their land but at the same time keeping

> them out' would be to ask them to make a nomination for this purpose, but we cannot risk their unfettered choice.[1]

When it came time for the 1953 tests at Emu Field, Titterton was once again the senior 'Australian' observer. Once again Australian access was limited. It wasn't until mid 1955, a year before the second series of tests at Monte Bello, that pressure started to appear for Australia to have some say over safety procedures at the British tests. Minister of Supply Howard Beale, the only minister in the Menzies government allowed to speak publicly about the British tests, constantly assured the Australian public that the tests were safe and posed no risk to humans or animals.

'The tests are quite safe,' Beale said dismissively in parliament. 'If they weren't safe they would not be taking place.'[2]

•

On 15 October 1953 the dawn sun crept over the horizon in central Australia, sending the sand a bright golden red. The crew of a waiting RAAF Lincoln bomber were assembled in the briefing room at the high security Woomera airfield. The skipper, Group Captain Maurie Onions, led a crack seven-man crew. Sergeant Edward Cheney was the youngest in the plane's crew, having joined the air force aged just seventeen. He'd spent the past twelve months fighting communist insurgents in the Malayan Emergency and was now, just turned twenty, an experienced navigator. Along with the rest of the crew, Cheney had put his hand up when the RAAF asked for volunteers for a 'special mission'.

'We thought it was something to do with Sukarno in Indonesia,' Cheney said.[3] 'They made a big show of having us sign the Official Secrets Act before they'd tell us where we were going. We'd already signed that sort of paper for the Malaya campaign as what we did there was pretty hush-hush. Then they said we'd be going to Woomera. I thought we had to be working with some sort of secret weapon.'

The crew spent three long months training at Woomera but the tedium of life in the dead centre of the vast continent was already getting to them. They knew they were to be used in surveillance for the atomic bomb tests, and were keen to do the job.

'We thought that would be interesting, flying around watching an atom bomb go off. Yes, a unique experience.'

But at this dawn meeting, Cheney was taken aback when a high-powered array of top military brass – even a British RAF air vice marshal – and senior scientists entered the briefing room to address them. The seven crewmen of the Lincoln snapped to attention when they saw the senior officers.

'The air vice marshal was dripping in military decorations. I think we were told he was a Lord something or other. Well, he thanked us for volunteering and said this atomic weapon test would put Britain in the top ranks of the world superpowers. I thought that's strange as we hadn't been trained to drop an atom bomb. I was the bombardier in this crew. My mind whirled. What could they have in mind for us?'

The scientists and top air force brass turned to exit the room, leaving the crew somewhat stunned. Then just as the air vice marshal was about to walk out the door, he turned back to the Australian crew and said: 'By the way, we don't know everything that is going to happen. It's a mystery as to what goes on inside an atom bomb's mushroom cloud. However there is one thing we are concerned about, and that is that it might affect your sterility . . . I think it is right at this stage to say if you want to pull out of the mission it is all right to do so. Well, good luck.' And with that the top RAF officer smiled and left the room.

'I looked left and right to the crew standing in a row beside me but not one had the guts to say to this bloke, "You can go and get stuffed if you don't know what effect this will have on us." I think they chose us because we were all veterans of war and we already had kids. I had a two-month-old daughter who was born while I was at Woomera and an older daughter. Maybe they thought it didn't matter if it turned me sterile as I already had two daughters.'

The crew remained silent after what had been said. They had little time to consider the RAF marshal's offer to pull out of the mission – they were immediately whizzed out to their waiting Lincoln plane.

'We did a thorough check and got ready for takeoff. We were dressed in the standard RAAF summer flying suit. As far as I knew we still hadn't been told exactly what we were going to do up there. We were only told we would be monitoring the atom bomb's performance from the air. That's all. We flew off towards Emu Field, the test site. We had eight hours' fuel. We flew around in big circles for hours. We had fruit cans the size of a tin of peaches screwed on to the plane's sides, wings, and one on the tail. There were about fourteen of them. We weren't told what they were for. We had no role in them at all. We didn't know a lot of the equipment they had put on board.

'Finally they told us to line up to fly south to north across the target, which is where the bomb would be detonated in thirty minutes or so. We were about fifteen to twenty miles [twenty-four–thirty-two kilómetres] away from the blast zone. We were told to do a circuit so when it went off we would be facing away from it. Over the radio we heard the countdown "10, 9, 8, 7, 6, 5, 4, 3, 2, 1" and then whoompa! There was this incredible white flash and then the shock wave hit us. It nearly tore the plane apart. The Lincoln is a very hardy plane that can take a lot of punishment. It was built for bombing raids over Germany and to withstand flak and fighter attacks. It's also very noisy and we didn't hear the explosion. But we felt it. The plane shook violently as though we were in a thunderstorm. I heard through the radio the base tell the skipper: "Turn and enter."

'Onions turned the plane around and from my position in

the canopy at the very front of the plane I saw this huge boiling mass of grey and brown crap shooting up into the air.'

Cheney's task was to take photos with a special aerial reconnaissance camera the scientists had installed in the plane. As they approached the column, Cheney called 'Cameras on' and the cameras proceeded to shoot – one directed straight down, one to the left and one to the right.

'I didn't see any flame in the mushroom cloud. It was this boiling mass of rising cloud of dirt and muck. We were at 20,000 feet and flew straight towards this rising column. It took just thirty seconds of flying to reach it. We hit it just under the mushroom cloud in the column that was still rising. It was like flying into a tornado. I had flown into storm clouds before to collect temperatures so I thought I knew what was coming. But this was something else. It was like flying into the gates of hell.

'We had the controllers in our ears all the time and the skipper was describing what he saw and what the plane was doing. We were an Australian Air Force plane operating under British command in Australia. These were British voices telling us to fly into the mushroom cloud column. At that moment I realised we were being used as guinea pigs.

'This was a boiling cloud of dust and crap. Immediately we entered the cloud, everything went black. At our speed it took just seconds and we were through and out the other side. I was very relieved. Then this Pommy voice comes over the radio: "About turn, and reenter."

'We looked at each other: "What the bloody hell? We just did that."

'The skipper asked them to repeat the instruction.

'They did, and the skipper turned the plane around and we went back into it.

'Again we felt the heat inside the boiling column. We were only in it for seconds and the air in the plane heated up very quickly. We went through it and flew at full speed back to Woomera.'

If being ordered to fly through an atom bomb mushroom cloud without any protective gear was madness, what happened next was staggering. The Lincoln landed at Woomera and the crew were told to park their plane at a far point on the tarmac.

'We got out of the plane. We were stunned at what happened next. A bloke in full white protective gear drove up, pulling a whole lot of trailers they usually use to pull bombs to the plane. On every little trailer there was a wood box about two feet long and a foot high.

'A group of scientists were waiting and they were dressed exactly like Neil Armstrong when he landed on the moon: helmet, gloves, sealed white overalls and boots. They all breathed through oxygen bottles. And there we were, standing around in just our regular flying suits. They didn't come near us.

'One of them had a long pole with hooks on it to reach the cans attached to the plane. Using the hook, he carried them over to these boxes. They used long poles to open the lid of the box and lowered the cans into the boxes then slammed the lid down. Clearly they didn't want to get close to the cans. We learned later the boxes were lined with lead.

'We just stood there watching. Nobody wanted to go near us. They loaded the trailers with the boxes and drove them straight over to a waiting silver British V Bomber. They were brand new planes and I really would have liked to look over it. But the V bomber took off immediately and flew direct to England with the cans. I didn't see the British RAF crew so I don't know if they had protective gear on. They were already on board.

'Once they'd taken all the cans and instruments off our plane the scientists got into a special bus and off they went, leaving us still standing by ourselves. We were at the far end of the runway and no other planes were landing or leaving. It was real quiet. We waited about half an hour or forty minutes. Finally a vehicle picked us up and we were taken to a decontamination area. They told us to strip off everything and took away our flying gear. We were hosed down with a high pressure hose. It was bore water, so hard you could cut it with a knife. They told us to clean ourselves and scrub thoroughly. They ran Geiger counters over us and if they beeped they told us to scrub and shower again.

'All this scrubbing and the sight of those Pommy scientists in protective gear made me think. We were up in the air for eight hours flying around. Whenever you do long-distance flying you carry a big thermos of hot coffee. It was strapped to the radar equipment. Beside it was a box full of sandwiches. All these were within arm's reach and it was my job to pour the coffee and hand out the sandwiches. We were eating stuff that had gone through the radioactive cloud. Oh shit! We were the lab rats for their test!

'They took our old clothes away and gave us fresh uniforms. We were a bit stunned by all this and sat silently when we finally got to the mess and sat down. We hadn't expected what they'd done to us. We thought we'd fly around the cloud, not right into it. We wondered what the hell that was all about. We hadn't volunteered – we'd been volunteered for a nuclear experiment.'

The next day, Cheney and the crew flew the Lincoln back to Amberley air base near Brisbane. When they landed they were ordered to park it in the far corner of a paddock.

But their mission with the nuclear cloud wasn't over. Cheney and his crew continued to fly missions following the spread of the nuclear cloud as it drifted across northern Australia. They were joined by an entire squadron of RAAF Lincolns.

After the explosion at Emu Field, the cloud had risen to 25,000 feet where it flattened out and drifted eastwards. Locating the cloud was fairly primitive science.

'In daylight it had this red colour,' Cheney said of the mission to follow the cloud across Australia. 'The only way to determine where it started and ended was to fly towards it until the Geiger counters on board started to go off. We'd fly straight through it and when the Geiger counters stopped clicking we'd know that was the limit of the cloud. I reckon we flew through that cloud forty to fifty times as we followed it across Australia until it drifted out to sea.

'We did this monitoring for two years. All this time we were sworn to secrecy. If I told you where it fell I could still be court martialed and jailed. But when I found the cloud hovered over one country town in Queensland for five days while it rained, I told my family never to go near the town. Years later I heard they'd detected a cancer cluster in that area.'

By 1956, three years after flying through that first mushroom cloud, Cheney had been promoted to pilot officer on Canberra bombers. Cheney and his skipper were called in by the CO and told they were being sent to Pearce base near Perth for a special mission. When Cheney got there he found he would be training British pilots to fly in Australian conditions.

'We didn't get on well with the RAF blokes. I found them a bunch of snobs. There's a tradition in the officers' mess that if a new officer enters the room an officer of equal rank must get up and welcome them, offer them a drink and introduce them around. Well, when we entered the mess for the first time the Brits would all be gathered together and you'd hear, just loud enough to pick up, them saying: "Oh, here come the colonials."

'This was despite us teaching them how to survive and navigate in Australia. We were winning all the competitions in which Brits were up against the Aussies. Yet still they looked down on us.'

After training they were all sent to Broome. Cheney knew he was going to have to fly through a nuclear cloud once again.

'I said to my skipper, "Do you think I should tell them I've already done this?" He said: "No bloody fear. I don't want anyone else with me on this flight."'

And so Cheney once again was volunteered to fly into radioactive clouds. It was his job as bombardier to work all the instruments and take all the measurements. This time the plane was to enter the mushroom cloud at 40,000 feet. Another bomb went off over Monte Bello Island on 19 June 1956, this time a massive sixty-kiloton bomb – the biggest ever exploded in Australia.

'We lined up and flew straight into the cloud. I was busy on the instruments. It was far more powerful than my first bomb. It threw the plane around like a cork. I reckon we were blown skywards by about 1000 feet. The heat was intense. I was glad we were in the more advanced Canberra jet and not the Lincoln, as the old bomber wasn't sealed and dust and air came in easily. But still the Geiger counters screamed their heads off. They went off the scale. It took just a couple of seconds to fly through the mushroom cloud, but then, just like last time, they had us turn around and fly through it again.

'This was far bigger than any previous bomb. That's why we were told to enter at a much higher altitude. The cloud continued rising to about 55,000 feet. After the flight we got hints from the scientists that it was really a hydrogen bomb, even though that was denied by the government. But we were bound by secrecy and couldn't tell anyone.'

Cheney landed at Pearce base after flying through the atom bomb cloud and the same thing happened as at Woomera three years earlier. The crew were in normal flying gear while scientists approached the plane in full white protective gear, helmets, gloves and all. They took away samples collected by the scoops attached to the plane and the instruments they'd installed. Once again they put the samples into lead containers and rushed them to a waiting RAF V Bomber to fly them direct to Britain for testing.

'We were taken to a hut on the far corner of the base. We had to strip down and they hosed us for over an hour, running a Geiger counter over us and then doing it all over again when it still clicked. This was June and it was bloody cold. I had a problem as some of the radioactive dust had disappeared up my crack and I had to wash and scrub it over and over.'

Cheney said several of his air force mates who had been at the atomic tests died of leukemia within a few years after their flight into the radioactive hell of the atomic clouds.

'I'm sure it was from Strontium-90, which we would have inhaled or ingested through the coffee or sandwiches on the plane. I saw a crew member a few years after the Monte Bello flight and he was really crook. He told me to tap his shoulder. It was like hitting a wooden door. He had to have two assistants to move him. They wrapped his body tightly and strapped him into a special chair just to hold him up. There's no other explanation for this high death rate apart from exposure to radiation.'

Cheney doesn't know why he came through unscathed.

'I had to be one of the very few who flew through an atom bomb mushroom cloud twice, but for some reason I am still alive. I'm sure they'd like to know why. There's no doubt we were all used as guinea pigs. They saw us as mere colonials and therefore we didn't rate. We have a big country and to them it didn't matter if radioactivity was spread across it.'

•

Lance Edwards was the radio operator on the same Lincoln plane as Ted Cheney for the Emu Field test in 1953. He flew into the mushroom clouds of both the first ten-kiloton bomb and in another plane for the second one two weeks later. It was smaller at eight kilotons.

'There was a radiation measuring instrument next to me on the plane and I saw it go off the scale as we flew into the cloud,' Edwards recalled in 2013. 'I don't remember being told of any health risks or that we could pull out of the mission, as we were volunteers. There was no way any of us could pull out. It just wasn't done. The truth was we were rather proud we'd been selected for this mission. But we had no idea what they were sending us into.'[4]

There were consequences for Edwards. He developed Hurthle cell carcinoma, a rare cancer of the thyroid that had to be surgically removed. His son, born in 1958, was just three months old when he was diagnosed with cancer of the bowel. Doctors removed 45.7 centimetres of the baby's bowels. Edwards said they later changed his baby son's diagnosis to a reduplication of the bowel, a rare abnormality caused by a defect in the father's genes. A second son born in 1960 had malformation of the teeth. Grandchildren have been born with the same problem.

Edwards, too, is convinced the air force crews were used as guinea pigs. Government scientists kept intermittent contact with him to record his health and that of his offspring.

'Scientists at the time must have known the dangers of being exposed to radiation. That's why they wore protective gear when they came near the plane. But they didn't give us that protection. We were the guinea pigs.'

•

Roy Cosgrove was in a different RAAF Lincoln bomber to Cheney and Edwards in 1953. His job was to photograph the atom bomb explosion from 8000 feet.

His plane was cruising forty kilometres from the explosion point. The countdown had begun when Cosgrove's skipper, Wing Commander Rose, told him: 'If you want to watch this thing I advise you not to. If you have to have a look at it, pick which eye you want to lose.'[5] Cosgrove later reported this conversation in a written statement to the Royal Commission.

Cosgrove thought he was joking, and aimed the camera with his left eye. 'We had no special goggles or protective clothing. The plane had to be aimed straight at the explosion because of the limited scan of the camera underneath the front turret. I couldn't close my eyes during the flash of the explosion because the camera was manually operated and I had to make sure it was properly aimed. I had to aim, shoot and wind on the film as quickly as possible in a constant motion. There was no electronic motor drive attached to the camera.

'At the moment of the explosion the aircraft was enveloped by a very intense white light similar to the beam of an opthalmoscope being shone right into your eyes. It was an eerie sensation. Being a Christian it is what I imagine the light of God being like. The light seemed to last for quite some time but probably it was only a second or two. There was no chatter among the crew. Everyone was in awe.'

Cosgrove continued shooting fifty to 100 pictures until the securing pin sheered off the camera. At the same time, Cosgrove saw a plane fly into the boiling atom cloud but he couldn't get the camera back up fast enough to get the photo. Cosgrove's plane didn't go into the cloud and they weren't tested for radioactivity and didn't have to shower when they landed at Woomera.

Two weeks later, Cosgrove was in another Lincoln with a different skipper – Flight Lieutenant Goldner. This plane was fitted with canisters suspended from the wings pointing in the direction of flight. They contained air filters and looked like large ham tins open at one end. The plane was also fitted with instruments to measure the radioactive cloud. Cosgrove was the instrument operator. At the pre-flight briefing he asked a British scientist what level of radiation could be expected.

'It will definitely be in the zero to ten bracket. It may go from ten to 100 but if it goes into the hundreds you will be unlucky,' the scientist told him.

Cosgrove asked what precautions they should take.

'What do you mean?'

'Will we be on full oxygen?' Cosgrove thought a mask would prevent them from breathing radioactive air.

'Sorry, we're short of oxygen.'

'Will we have protective clothing?'

'There is none available.'

With that dismissive tone from the British scientist ringing in Cosgrove's ears, they took off six hours after the atom bomb exploded at Emu Field. After two and a half hours flying they found the radioactive cloud.

'We flew the length of the cloud to take a time and distance measure and then flew across the top of the cloud. We measured how deep it was with an altimeter. All these details were logged by the navigator. I was in the main spar of the plane and couldn't see outside. The captain said we were coming up to the cloud and were about to enter.

'Immediately the radiation recordings jumped to full. Even after we left the cloud five miles [eight kilometres] behind, the readings were still hitting maximum.'

After they landed, the canisters were removed by ground crew. They were dressed only in shorts and shirt. The canisters were loaded into a jeep and taken to a storeroom where Geiger counters were run over them.

Cosgrove said the counters 'went berserk'. Senior officers ordered the ground crew to take the canisters straight back to the parked Lincoln where they remained untouched for several days. Cosgrove and the crew were taken to a hangar where a Geiger counter was waved over them. Some of their clothing, such as flying boots and parachutes, was put aside for destruction.

'We weren't required to shower although we were told that when washing the clothes we had worn on the flight we should wash them ourselves by hand. We had to rinse the clothes thoroughly, and make sure our wives and children were not present. We were given no reason for that instruction.'

Cosgrove told the 1984 Royal Commission he suspected the British scientists did not expect the bomb to be as dirty as it was. If they knew it was going to have higher radioactivity they would have increased the limits on the radiation instruments on board the aircraft.

Soon after the mission Cosgrove experienced severe stomach problems and dizzy spells. Years later he had a severe intestinal haemorrhage. Doctors couldn't find a cause. Cosgrove said when he told them he'd been involved in the atomic tests they didn't want to know about it.

Despite his experience and health problems after the tests, Cosgrove told the Royal Commission he was in favour of atomic energy and uranium mining, and believed Australia should have its own atomic weapons.

•

While safety precautions for Australian aircrews were practically zero, British and American air forces insisted on far stronger controls for their own men monitoring the Australian tests. There was good reason. Before the 1952 Monte Bello explosion, the British had been warned against flying into the nuclear cloud. Dr W.G. Marley, head of the UK Health Physics Division, told the British Air Force that exposure from flying through a radioactive cloud would not be lethal – so long as it was more than fifteen minutes after the explosion. Marley added, though, that contamination of the aircraft would be likely to cause radiation exposure 'quite as serious as that arising from direct exposure from the cloud'.[6] Marley warned 'aircraft must avoid flying through the visible cloud following an atomic bomb explosion'. The Australians were never given that message. The RAAF was told: 'The radioactive hazard to aircrews in flying through this cloud is negligible and there is no fear of the aircraft becoming contaminated.'[7] Deliberate or a stuff up? Either way, it saved the RAF from doing the dirty work. After all, the Australians were only colonials.

The US had asked if it could monitor the 1953 tests at Emu Field using its own air force planes. The British, still keen on being permitted to participate with the American nuclear weapons testing program, quickly agreed. The British wanted to impress the Americans with their atomic acumen, even sending a film of the Monte Bello test to Washington. By this time the US had exploded forty-one nuclear weapons at its test sites in Nevada and the Marshall Islands in the Pacific. The Americans saw the British tests as a chance to practise techniques for monitoring Soviet nuclear bomb tests. They asked for permission to land USAF B-29s in Australia and to fly over Australian territory to follow the atomic clouds at a distance.

As soon as the British said it was OK for the Americans to join in the sampling of the atomic cloud from the series of Totem tests at Emu Field, Australia immediately gave permission for two B-29 long range bombers to land at Richmond RAAF base near Sydney. The B-29s were equipped with highly sensitive radiation-measuring equipment – far more sophisticated instruments than anything the Australians and British had. The USAF planes were to stay at least 640 kilometres downwind of the Totem explosions; only RAF and RAAF planes were to go near the mushroom clouds after the explosion. The Australian government sought to hide the true mission of the huge USAF planes, issuing a press release saying they were simply 'flying meteorological laboratories'.[8] The British weren't keen on the USAF planes getting too close to their own planes, and told the Australian government nuclear cloud samples should not be transferred to the USAF at the Pearce RAAF base. Britain wanted the transfer to take place at the Perth civil airport and at Sydney civil airport as the US would probably use civil aircraft to carry the samples to the United States.[9]

The first plane to fly into the atomic mushroom cloud after the Totem explosion was to be a British air force crew in a Canberra bomber. Six minutes after the explosion, the RAF crew took the Canberra into the rising tower of dirt and radioactive material at 9000 feet. It was so dark inside the boiling cloud the crew had to turn the lights on in the cockpit. But unlike the Australian Lincoln bombers, the RAF Canberra had been completely sealed with tape to stop radioactive dust getting to the men inside. The British airmen were told to wear oxygen masks throughout the flight. Not so the Australians. The British crew had radiation badges that would show the level they were being exposed to. The Australians had nothing like that. They weren't even tested when they landed.

The American readings of the radioactive cloud showed it was the most intense they had ever encountered – it had gone off the scale on their sensitive equipment. The Australians and Americans picked up conflicting directions for the nuclear cloud. The Americans said it was breaking up and drifting towards Brisbane. The Australians said they tracked it heading towards Darwin.

One of the RAAF Lincolns following the cloud was running very low on fuel and was forced to land at Williamtown air base – about 120 kilometres north of Richmond where the USAF planes were based. The crew was ordered to stay with the plane. The base put armed guards around the Lincoln to prevent anyone going near it. The next day the RAAF crew invited one of the American pilots to join them for the short flight from Williamtown to Richmond. The American had his own Geiger counter and he walked around the Lincoln checking the fuselage, wheels and the interior. One of the RAAF crew, Bruce Stein, heard the American muttering to himself, 'Oh shit, oh shit', as he read his Geiger counter.

'So, would you like a lift back to Richmond?' he asked. 'Christ no!' the American replied. 'That bloody machine is hot. I'm not going anywhere near it.' The American caught a train back to Richmond while the Aussies flew in the contaminated plane.[10]

•

Squadron Leader Geoffrey Tuck was one of the RAAF's most skilled and respected airmen. During the Second World War he was awarded the Air Force Cross for gallantry. In March 1952 he flew from London to Melbourne in the record time of twenty-four hours and twenty minutes in a new Canberra jet bomber. A happy photo of the 31-year-old officer being greeted at Melbourne airport by his wife, Edith, and two-year-old daughter, Jenny, made the newspapers.

In October 1952, Tuck was put in charge of the RAAF Airborne Radiation Detection Unit at Woomera. The unit's ten Lincoln bombers and two Dakota transport planes were ordered to fly into the atomic mushroom clouds of the two bombs exploded at Emu Field and follow the radioactive clouds as they drifted eastwards.

Less than three years later, Tuck was dead. He died of a rare form of testicular cancer, but his body was riddled with the disease. He was just thirty-four years old. For years his widow tried to get answers from Defence officials about what could have happened to him. He was fit and healthy before he went to Woomera, but fell sick soon after he returned. Defence would say only that the information was classified. A blanket was thrown over his records. Tuck died on 8 April 1955. He is listed on RAAF records as being officially discharged the next day, on 9 April.

When Jenny reached adulthood, she joined her mother searching for answers. She suspected her father's death had something to do with his service at Woomera during the nuclear tests. For forty-six long years, Defence officials refused to answer the family's questions, citing the Official Secrets Act.

It wasn't until 2001, when the government released the nominal roll of people who served at the nuclear tests, that the family finally discovered Squadron Leader Geoffrey Tuck had been part of the RAAF unit ordered to fly into nuclear clouds.

'The lies and deception have been just unbelievable,' Jenny Carson told the Adelaide *Advertiser*'s Colin James, who wrote a series of hard-hitting stories in 2001 revealing the extent of the official cover up of the British tests.[11]

'These guys served their country and this is how they and their families have been treated.'

•

The Americans had a lot more experience with radioactive clouds and took far more precautions than the Australians were instructed to. They were on oxygen from the moment they came into contact with the clouds until they landed. They were forbidden from eating or smoking the entire time and their aircraft were thoroughly sealed to prevent radioactive dust getting in.

Documents later unearthed by the Royal Commission revealed the British had told Australian air force chiefs there was little chance of contamination to either the planes or their crews.[12] So the RAAF did nothing to protect their men. It was only after complaints from Cheney's crew that measurements were taken of their plane. The tests found the plane was heavily contaminated and it was ordered to be cleaned. Both British and Australian scientists summoned to test the planes admitted they didn't even know RAAF Lincolns were being ordered to repeatedly fly through nuclear clouds. It was very much a military operation. Nine out of ten Lincoln planes used in the monitoring were found to be contaminated – several of them to a dangerous level.

The amount of time the RAAF Lincolns spent in the radioactive clouds was simply shocking. Planes sent into the cloud shortly after the explosion spent a total of ten minutes inside the radioactive dirt. Other planes spent thirty, forty-five and fifty-five minutes inside the clouds as they drifted across northern Australia.

•

If health protection was slack or non-existent for Australian airmen flying through the radioactive clouds, standards were just as low for RAAF people on the ground.

Frank Bingham served in the wartime British Royal Navy and was involved in the Allied landing at Normandy. After the war he moved to Australia and got a job as a mechanic with the Department of Supply at Emu Field. In 1984, he told the Royal Commission he was at the control base for both 1953 tests. He was never told he could be at risk from radiation or to stay out of certain areas.

Just before the first bomb went off, the men in the control base turned their back from the blast. The first blast – called Totem One – was less than half the size of the first test at Monte Bello the previous year. Scientists assumed they were safe at the base just 6.5 kilometres from the blast site.

After the blast, Bingham was invited by a scientist to go with him to see the crater. 'We put on a "goon suit" but no respirator. I was also given a dosimeter badge [a device that measures exposure to ionising radiation] that I gave back after the visit to the crater. I'm told it read forty millirems.'[13] This is the equivalent of four chest X-rays.[14]

After the first bomb on 15 October 1953, Bingham and other workers followed a sergeant into the site to remove sandbags from a bunker full of scientific gear. 'None of us had any protective clothing. We waited for the signal to start work when word came over the radio the area was too hot to touch and we should leave immediately. We left, but no radiation checks were done on us or the truck. This truck was used by us every day and as far as I know, it was never checked for radiation.'

They turned their backs for the flash of the second explosion on 27 October then turned to watch the cloud head south-east, towards the camp. It didn't look like the previous atomic clouds.

'The cloud looked like a heavy rain cloud. It was like a wall moving over the desert. We could see stuff falling to the ground inside the cloud. Two days later we were suddenly ordered to pack up our gear and get out immediately. They said to leave everything, like batteries and the generator, in the field. We were flown to Adelaide the next day.'

Bingham was puzzled, as they had been told they would be in Emu Field until Christmas. The sudden departure had all the elements of a panic. Something must have gone very wrong.

'They got us out as fast as they could. No one expected us when we reached Adelaide. One man threw up on the plane.'

Bingham pocketed rolls of unused film still in their original packages he'd seen at the base. He later found they had been exposed even though they were still in their packaging, a sure sign of radiation.

'Very soon afterwards I fell very sick. The doctor didn't know what was wrong. A year later when I went back to Woomera my teeth started falling out. It was so bad I couldn't eat. I got dentures in the Woomera Hospital. I also had a bad skin rash. For years I had dermatitis on my feet. My toenails fell out. When I left Woomera in 1955 I was constantly sick, tired and listless. I felt nausea constantly. In the 1960s, boils broke out all over my body.'

•

Merv Bale was a 21-year-old RAAF mechanic sent to Woomera in 1953 to clean and refuel planes. When the Lincolns finished their flights into the nuclear clouds, Bale was ordered to clean them as they sat on a distant part of the airfield. He was in shorts and boots. He wasn't warned about contamination or given any protective clothing.

'We knew they'd been through radioactive clouds but they said not to worry. We didn't know any better. We just did the job. But while I was cleaning the plane I suddenly felt dizzy and nauseous. I staggered over to the hangar where the Geiger counter team was, and I collapsed in front of them. By the time they got me into hospital, I'd passed out.

'I regained consciousness in Woomera Hospital forty-eight hours later. The medical orderly had to keep sponging me to get my temperature down. I was told I reached 104.2, which is life threatening.'[15]

Bale was moved away from Woomera shortly after this incident. Many years later he tried to find the medical records of his time in the hospital.

'They couldn't find them. The Department of Veterans' Affairs said all records from Woomera Hospital had disappeared. They wanted to keep it a secret that I had fallen sick while cleaning the plane. All hospital records disappeared. There were no records of anyone falling sick after coming into contact with those contaminated planes. It was deliberate cover-up of anyone who got sick.'

•

In 1954, Michael Hubert was a twenty-year-old national serviceman doing his time in the RAAF at Amberley air force base near Brisbane.

Hubert and a group of young 'nashos' were asked to volunteer for what they were told was 'aircraft duty'. They were handed buckets, brooms and soap and told to wash down a group of planes parked in a remote corner of the base well away from other planes. They were told these were special planes that had been used in the atomic tests and were in a quarantine zone.

'No one said they were radioactive and it didn't occur to us they might be dangerous. We didn't even know what radioactivity was. We thought it was just training on how to clean planes – where to stand on the wings and fuselage and so on. Anybody could walk up to these planes. There was no guard or anything to stop people going up to them. We weren't given protective gear or anything like that.'[16] As they scrubbed their way through the planes, Hubert and his mates discovered rations were still on board. 'We took the chocolates and ate them. We didn't ask, and nobody told us not to touch them.'

Dirt and muck from the plane washed over them as they scrubbed away. They were soaked by water as they stood underneath the wings and belly of the plane, reaching up with brooms to wash the fuselage.

'I thought at the time it was odd that no regular RAAF guys came near us. But we were nashos and that's pretty normal. They never tested us with Geiger counters or anything like that.'

Years later, Hubert developed serious skin cancers. He was twenty-five when he had his first operation, and has had forty to fifty operations since then. Strangely, his son also developed skin cancers at age thirty. Doctors said the contact with contaminated planes may have been the cause, but it might also be the Australian sun.

4
THE MYSTERY OF THE BLACK MIST

While Ed Cheney and his crew were preparing to fly into the atomic cloud of the Totem One bomb at Emu Field early in the morning of 15 October 1953, 173 kilometres to the north-west, eleven-year-old Yami Lester was playing in the red dust at Wallatinna, an isolated cattle station homestead. The Aboriginal boy filled a tin with red dust and rolled it around, keeping it going as long as he could before the dust trickled out. It was a simple game but in the flat, stony, desert country of far north South Australia, a boy had to make his own toys. Yami Lester was with his family in the heart of his Yankunytjatjara tribal land, and many Aboriginal people were at the camp near the homestead.

Most were just getting up. One was boiling the billy on the camp fire for the morning tea. Some had already left for work on the cattle station.

Suddenly Lester heard a huge bang in the distance. It was like an explosion, but Lester had never heard anything like it. It was a deep rumble, as though coming from the very bowels of the earth, almost like three or four bangs in quick succession. He stopped and listened to see if there would be another bang.

The noise had come from the south. But there was nothing out there that could make such a noise.

Puzzled adults in the camp asked each other what it might be. One suggested the army had fired a cannon. They'd heard the noise made by explosive testing coming from the Woomera testing range before, but that was too far away from Wallatinna for noise to reach. Lester shrugged and went back to playing until his mother had made damper for breakfast. Lester loved the warm, fresh bush bread and sat down with his mother, Pingkayi, and father, Kanytji, to eat.

The next morning, Lester noticed a big black cloud appear low on the horizon. It was rolling in from the south and was behaving very strangely. It wasn't like any other cloud Lester had ever seen. It was black, greasy looking and the sun shining on it glinted back, like it was reflecting off something solid. It was more like a black mist or dust storm. But there was no wind. Everything was quiet. Others noticed the low cloud too, and stopped what they were doing to watch it advance slowly and steadily towards them. It was very dark and made a whispering sound as it slowly rolled through the mulga trees.

'It stretched as far as I could see,' Yami Lester told the Royal Commission when he gave evidence in 1985.[1]

'As it came over the camp it blocked the sun. Everything went dark. It was like a thick black mist rolling along. It took a long time to pass over the camp. The old people were frightened as they'd never seen anything like it before. They thought it was "Mamu". It's a word that doesn't translate directly, but applies to something strange you don't understand that could be a bad or evil spirit. Mamu is frightening.'

The older men waved their woomeras at the cloud, trying to scare off this Mamu devil spirit. Aboriginal lore says if you wave your throwing stick at Mamu, it takes fright and goes another way. But this black mist just kept on coming. Women furiously dug holes to climb into as the black mist passed over them, telling the kids to get in and lie low. The black mist had a nasty metallic smell, like you get from smelter factories. Lester climbed into a hole with one of his relatives. It wasn't very deep and Lester could feel sticky dirt from the strange black mist and heard the faint hiss of it settling all around him.

'The cloud went over us and it kept on going for some time and then it was over.'

Kanytji Lester thought the noise was the sound of Wanambi, the water serpent of the Dreamtime, thumping the ground as it made water holes. Pingkayi remembered the cloud had a really strong pungent smell that made her vomit. A black, moist, sticky substance was left on the leaves of bushes, on their huts and on the ground as the cloud passed over them.

Pingkayi said that within a day several people in the camp fell sick. Their eyes became sore and watery. They had intense stomach pains with diarrhea and vomiting. Skin rashes appeared on many of the people touched by the black substance. Yami Lester started vomiting and had diarrhea. His eyes were incredibly sore and weeping.

Lester told the Royal Commission he thought several people died over the next few days. He couldn't be sure how many as they all moved camp. They moved several times over the next weeks. It's difficult to know how many died as Aboriginal people don't talk of the dead, moving on each time they bury a body.

'When a death happens the young people are not supposed to know about it. I was young at the time and I only guessed because people were upset and crying.'

Pingkayi said 'one thousand people' died.[2] The translator for the Royal Commission explained this was not a literal number. Pingkayi was just explaining that many people died. Many other Aboriginals said they knew people who died in the next few days after the black mist passed over Wallatinna. Some said a dozen old people and children died. Others said about forty. No doctor or medical official came to Wallatinna and the people in the camp quickly moved away.

Lester was frightened, as within days his eyes closed and he couldn't see. He eventually received treatment at a hospital and sight returned in his left eye, but everything at a distance was a blur. He was completely blind in his right eye. One morning he woke up and he was blind in his left eye too.

Doctors dismissed Lester's questions years later about whether it could have been caused by the black mist and exposure to radiation. They said the blindness came from him having measles as a child. But Lester said he never had measles.

Renowned eye doctor Professor Fred Hollows said it was unheard of for a person Lester's age to get a trachoma that causes blindness. He said if Lester was exposed to whole body irradiation between the ages of eight and twelve it was possible his immune system could be so depressed it might blind him in his teenage years.

•

The same morning Lester was playing in the dirt, Lalli Lennon was looking for opals at Mintabie, a remote camp east of Wallatinna. She sold the uncut opals to the miners at Coober Pedy. She was significantly closer to the Emu Field site. The Aboriginal officer had told them not to go near Emu but he seemed satisfied they would be all right at Mintabie.

Suddenly she heard 'a big bang like a thunder storm, then it got louder then it just vibrated. We were all very scared.'[3]

She saw black smoke rising in the south. She watched it with the other opal hunters as it grew and moved towards them.

'We were scared. We did not know what was going to happen next. We heard on the radio that a big bomb was going to go off. The noise and shaking really frightened us. We thought the ground was going to cave in. After a while when nothing happened we went back to looking for opals.

'Then we saw the black cloud low on the ground coming through the trees. It came quickly. We thought we were going to die. We got into a tent and covered up but then when nothing happened we got out. Dust was everywhere.'

That night the children fell ill. One was feverish. Another had a headache. Then they all got diarrhea and started vomiting. Skin rashes appeared on several of them. Eyes became very sore.

'The kids started having fits. We took them into Coober Pedy to the medical centre. But there was no doctor there. All were sick with upset stomachs. Their skin became dry and scabby. Sores broke out on their head and spread over their body. My son got it too.'

The rash also started on Lalli Lennon. 'I never really got rid of it. It comes and goes.' Doctors were at a loss to explain it. For many years doctors didn't know what it was before they finally wrote it down as psoriasis.

•

Meanwhile Almerta Lander at Never Never, a camp about 200 kilometres north-east of Emu Field, was puzzled why the birds were silent that morning. Usually there was a chorus of squawks and whistles to greet the new day. She then noticed low on the horizon a big dark curtain of cloud rolling towards them.

'It was the colour of a rain cloud, darkish. It didn't have the compact, rolling look that a rain cloud would have. It was just a sort of a mass and at the top of it was something most unusual like a banner that stretched upward from the top right across it. It wasn't like a cloud, more like a big banner with tendrils coming off it. There were no other clouds in the sky.'[4]

The base of the cloud reached down to the height of a short mulga tree. It stretched across the horizon heading east. She watched as the sinister-looking cloud came creeping towards her and went right over the top of the caravan. Dust drifted down from the cloud and landed on top of her.

'It was eerie as there was no wind, so it could not be a dust storm. The grey dust that fell was very sticky; very, very fine, soft and sticky. It was so fine that when you brushed it away it just rose up and settled down again. It was a beige-brown colour. We had to use a wet cloth to get it out of the caravan but it just smeared everywhere. I've never seen a dust storm like it.'

The family dusted off the pots and pans and cooked their dinner. There is no doubt they would have ingested some of the dust as it had settled on their food as well.

Her son later developed a severe lung complaint. No doctor could explain it. Lander developed a severe rash that wouldn't go away.

•

Shortly after the first atom bomb was exploded on the Australian mainland at Emu Field, Menzies was asked in parliament whether a thorough investigation could be made into the bomb's effect on human, animal and plant life in Australia. Menzies dodged the question. 'It has been stated most authoritatively that no conceivable injury to life, limb or property could emerge from the test,' Menzies thundered in the most imperious tone he could muster.[5] He went on to attack anybody who might question the ongoing nuclear program. He made no mention of Aboriginals who might be in the path of this deadly atomic experiment.

'I should like to say that it would be unfortunate if we in Australia began to display some unreal nervousness on this point,' Menzies scolded. 'The tests are conducted in the vast spaces in the centre of Australia and, if it is to be said however groundlessly, that there are risks, what will be said in other countries? Are we then to reach the position in which we shall not conduct these experiments? Believe me, the enemy will conduct them. If the experiments are not to be conducted in Australia with all our natural advantages for this purpose we are contracting out of the common defence of the free world. No risk is involved in this matter. The greatest risk is that we may become inferior in potential military strength to the potential of the enemy.'

•

The black mist receded into Aboriginal folklore. Stories of the terrifying creeping black cloud that brought pain and death was limited to low-voiced talk around camp fires in the outback. Aboriginal custom not to mention the dead helped keep the story from the ears of outsiders. Besides, what proof was there to link the deaths, rashes and blindness to the mysterious black mist? No scientists or doctors were asking or making the connection. In 1970 anthropologist Annette Hamilton heard stories of the black mist from Aboriginals, but didn't connect the story to the atomic tests until she saw it in the newspapers ten years later.

It wasn't until decades after the tests that the mystery of the black mist came to the attention of people in the big cities. In 1980 Yami Lester, by this time totally blind and an Aboriginal leader in central Australia, heard Titterton on radio talking about 'the Aboriginal people we looked after'. Lester was so angry he rang the Adelaide *Advertiser* newspaper to tell what had happened to him twenty-seven years earlier. Reporters Robert Ball, Peter De Ionno and David English investigated Lester's amazing story. Their front-page report 'A "Black Mist" that brought death' caused a nationwide sensation.[6] The report said that within hours of the mysterious black mist rolling over the camp, everyone was debilitated by uncontrollable vomiting and diarrhea. The group almost starved because they were too sick to gather food or go hunting. Within seventy-two hours healthy children went blind. Many never regained their eyesight. 'Within five days the old and the frail began dying. Some lingered for twelve months.'

Lester told the reporters Aboriginal people knew at the time that 'white-fella government business' was going on south of them. He had chosen to speak out about it because he'd heard government people claim Aboriginals were properly looked after during and after the blasts. 'I say bullshit to that.'

The reporters also tracked down 74-year-old Mrs Ellen Giles who, at the time of the blasts, ran the Welbourne Hill Station, north-east of Wallatinna, with her husband.

'I remember a cloud coming in – the dark girls ran to tell me a dust storm was coming,' she told the reporters.

'We shut up the house, closed windows and everything and waited for the storm to hit. But it was unusually quiet. Normally a dust storm roars, but this was quiet. There was no force. Yes, it was rather eerie . . . just a big, coiling cloud-like thing. We all stayed inside. Not even the black girls went out. After it had gone we went outside and the orange and lemon trees were coated in this dust. It was an oily dust. You could see it on the walls too. We tried to hose the trees down, but they just withered and died.'

Her husband and two employees died of cancer ten years later.

After the *Advertiser* story, more people came forward, some with stories of radiation contamination falling in the far north of Australia. The stories sparked a national outcry, increasing pressure on the Liberal government of Malcolm Fraser to investigate. South Australian Health Minister Jennifer Adamson ordered a check on Aboriginals in the far north of the state to see if the atom bomb tests had caused health problems. Federal Opposition health spokesman, Dr Neal Blewett, said the black mist report confirmed Labor's view there should be a thorough check on the health of people possibly affected by British atomic tests in Australia.

Days after the story appeared, Labor Senator Jim Cavanagh – a former Aboriginal Affairs Minister – told the Senate: 'We must have some clear investigation. The Aboriginals are deserving of consideration. We must find out whether that incident is the cause of the blindness that one can track from Emu through to the north of Australia and Darwin. There is more incidence of blindness among Aboriginals – what the medical profession is treating as trachoma – in that area than there is outside the passageway [the path of fallout]. Should this not be investigated?'[7]

The *Advertiser* followed up with another front-page story on 12 May 1980, declaring, 'A-Test "Mist" may have killed 50'. Doctor Trevor Cutter, sent by the South Australian government to investigate the paper's earlier report, made the alarming finding that at least thirty and possibly fifty Aboriginals could have died after contact with the black mist. He said cancer rates in Aboriginal communities had risen after the atomic tests from one in five years, to two every year.

'This thing is so much more widespread than we first thought,' Cutter said. 'We could be looking at 1000 people affected directly, more if there are genetic problems.'

He said there were stories of wandering Aboriginals encountering white men in white protective clothing and planes dropping 'cough medicine' to Aboriginals who fell ill after the black mist and a white station manager making them take the medicine. Cutter said there were reports from Aboriginals who were near Ernabella when an airplane took away the corpses of two Aboriginals, as well as unconfirmed reports of a mass grave containing Aboriginal bodies.

Despite the pressure, the Liberal government refused to budge. Prime Minister Fraser's Energy Minister, Senator John Carrick, said there was no need to order any investigation into the health of those who might be affected by the British tests. Carrick, who helped Menzies establish the Liberal Party, told the Senate there was 'no evidence of exposure to nuclear radiation significantly above the natural background level or that cancer rose from other than natural causes'.[8]

Titterton was utterly dismissive of the whole notion of black mists and radioactive clouds reaching human populations. As the uproar grew, he said on ABC national radio: 'No such thing can possibly occur. I don't know of any black mists. No black mists have ever been reported until the scare campaign was started.

The radioactive cloud is in fact at 30,000 feet, not at ground level, and it's not black . . . If you investigate black mists sure you're going to get into an area where mystique is the central feature and you'll never be able to establish or not.'[9] Titterton said an investigation 'would be a complete waste of time and money'.

Despite all the public assurances from Menzies and Titterton that everything had gone to plan at Emu Field and there was no danger, the evidence is clear that something went terribly wrong with the first two atomic bombs exploded on Australia's mainland under Operation Totem in October 1953.

Was there really a deadly black radioactive mist that spread hundreds of kilometres from the blast zone?

Was it the right weather to explode the first bomb?

Were there political pressures to explode the bomb on 15 October, just before Britain was to go into a major international arms conference with the Soviets?

Why did the scientists suddenly order the entire Emu Field camp be immediately abandoned and everyone flee after the second explosion on 27 October?

•

From the start, Operation Totem was a rushed project. Penney admitted as much to the Australian government chief scientist Alan Butement while they were looking for a new permanent testing site to replace Emu Field. On 20 October, seven days before the second Emu explosion, Penney told Butement in a conversation that was recorded and later revealed to the Royal Commission: 'The investment at Emu is part of the price that we have to pay for rushing the Totem trials.'[10]

A secret file prepared by British scientists five months before Totem One shows they didn't really know what sort of contamination they could expect from the atom bomb. Titled 'High Explosives Research Report No. A32', the file tried to estimate the rate contaminated particles fall back to earth after the explosion. It concluded contamination would be worst where a steady wind blows in the same direction at all heights of the bomb cloud. This would concentrate contamination in a narrow band for up to 190 kilometres.[11]

The A32 file, uncovered at the Royal Commission, predicted the blast for Totem One would be five kilotons. It ended up being twice that size. Weather conditions at the time of the blast were exactly what A32 said would produce the highest concentrations of contamination. So the scientists knew at the time that Totem One could produce a band of concentrated contaminated cloud that would stay intact for a couple of hundred kilometres, spreading radioactive material in the direction of the wind. No one checked to see if humans were in that potential danger zone. No one thought of the people at Wallatinna and Mintabie.

Months before the Totem trials, Penney assured Titterton and Martin, Australia's official observers at the trials, there was no possible risk of contamination in areas of settlement. Penney said winds would limit the nuclear cloud to below 30,000 feet and he was confident meteorological information would ensure no possible risk of danger to health. After this briefing, Titterton and Martin sent Menzies a top secret note in June 1953, four months before the scheduled Totem trials, guaranteeing the safety of the tests: 'We are able to assure you that the isolation of the site of the trials precludes any possible damage to habitation or living beings by the "shock" wave, thermal radiation, gamma rays and neutrons. It is possible for us to assure you that the time of firing will be chosen so that any risk to health due to radioactive contamination to our cities, or in fact of any human beings, is impossible. To sum up, on the basis of information before us, we are able to assure you, Sir, that no habitations or living beings will suffer injury to health from the effects of the atomic explosions proposed for the trials.'[12]

The first test was due to take place on 7 October, but it had to be postponed due to bad weather. Rain over the test site and the area meant it would be a week before there could be another attempt. This was annoying and embarrassing for Penney and his team because Churchill's top atomic adviser, Lord Cherwell, and other senior officials had secretly arrived at Emu Field to witness the explosion.

Cherwell was an arrogant aristocrat with some extreme racist beliefs. The teetotalling, non-smoking vegetarian regarded himself as superior to all others and hated being kept waiting while scientists dithered. Cherwell, like the British Royal family, was from German stock. He was born in Germany and studied physics in Berlin. He was a very close friend of Churchill, serving as his science adviser during the war. He advocated the blanket bombing of Germany, arguing destroying cities would break the will to fight. It wouldn't have been fun stuck with Cherwell in the outback; he believed an elite order of aristocrats and the intelligent should rule the world, advocated sterilisation of the mentally incompetent and argued for creating a lower class of slave humans controlled through drugs and brain surgery. Cherwell despised homosexuals, blacks and the working class. He never married and was always accompanied by his valet. An atom bomb would have been preferable company in the tent town at Emu Field.

Penney must have been relieved when Totem One was finally fired at 7 am on 15 October 1953. The ten-kiloton explosion sent up a cloud 15,000 feet – half the predicted level. Weather conditions were calm. The cloud dispersed slowly and drifted north-east – towards Wallatinna. Observation crews said the cloud remained very concentrated. It could even be seen at night. American air force pilots, experienced in following radioactive clouds from nuclear blasts, later told Australians they were staggered at the intensity of the radioactivity in the cloud, telling them it was the most intense they had every encountered. Their measuring instruments had gone off the scale.

When reports of the black mist first became public in 1980, the UK Ministry of Defence denied there could be any connection with the Totem One bomb. But, secretly, the British atomic weapons research facility commissioned meteorologist William Roach and radiologist Derek Vallis to see if the black mist story could be true. They examined the cloud shape, levels of radioactivity at the site, volume of soil swept up into the cloud and size of radioactive particles that made up the cloud. They reported a black mist after the blast was possible and could have travelled to Wallatinna, but that it couldn't have caused health problems so far away.

Vallis later admitted to the Royal Commission that their conclusions weren't based on any scientific measurements taken at the time simply because no readings had been taken.[13] There was no data whatsoever on how far the fallout had spread from Totem One. The cloud itself had been traced by aircraft all the way across Queensland and out to sea over Townsville. But no measurements were taken on the ground over that path. There were no medical records of Aboriginals in northern South Australia in the 1950s. It is taboo for Aborigines in that area to mention names of dead people, so it was almost impossible to trace who might have fallen victim to the black mist. Some medical researchers suggested Aboriginal people might have immune systems more vulnerable to low-level radiation, therefore the black mist could have been more deadly for Aboriginal people than the white population.

Finally, after much public pressure to investigate, in September 1980 the Australian Fraser government ordered the Australian Ionising Radiation Advisory Council (AIRAC) to investigate the black mist mystery. Three years later, just before the Fraser government went to an election, the council came back with a report. In a conclusion that surprised no one, it totally cleared safety procedures at the tests. The report, called AIRAC 9, concluded there was 'no evidence that any Aboriginals were injured by the nuclear tests'.

Labor won the March 1983 election and a year later set up the Royal Commission into the British Nuclear Tests in Australia. The Royal Commission got hold of AIRAC's internal notes on discussions with the Fraser government and found investigating officials had made up their minds before they even started. One of the AIRAC investigators noted 'the black mist question appears to be a myth in the making'. Investigators complained of the difficulty of getting first hand evidence from 'responsible persons'.[14] AIRAC would prepare a report that would 'allay public concern'. Investigators didn't talk to any people who had actually seen the black mist. Instead they spoke only to experts such as Titterton, who had already rubbished the black mist stories. AIRAC treated Titterton with kid gloves – he was even allowed to edit the transcript of his interview. The Royal Commission concluded AIRAC 9 was not an adequate scientific account of the safety program at the tests and investigators 'failed to make adequate inquiries before offering its conclusions'.[15]

That's a lawyer's way of saying the report was a total whitewash. The Royal Commission concluded scientific modelling showed the black mist could have happened, that there was no reason to disbelieve the black mist stories from the Aboriginal people, and that Aboriginal people at Wallatinna did receive radiation fallout. 'This may have made some people temporarily ill,' the commission concluded. But it said there was not enough evidence to say whether or not it caused other illnesses or injuries.

'Given the historical uncertainties and the current state of scientific knowledge, the evidence presented does not enable the Royal Commission to decide one way or the other whether the black mist caused or contributed to the blindness of Yami Lester.'

•

If Totem One had been rushed and exploded in less than ideal conditions, Totem Two was far worse. The bomb was exploded twelve days later in a tower in exactly the same weather conditions. It was slightly smaller, eight kilotons. Just like the first bomb, the mushroom cloud started drifting in a north-easterly direction. Suddenly, to the horror of watching scientists and military men, the wind shifted to the opposite direction. It was bringing the radioactive cloud right back over the blast zone and towards the makeshift camp where they were all watching. The alarm went off and everybody dropped what they were doing, jumped into vehicles and got the hell out of there.

This wasn't in the official accounts of what happened at Totem Two – it was all hushed up. But it does explain the 'Marie Celeste' atmosphere of the Emu camp discovered three years later by Australian military men who wandered over from where they were working at Maralinga. Like the empty ship of legend, everything at Emu had been abandoned: tools, food, tents, tables and equipment were all lying around exactly as they had been left three years earlier.

After abandoning Emu Field, British military experts looked around for a new atomic testing site. They had drawn up a long list of possibilities around the world, but like the porridge of the three bears, nothing was quite right. The Indian Ocean had a few nice islands but the Seychelles were too populated. Diego Garcia had no available land. Addu Atoll south of the Maldives unfortunately belonged to Ceylon (today's Sri Lanka). British territories in Africa were evaluated, but the best, British Somaliland, had a nomadic population hard to keep track of and winds could shift (just like Australia). In the Atlantic the Falkland Islands were deemed too remote and difficult to access, while the Bahamas had unsuitable winds. Besides, Americans might not be too happy having their holiday resorts blown up. Australia, of course, was Goldilocks land – everything was just right.

The British told RAF Air Marshal Sir Thomas Elmhirst to look around Australia for a good spot to explode an atom bomb. Elmhirst sat down for a cup of tea with Lord Cherwell, Churchill's odious atomic adviser. Cherwell said he liked islands and he'd looked at a few maps and thought Groote Eylandt off the coast of the Northern Territory looked about right. Advisers said the problem was people in the area called it home, and it got inundated in the wet season. Fine, said Cherwell, and turned the map around to the south. He pointed to Cape Barren Island off the north coast of Tasmania. Let's have that one. Elmhirst pointed out there was a sheep station on it. That didn't deter Cherwell. 'Pay them and get them off the island' was Cherwell's attitude.[16] Cape Barren Island escaped being turned into a nuclear test site when they discovered it is one of the windiest places in the world.

Len Beadell, an outback bushman and surveyor who had explored Emu Field for the Totem tests, explored areas near Emu never seen before by white men. About 200 kilometres south, he found a large area of mulga scrub land that seemed ideal. It was remote, had bore water and low, undulating hills that could protect men from the shock wave from atomic blasts. Penney came in for a secret inspection. He met up with Beadell and Australia's chief scientist, Alan Butement. Penney agreed it was suitable for a permanent nuclear-testing base. It was thirty-five kilometres north of the east–west railway line and there was a siding at the tiny settlement of Watson that could act as the gateway to the large camp that would be needed for the coming atomic tests.

Penney did ask whether there were any Aboriginals nearby. Beadell had seen signs of Aboriginal pathways in the area. He was excited when he drove to the top of a plateau and found an extraordinary ancient ceremonial ground unlike anything ever discovered. Sixty vertical shale slabs, nearly identical in size, stood at regular intervals in a line stretching 120 metres.

Half-a-dozen larger clusters of shale slabs stood like pyramids about one metre high. One pyramid built on rock stood taller and apart from the others. No white man had seen anything like this before. Beadell dubbed it the Aboriginal Stonehenge. 'It was obviously an ancient Aboriginal ceremonial ground built by those primitive stone-age nomads in some distant Dreamtime,' Beadell later wrote in his memoir.[17] Its purpose was a mystery but clearly it was a sacred site. Beadell found charcoal under the surface proving it had been a camping site for Aboriginals.

'There was an ironic clash of old and new here, as only a few short miles away the first mighty atom bomb ever brought to the mainland of Australia was to be blasted into immediate oblivion in several weeks' time . . .' Beadell wrote.[18]

The area was clearly important for Aboriginal heritage, but this wouldn't stop the nuclear scientists.

Butement and Penney were with Beadell at the time and looked over the exciting discovery. Butement later put down on paper in a letter to Penney: 'I am given to understand that this area is no longer used for Aboriginals. There was a track from Ooldea up to the north through the area roughly where Emu is now, but here again I understand that this is now not used except by one or two elderly blacks and then on rare occasions and that there is no need whatever for Aboriginals to use any part of this country around the proposed area.'

Penney replied: 'That sounds very satisfactory.'[19]

They stole Aboriginal land, so why not steal Aboriginal language? They named the new atomic bomb site 'Maralinga', a Pitjantjatjara dialect word for 'field of thunder'.[20]

5

A 'BEAUTIFUL' BOMB

In 1956, two and a half years after the blasts at Emu Field, the British returned for a third series of atom bomb tests in Australia. It was to be a bumper year for atom bombs – the British planned to blow up a total of six on Australian soil. The first two, codenamed Operation Mosaic, were to be exploded in May and June in a return to the Monte Bello Islands. Britain wanted the isolation of the remote islands for these two as they were planning a truly monster bomb, the biggest they had ever exploded, one that would put Britain up with the Americans and Russians.

In London, Churchill was keen to expand the British nuclear weapons program as fast as possible. Military chiefs and Churchill's atomic adviser, Lord Cherwell, had been pushing for a stockpile of 200 bombs so that Britain could be regarded as partners with the United States in containing the Soviet communist menace. Churchill told his cabinet Britain could not maintain its influence as a world power unless it had the biggest and newest weapons. If Britain wanted to prevent war, he said, it had to be made clear to potential aggressors they would be met with devastating retaliation from British nuclear weapons.

The prospect of the Cold War breaking into a hot war seemed very real in the 1950s. International events were moving fast.

The arms race madness was out of control as each side struggled to produce bigger and more powerful nuclear bombs. Both sides were working on the next generation of nuclear weapon, the thermonuclear bomb, also called the hydrogen or fusion bomb. On paper, the explosive power of this type of bomb was limitless. The atom bomb got its energy from splitting the atom of heavy elements like uranium and plutonium, a process called fission. The thermonuclear explosion was based on fusion, joining together isotopes of the lightest element, hydrogen. The energy released by this process was far bigger. It needed the power of an atom bomb just to act as the trigger to provide the heat needed to create fusion of the hydrogen atoms.

Just two months before the 1953 British tests at Emu Field, the Soviets stunned the West when they exploded their first hydrogen bomb. It was the biggest blast to date, at 400 kilotons – forty times more powerful than the British bomb at Emu. But it was mere fireworks compared to what was to come.

In 1954 the US hit back with its first thermonuclear blast at Bikini Atoll in the Pacific Marshall Islands. It had the incredible power of 16,000 kilotons – 900 times more powerful than Hiroshima. The size of the blast shocked even the scientists. They were expecting an explosion half that size – around 8000 kilotons. It was the dirtiest bomb ever exploded, spreading radioactive clouds around the globe.

People the world over shook their heads in horror. This was far bigger than was needed to destroy any city in the world. Mankind now had the ability to destroy itself. Some cried 'Enough!' Stop the Bomb protests grew. But the peaceniks were up against the Cold War in deep freeze. The Bikini Atoll blast sent the Soviets racing to build an even bigger bomb. In Washington, Senator Joseph McCarthy was discovering Reds under every bed, creating a climate of fear and suspicion that few dared oppose. Menzies whipped up Australia's own anti-communist hysteria with the defection of Soviet spy Vladimir Petrov and his wife's dramatic rescue by Australian security agents from an airplane taking her to Moscow. The Labor Party split, with the anti-communist Catholic right wing of the party breaking away to form a new party, the Democratic Labor Party. All this conveniently just before the 1954 election. Menzies was on a path to losing until the Petrov excitement and the Labor Party split gave him victory.

For some the Cold War was terminally hot. The Korean War raged from 1950 until the armistice in July 1953. Menzies heavily committed Australia to the Allied fighting force. Australian casualties numbered 340 dead and 1500 wounded. Despite pressure from US military commanders, America did not use the atom bomb during the war. When President Eisenhower was elected in 1953, he considered using atom bombs to break the communist front line. But the death of Stalin in March, and the lack of a winning strategic target for an atomic strike, enabled Eisenhower to do what he wanted after losing 36,000 troops: strike a ceasefire agreement and get out.

Menzies also had Australian troops engaged against communists in the Malayan Emergency – the RAAF from 1950 and the Army from 1955. Cold War dirty tricks were in full play when the CIA toppled the democratically elected government of Iran in 1953 and installed a puppet regime under the Shah. In 1956 the UK, France and Israel attacked Egypt to stop nationalisation of the Suez Canal. Soviet tanks crushed a pro-West uprising in Hungary.

Britain saw Operation Mosaic at Monte Bello as essential to developing a British thermonuclear bomb. Not that the Australian public at the time knew any of this. They were told only that Monte Bello would again be used to test British atomic weapons. The Australian military would be involved in the physical work of laying out the ground-monitoring stations, flying through nuclear clouds and cleaning up afterwards.

Australian scientists were barred from any detailed knowledge of the bombs. Documents written before the 1956 Mosaic and the Buffalo series of tests at Maralinga show the British were intent on covering up what was really going on. On 22 December 1955, five months before the Mosaic tests at Monte Bello, Sir William Penney wrote a secret memo to Sir Frederick Brundrett at the UK Ministry of Defence: 'We think it likely that the Australians will ask us for filters which have been flown at Mosaic and Buffalo. While I am not keen on giving them samples, I do not see how we can refuse. I am recommending that, if they ask us, we give them a little piece of the filters, but we wait a few days so that some of the isotopes have decayed a good deal.'[1] The nice 'Call me Bill' Penney didn't want his hosts to know how much he was poisoning their country.

Britain did not want Australians to know that Operation Mosaic actually involved testing triggering devices for hydrogen bombs. They kept from the public that the second Mosaic bomb would contain components of a fission-fusion thermonuclear bomb, something Australia had not known about or agreed to.

The Soviets weren't the only reason the British felt in a race against time. For the first time the anti-bomb movement in the West was gaining traction. In March 1954 the Americans detonated their first fifteen-megaton hydrogen bomb at Bikini Atoll. Horror stories of radiation fallout spreading around the world from the massive bomb sparked widespread public opposition to atmospheric nuclear tests. A large number of MPs in the British Labour Party called for an end to such tests. In July 1955 British philosopher Bertrand Russell and renowned scientist Albert Einstein signed a manifesto highlighting the dangers posed to humanity by nuclear weapons. Thousands marched against the bomb in capitals around the world.

In April 1955 Churchill stepped down as prime minister due to ill health. Menzies was devastated – his hero had left the stage. They kept in close touch and Menzies continued to consult Churchill, particularly about Commonwealth matters. Perhaps Menzies lamented what might have been: if he had taken up suggestions made to him in the late 1940s to leave Australia and take a seat in the House of Commons, he might have been Churchill's successor as Prime Minister of the United Kingdom. It would have meant weekly chats with the Queen.

Churchill's successor, Anthony Eden, continued Britain's atomic policy. Eden wrote to Menzies explaining the Mosaic tests would 'consist of atomic explosions with inclusion of light elements as a boost. It would of course be made clear in any public announcement that explosions were atomic and not thermonuclear.'[2]

Thus the cover-up of the true nature of the Mosaic tests started long before the bombs exploded. The use of 'light elements' to boost an atomic explosion turns it into a thermonuclear bomb. An internal British secret cable a year before the Mosaic tests warned 'any mention of thermonuclear is political dynamite and must be avoided in announcements of trials'. Another secret message inside the UK Ministry of Defence said: 'The greatest difficulty relates to the reason we give to the decision [for the Mosaic tests]. We cannot avoid telling the Australians that the bombs fired will contain small quantities of thermonuclear material. In the statement attached, the reason for the trials is linked with the development of small atomic bombs, the yields of which are boosted by using small quantities of thermonuclear material . . . The correct reason is to obtain early information on the likelihood of success of the one megaton [1000 kilotons] weapon as conceived at present.'[3]

Eden told Menzies the second round of atomic explosions at Monte Bello would be, at most, two and a half times the force of the first blast in Operation Hurricane. But Britain had never officially told Australia the size of the Hurricane blast. The fact it was twenty-five kilotons didn't come out until years later.

Despite indications Mosaic would be a much bigger thermonuclear blast, it took Menzies just five weeks to give it the green light. Menzies even apologised that the Australian military might not be able to provide all the logistical assistance Britain might want at Monte Bello as Australian troops were already committed to supporting Britain in the Malaya Emergency and preparing for tests at Maralinga.

In September 1955 Eden and Menzies released a joint statement that new trials would take place at Monte Bello in April 1956. None of the blasts, the statement said, would exceed 'a few tens of kilotons'. Just in case pesky reporters or subversive anti-nuclear types weren't satisfied by this bland announcement and asked awkward questions, the helpful British Defence Ministry provided a list of answers to questions that might be put to Australian government ministers in Canberra. It was masterful misleading spin and obfuscation:

'Q: Have any of these tests any connection with an H-Bomb?

A: There will be no explosion of an H-Bomb nor any explosion of the character or magnitude of that bomb, but all atomic tests contribute information to the development of H-Bombs.

Q: Are these actual weapons or are they test equipment which may be used in various types of weapons?

A: No statement can be made.'[4]

The Menzies government set up a formal safety committee to determine whether safety precautions at the tests were adequate. The first chairman was to be Leslie Martin of Melbourne University, with Titterton and several other Australian scientists on the committee. Within two years, Titterton replaced Martin as chairman. Australian scientists' knowledge of the real nature of the Mosaic bombs was extremely limited. But for the first time in the series of atomic tests, Australia's chief scientific representatives at the Mosaic tests – Titterton, Butement and Martin – would be the official safety committee. Until now they had only been permitted to attend as observers. Now their role was to safeguard the safety of Australians – both military people and civilians at the blast site as well as citizens across the continent. Officially they had the power to call off a blast. They never did. As for protecting the wellbeing of Australians across the country, that came a long second to making sure Britain's bombs went off as planned.

•

Eighteen-year-old Australian sailor Doug Brooks had a close encounter of the deadly kind with the Cold War even before he reached Monte Bello. He was fresh out of training in Sydney in March 1956 when he was 'volunteered' for a top secret mission.

'All we were told was that half-a-dozen of us ratings would be flying out of Sydney that night and we weren't to tell a soul,' Brooks later recalled.[5]

'We boarded a plane and after a few stops landed in Hong Kong. We didn't know what it was all about until they told us we'd been seconded to a British navy frigate, HMS *Alert*. We got a rather curt, cold greeting from the officer of the watch telling us we were late and had held up the ship's departure. I thought, "Welcome to the Royal Navy."'

Brooks was surprised to discover the Australian sailors had been brought aboard the RN ship to replace Chinese crew members who'd been used for menial tasks such as washing clothes, cleaning toilets and the like.

'They'd been offloaded at Hong Kong. The British didn't want them on board for where we were going.'

To Brooks and the other young Australian sailors, their destination was a mystery. They sailed to Singapore navy base and for days helped load crates and boxes aboard. He figured with all these provisions they would be at sea for some time, but he still had no idea of their mission.

Brooks and three other Australian sailors were given a break from this menial work and told to report for duty in Singapore.

They got on a civilian bus to go into the exotic city. Dressed in navy whites and crowded in by locals, it was Brooks' first taste of the Orient and he found it all very exciting. The bus left the navy base and chugged through hilly jungle country. Suddenly gunshots shattered the bus windows.

'We threw ourselves on the floor of the bus. We knew there were communist insurgents in the region, but we had no idea they were right inside Singapore. I looked around. Everyone else was on the floor but we were huge targets in our dress whites.'

Machine-gun blasts continued to rake the side of the bus. Glass showered down on the people inside.

'The locals were screaming and some tried to escape by running out the door at the front of the bus. We kept our heads down and flat to the floor of the bus. We knew they'd kill us if they saw us.'

Brooks heard people outside screaming in terror as the gun blasts continued. And then the firing stopped. Brooks never saw the attackers. Military vehicles raced up. Armed soldiers poured out and ran into the jungle after the communist insurgents. A British major waving a pistol entered the bus and told the sailors to stay low until they cleared the area. After a while they were told to get off the bus and into jeeps to go back to the navy base.

'The scene that greeted us outside was horrific. Several bodies lay strewn across the road and blood ran in little rivulets down the gutter.'

It was a rough introduction to the Cold War for the young sailors. HMS *Alert* was at battle stations and left harbour in the middle of the night.

It wasn't until they were well out to sea that the ship's captain addressed the crew. He told them they were heading for the west coast of Australia to provide logistic support for the next British nuclear test. He ordered all cameras confiscated and told them letters home would be heavily censored.

Brooks was horrified. In quiet tones, he talked with other crew, who were also mortified at the prospect of being struck by radiation.

'I'd heard radiation could make you sterile. I hadn't volunteered for this.

'Morale on board was really low. Some even talked of deserting the ship if they had a chance. I knew this was ridiculous and I told the Poms that even if the ship touched land there was simply nowhere to go in north-west Australia. It was all desert.'

When HMS *Alert* pulled into the lagoon of the Monte Bello Islands, men were already erecting huts and bunkers on the white sands.

'We were told we could go on to the islands for a bit of R&R. There was a canvas shelter dubbed The Lido where we could get a cold beer. This was most welcome because when I was on HMS *Alert* I wasn't allowed to join the traditional Royal Navy daily tot of rum as I was underage.'

Brooks and other sailors swam in the lagoon during their time off.

'But the mood changed when we discovered signs suggesting the area still remained radioactive from tests conducted there four years earlier. Nobody warned us before we went ashore.

'We asked ourselves if we were intentionally being exposed to residual radiation to see how it affected us. There were a lot of unhappy sailors on board and some talked of jumping ship if they got the chance. I didn't agree with them, but I could understand why it would be better to spend time in the slammer than be used as guinea pigs exposed to radiation to see how quickly it kills you.'

Brooks was ashore when a helicopter swept in and it was announced there was a surprise visit by the First Sea Lord, Earl Mountbatten.

'We were mustered on a sandy tract of beach and Mountbatten

stood on top of a rock and told us what a great job we were doing. He got back in the helicopter and was gone in a flash.'

A few days later HMS *Alert* sailed to Onslow to pick up supplies and several scientists. Brooks went ashore with a few others for a quiet beer.

'Two Pommy sailors in the pub said they weren't going back to Monte Bello and would try and get to Perth. I told them they had no chance as it was 1400 kilometres and bugger all in between. I heard they were picked up the very next day trying to hitchhike south. They were flown back to England for whatever punishment awaited them. At least they wouldn't have to face what was going to come our way in the days ahead.'

When 16 May rolled around Brooks was assigned to duty below decks. HMS *Alert* was nine nautical miles from ground zero when the fifteen-kiloton atomic bomb dubbed G1 exploded.

'We were at action stations and my post was the forward magazine. I knew the bomb was about to go off and I was in a cold sweat. Yes, I was scared. Not being able to see what was going on made it even worse.

'Suddenly a great tremor shook the ship, followed by a very loud bang. I thought of deserting my post but there was nowhere to go. There was dead quiet after that until the captain announced a return to normal. I climbed to the deck and one of the sailors said we'd switch for the next bomb – I'd be up top and he'd be down below. I didn't like this at all. Why expose all of us? What good could come of rotating the crew so we could see the atomic mushroom cloud?'

Brooks' apprehension grew steadily over the next four weeks as HMS *Alert* ferried equipment and scientists back and forth. Then early in the morning on 19 June, Brooks was issued a radiation detector badge and the crew was instructed to turn their backs and close their eyes before the bomb went off.

'They'd been waiting for the wind to be in the right direction, to blow the radioactive cloud to the north and away from the mainland. But I knew, as did all the other Australians, that prevailing winds over Australia are from west to east. This would take the cloud right over Australia.'

HMS *Alert* moved to the same position it had for the previous test – south of the islands and nine nautical miles from ground zero.

The ship's address system was patched into the master control system so the crew could listen to the countdown. Brooks joined other off-duty crew on the forward deck. He was dressed in just shorts and sandals.

'Why haven't we got any protective gear? The bastards are using us as guinea pigs,' Brooks thought to himself. Speaking quietly to other crew members Brooks discovered many agreed with him.

As the countdown reached the last thirty seconds the men were ordered to face away from the blast and cover their eyes with their hands.

'As the count went from ten down to one, I was overcome with fear. Suddenly on zero there was an enormous flash of white light. It was so powerful I could feel it burning my neck. I could see right through my hand and saw the bones of my fingers as in an X-ray.

'Almost immediately after the bright flash a great thunder clap hit my ears, followed by a rolling tremor that vibrated the deck, causing me to lose my footing.'

In less than a minute the men were ordered to turn around. Brooks' legs were wobbling like jelly as he turned and opened his eyes.

'I was awestruck – a great black billowing mushroom cloud was rising into the air. Inside it I could see a huge boiling fireball climbing up with the cloud. I stared. I couldn't take my eyes off it. I saw what looked like walls of molten glass rolling out towards the horizon.'

Brooks saw two specks high in the sky heading straight towards the mushroom cloud.

'I couldn't believe my eyes – two planes were heading straight into that boiling hell. This is madness!'

Brooks watched intently as the first plane flew straight into the cloud. Within seconds it came out the other side. He didn't realise it, but he'd been holding his breath the whole time. He let it out when he saw the plane emerge from the huge mushroom cloud, but he was almost sick to the stomach over what he had seen. He turned to go below deck, not wanting to see any more of this bizarre display of atomic power.

'Just as I started to move away a triumphant voice came over the ship's address system. The boffins were announcing they had got the result they had been hoping for. The yield from G2, as they called it, was the equivalent of ninety-eight kilotons and would facilitate ongoing tests and allow for the detonation of a thermonuclear device.'

Brooks turned to the sailor next to him and muttered: 'Heaven help us all.'

He was mortified when a few hours later the ship steered north and headed straight towards the channel between the Monte Bello Islands that led to ground zero.

'We were nudging forward at about five knots. Dead fish were floating on the surface all around us. Hundreds of them. Sea turtles lay upside down, their gleaming shell backs reflecting the sun high overhead. It was a nightmare.'

Someone at the bow yelled to lower the cutter and pick up the easy catch. For once Brooks was pleased to hear the order from the captain. 'No, we will not eat the fish.'

Normally this devastation would be a feast for sea birds. But there were none around. The place was eerily silent. As they approached the island Brooks was stunned to see that a big chunk of land was simply gone. Clouds of steam rose from the sand that was still glistening from the heat of the blast. It was shiny, as though the sand had been turned to glass.

Within minutes of dropping anchor, the crew were ordered to lower the ship's cutter: the scientists on board were keen to retrieve their instruments. The crew and boffins wore white overalls and rubber boots. Brooks was surprised they hadn't been issued breathing gear too.

'Within an hour we saw the cutter racing back, people on board waving their arms. They seemed to be in a bit of a panic. When they got close enough they shouted they'd snared the boat on some floating debris and contaminated their craft.'

Brooks helped raise the cutter from the water and the crew trained sea-hoses on the boat, washing it down. Scientists waved Geiger counters over the vessel and registered very high radiation. Brooks thought of deserting his station and hiding in a deep hole, but there was nowhere to run to. The crew were swearing under their breath. They weren't happy at bringing this radioactive boat on board. HMS *Alert* raised anchor and sailed back out the channel. The ship stayed in the area for a few more days as scientists carried out their work.

'Several members of the crew fell sick, vomiting violently and constantly nauseous. The skipper was flown off sick. We had all been using sea water turned into fresh water. I thought it had to be contaminated.'

Eventually the ship sailed to Onslow to offload the scientists. The crew were told their tasks at Monte Bello had been fulfilled. Brooks said by this time several members of the crew were feeling sick. He thought it might be from radiation, but he didn't know for sure. They couldn't tell how much radiation they'd received: none of the radiation badges had been collected.

'They were a waste of time. Or did they not want to know? We'd gone in to the blast zone very soon after the atomic bomb and we'd been able to function as a ship's crew. Was that the real experiment? Were we all used as guinea pigs to see how soon we could enter the area after an atom bomb?'

Life didn't go well for Brooks after Monte Bello. He was only eighteen at the atomic blast but his life changed that day. He left the navy in 1961, hit the grog pretty hard, married in 1963, but had difficulty working. He had a breakdown in 1991 and was diagnosed with bone disease and PTSD. He'd be drunk by 11 am and staring out the window in his dressing gown.

'I watched a science fiction film about life after a nuclear holocaust and I just collapsed in a heap. I had nightmares about that nuclear cloud.'

His wife helped him get back on track. His first son was born with mild spina bifida, but his two other children and six grandchildren are OK.

'I was on edge every time the family was having a baby, out of fear they might have health problems or deformities caused by my exposure. It's had a terrible impact on my life. I've contemplated suicide many times as I felt I was a burden on my family. All I want is an apology from the government for how we were used.'

•

Sub-Lieutenant Bob Dennis was a 22-year-old navigating officer on HMAS *Karangi*, an odd-looking wartime boom defence vessel brought out of mothballs specially for the 1956 Monte Bello tests. *Karangi* had been bombed in Darwin in the Second World War but was now stripped of most of her gear, including hatch covers and hoses. She could manage just eight knots but the gutted 400-ton ship, which had absolutely no protection against radiation, was deemed suitable for transport purposes at Monte Bello.

'We were far away at Onslow when the bomb went off and we didn't see it, but we were at Monte Bello later the same day and we sailed right in to the lagoon,' Dennis said later.[6]

'I'm sure we were the first there. I don't remember seeing another ship until the next day when one of the boats from HMS *Narvik* came in. We all laughed as they were dressed in protective gear and white overalls while we had none. All we had were boots and shorts. Most of us didn't wear a shirt. I was wearing a shirt and cap as I was an officer. We knew nothing about radiation and the dangers we faced entering the blast zone.

'HMS *Narvik* and HMS *Alert* came into the lagoon after that and we were assigned to help ferry the boffins and their marines around the lagoon. I was in charge of a landing craft with about twenty British Royal Marines and engineers. We went in to salvage any pieces we could find, such as generators and jeeps left on the islands. All this debris was taken on board *Karangi* as deck cargo. It would be offloaded in Fremantle. Everything was covered in dust, but we had no hoses to clean them off. Throughout the entire week we were at Monte Bello we had no protective gear at all. We had no wash-downs, no anti-radiation measures whatsoever.'

Dennis said they were issued film badges that were exchanged twice a day, but they weren't told the results of the readings.

'We walked over ground zero several times but we were never warned about the dangers. The sand was black and brittle like flakes of glass, crackling underfoot as we walked over it. The sand had fused together in the heat of the explosion.' Dennis said the Royal Marines they were working with also had no protective gear, no warnings about radiation, no wash-downs and no Geiger counters run over them.

'It was stinking hot so we swam in the lagoon on our time off. We even caught fish to eat. No one told us we shouldn't swim or eat the fish.'

Dennis was invited to HMS *Alert* for a thank-you dinner with the scientists. Penney thanked them for their hard work. Two days later they left for Fremantle. Dennis didn't think much about his time on Monte Bello until about seven years later.

'I suddenly developed this unexplained bleeding from my nose and mouth and it went on for years. Doctors couldn't explain it. They gave me urine tests that showed blood. I had nausea and vomiting. I don't know if it was from radiation exposure. Nobody could tell me.'

His wife had a miscarriage. Their first son born in 1960 had psoriasis. Their second son had diabetes from age eleven. Their third son had eyesight problems.

'I didn't really connect any of this to my time at Monte Bello until I saw a *60 Minutes* program on TV in about 1982. They interviewed Howard Beale, who was Minister of Supply at the time of the tests and he said all Australian servicemen were supplied with protective clothing at the tests.

'I was furious as I knew this was a lie. I rang Channel 9 and told them. I never heard back from them. It turned my whole thinking around. I wondered what other lies they were telling us about the atomic tests. I talked to the Royal Commission but the navy wasn't interested in what I had to say. The navy acted like a door had been slammed shut on what happened at Monte Bello.'

•

Bill Hunter was a young physicist working for the Department of Supply assigned to Operation Mosaic. His task was to see if it was possible to tell the size of an atom bomb by measuring the amount of electromagnetic radiation it released.

'There were a few of us doing the tests and I was positioned by myself about sixty kilometres from the Monte Bello detonations on the mainland at Mardie sheep station.[7]

'When the first bomb went off on May 16 we were told the wind would take the mushroom cloud debris to the north-west. I was inside the caravan taking measurements on the instruments when it detonated.

'About a minute after the explosion I went outside and saw the mushroom cloud rising to a certain height and it was going out to sea. An hour or so later I saw the cloud turn around and come back right over me.

'I never thought of danger. I was just twenty-four. But I watched it go over my head and I felt a sudden nausea. I knew it was a classic symptom of radiation. I didn't feel any dust or dirt land on me. I was the only human being around for the next few hundred kilometres so there was no help.

'They'd given me a supply of sticky flypaper-type badges to hang up around the place. At certain times I was to take them down and post them off to the radiation lab in Melbourne.

'I never got any feedback from them, but they must have known fairly soon after that first bomb test that there was a bit of danger. I never had any other symptoms even though when I was at Maralinga I was even closer to the explosion.'

While Hunter was at Monte Bello he met a navy commander who said he had walked right up to the crater hours after the explosion and looked down into it.

'I thought at the time he was a bloody idiot. He would have got a fatal dose. Three months later I heard he was dead.

'There was no warning of radiation dangers after the explosion, and I knew as a physicist it would be deadly. I don't think the nuclear scientists even knew I was there at Mardie. Everything we were doing was secret and we didn't mix or compare notes. I'd signed the Official Secrets Act so couldn't say anything to anybody. But they must have known pretty soon afterwards that the cloud blew over Mardie. Prevailing winds always go east in Australia. The radiation did go east with the wind and they must have recorded it.'

When Hunter recounted his story in 2013 the cancer that had gripped him in 2000 was taking its toll. 'I have non-Hodgkin Lymphoma – a type of cancer that can be caused by exposure to radiation. But there's no way to prove my exposure to the Monte Bello bomb in 1956 caused me to develop cancer forty-four years later.

'We trusted governments to look after our welfare much more then than we do today. We've learned not to be so trusting.

There's no doubt back in the 1950s we saw the atom bomb as protecting us from the Soviets. I thought I was doing my bit for Australia's defence. I now realise we were being used as guinea pigs.

'But at the time they had to make decisions like that as we needed to know the effects of exposure to atom bombs. It was a different era. You couldn't do that sort of testing on humans now.'

•

David Brennan was a nineteen-year-old doing his national service as a sailor on the corvette HMAS *Junee*. In 1956 the old wartime minesweeper was being used as a training ship so it had a crew of young, inexperienced sailors on board. The ship sailed up the coast from Fremantle and put in at Onslow.

'We took civilians on board. I later found they were English scientists. We were told nothing until we were mustered on deck and one of scientists lectured us on what makes an atom bomb. He told us how it works and what sets it off. We thought this was exciting, but we still had no idea what we were going to do. We knew there had been tests at Monte Bello in 1952. I thought they were going to have a look to see what was still there four years later.[8]

'When we got to Monte Bello there was a whole fleet of ships. The British navy ship HMS *Narvik* was HQ for the scientists. A destroyer patrolled for security and small landing craft zipped back and forth.

'We still weren't told what our ship would be doing. They'd already had one atomic bomb go off a few weeks before we got there. Obviously they were preparing for a second one. Onslow was a shallow water port and corvettes are small warships so we were one of the few that were able to dock there. We spent a long time ferrying stuff out to the islands including food, people and crates of equipment.'

Junee anchored in the lagoon. Brennan and other sailors climbed into a landing barge in shorts and sandals and were taken ashore.

'We spent a few days manning a very large concrete mixer. There were bits of molten metal everywhere and it was obvious the island had been devastated.

'The other thing was the British scientists were coming ashore in full protective gear, glass visors and respiratory gear. They walked around with Geiger counters. They never came near us while we were on the island. They were working about fifty to 100 metres from us while we built a big concrete base. The blast zone from the first atomic test a few weeks earlier was about 300 metres away. They gave us some badges to wear all the time. They said if we were to be exposed to any radiation, which is highly unlikely, then the badge would change colour.

'We thought that's interesting – what happens then? But these badges were never checked or collected. Most of them were lost or fell off. No one collected them. When we got back to Perth most of us threw them in the bin.'

Brennan's account of the way the raw sailors of the *Junee* were allowed to spend their spare time is alarming.

'We weren't told not to fish or swim or drink desalinated water. Our skipper was a keen fisherman and he spent half his days fishing and he got the cook to serve up his catch for dinner.'

Brennan bumped into the officer about ten years later. Brennan said he was very ill and riddled with cancer and died soon after.

'We were eventually told there would be another test. We anchored about seven nautical miles away. We got the countdown. Then there was an incredible bang. We turned our backs and after counting to five we turned around and saw the ball of fire and smoke. The boiling mass spread over the island and then went up in this huge column and formed the mushroom cloud.

'Then the pressure wave hit us. We had our stern to it. There wasn't a ripple on the water. No one said a word afterwards. We were all just in awe. We watched it [the mushroom cloud] rise for about forty-five minutes to an hour.

'I saw this plane fly right in to the mushroom cloud. I couldn't believe it. I wondered who those poor bastards were. I thought they must be collecting samples, but I thought it was madness. I wondered whether the plane would conk out from the heat and dirt.

'It was the most horrific thing I had seen in my whole life, and I hoped I would never see anything like it again. My thoughts went to Hiroshima and Nagasaki and I wondered why we were exploding that sort of bomb in Australia.'

Afterwards the crew was told to wash down the ship, but the fire hoses and pumps were old and didn't do the job properly. Brennan says the crew was never told to take showers to avoid contamination.

'The wind was blowing away from us so maybe they thought it wasn't necessary. Nobody really talked about what we had witnessed. We were all a bit speechless. We sailed back to Onslow, dropped some gear and then on to Fremantle. I left the navy four years later.'

Since then he's had a lot of skin cancers removed and operations for bowel cancer. His daughter suffered three miscarriages. Doctors didn't know why.

'We had a fifty year reunion of the national service navy intake from my year. Half of us had been posted to HMAS *Fremantle* and half to her sister ship, HMAS *Junee*. I found nine guys from *Junee* had died – none from *Fremantle*. The only difference was *Junee* had been at Monte Bello.

'At our next get-together a dozen or so years later, thirteen from *Junee* were dead and just one from *Fremantle*. I learned many years after we were at Monte Bello a warning had been sent to the fleet not to eat fish, drink desalinated water or swim in the lagoon. For some reason it never got through to us.'

•

Three days after the first Mosaic test, James Hole, a British radiological safety officer on board HMS *Narvik*, took a radio call from a colleague at RAAF base Pearce near Perth.

One of their transport planes had just flown in from Onslow. It was heavily contaminated. Hole was worried. The plane shouldn't have been exposed to radiation at all as the cloud from the Mosaic blast had been observed heading west out to sea. All this plane had done was fly between Onslow and Pearce.

Hole decided to investigate himself. He dressed in nondescript grey overalls, gathered radiation-measuring equipment and put it in a picnic basket. He thought there was no sense alarming everyone by going into town in white radiation-protective gear waving Geiger counters.

He got a lift to Onslow on a helicopter and then persuaded an Australian security officer to load a mattress into the back of a Holden ute. Hole climbed in and had the man drive around the airport while he held up the radiation-measuring device. To Hole's surprise he detected patches of contamination on the tarmac.

They drove around the outskirts of Onslow and Hole found more patches of contamination that shouldn't have been there. He then casually wandered into Onslow's only bar and sat quietly in a corner sipping a beer while secretly reading for contamination. Nobody noticed him as the town had seen a lot of strange boffins, military men and reporters during the tests. The bar wasn't contaminated. Hole had another beer and slipped out unnoticed. But he was concerned – somehow the mainland had been contaminated when it shouldn't have.

As readings came in from across the mainland, what Hole and others found out was that while most of the cloud from the first blast, G1, had gone out to sea, a portion of the cloud was blown the other way and dropped low-level fallout across northern

Australia. It was recorded all the way across the Northern Territory and finally at Cairns, Townsville, Charleville and Brisbane. The highest recordings were at Broome and Onslow. The readings were all below the level set for the tests by the health physics scientists as being safe for the public.

Thirty years later Hole told the Royal Commission the measuring equipment was faulty. When he got back to England and conducted further tests he found the real level of contamination on the ground and in the planes flying through the radioactive clouds was ten times higher than the instruments recorded.

So Australia had received a far higher dose of radioactive contamination than anyone knew or admitted at the time.

Hole certainly wished he'd known about the underestimated readings at the time. After the second blast, G2, as safety officer he had to escort a scientist ordered to go into the crater left by the blast and collect samples.

'It was virtually like a skating rink. The sand obviously had been glazed and there were lots of colours in it. One of the problems standing in the crater was you could get fascinated and forget you were receiving a dose. It was very pretty.'[9]

•

Titterton fell in love with G2, the second Monte Bello bomb, as soon as his eyes fell on it. The British allowed Titterton and the two other 'Australians' present – Butement and Martin – to gaze upon the deadly weapon in the 100 feet–high tower before it was exploded. Titterton's comments twenty-nine years later to the Royal Commission about that moment showed his heart was still all aflutter.

'We stood, if you like, and admired it. I do not want that to be misunderstood. But in truth, that weapon was a very beautiful piece of highly sophisticated engineering. I think the only word to describe it is beautiful.'[10]

Titterton was furious when Supply Minister Howard Beale ordered that the planned Sunday detonation of G2 be postponed by a day. The weather and wind direction was just right, but it was a Sunday and Beale wouldn't tolerate the day of the Lord being disturbed by exploding atomic bombs.

It took several days before the weather was right again and on Wednesday 19 June 1956 the bomb was fired. Everyone present was stunned at the power of the blast. Buildings shook at Onslow more than 100 kilometres away. In the mining town of Marble Bar, 400 kilometres inland, windows and roofs rattled.

Officially G2 exploded with the force of sixty kilotons – more than three times the power of Hiroshima and the biggest nuclear bomb ever exploded in Australia. Initial reports had it as ninety-eight kilotons, but that would have revealed G2 was a thermonuclear bomb.

So, officially G2 wasn't as powerful as the American thermonuclear bomb exploded at Bikini Atoll in 1954 but it meant Britain had taken the first step to joining the exclusive thermonuclear club with the US and the USSR. Unable to explode an official thermonuclear or hydrogen bomb in Australia, they moved this part of the British nuclear weapons project to the middle of the Pacific Ocean at Malden Island and Christmas Island, an atoll now called Kiritimati. (Not to be confused with the Christmas Island in the Indian Ocean now in the news with asylum seekers.)

Using knowledge gained from the Monte Bello blasts, the first British thermonuclear bomb in the Pacific, Grapple 1, was dropped at Malden Island just under one year later, on 15 May 1957. The British were disappointed that it had the explosive power of only 300 kilotons – far less than the Americans were dropping on a regular basis. British scientists boosted the power of their bomb and, over eight tests in just twelve months, dropped a thermonuclear bomb reaching 3000 kilotons.

If the primary aim of the British nuclear tests was to explode such powerful hydrogen bombs, the Australian government should have been asking why they still needed to explode their nuclear bombs in Australia. Was Maralinga still necessary? Protests were starting to mount against the bomb.

The Menzies government appeared to have been caught out by the size of G2 – Beale had said that it would be smaller than G1. The day after the explosion, some press were accompanying Beale on a trip to Woomera to see progress at Maralinga when news of the size of the bomb reached them. News was also leaking out from Onslow that the huge mushroom cloud had drifted towards the mainland.

Then on 21 June, two days after the explosion, a mining prospector called Jack Tunny in remote back country near Kuridala in Queensland – about 100 kilometres south of Cloncurry – was surprised when his Geiger counter suddenly clicked furiously. It was raining and Tunny, having heard on radio that the radioactive cloud was drifting east, decided to test the rainwater.

'This morning I measured the ground around the camp and it registered a normal count of fifteen,' he told a newspaper reporter. 'But when rain began to fall I tested it as it came off the roof and the counter leaped to 2000.'[11]

Tunny called uranium miner Clem Watson at Mt Isa and asked him to check his readings. Watson immediately confirmed the radioactivity.

Tunny called a reporter and the story hit front pages around the country. 'Atomic Rain in Qld' screamed the front page of the Adelaide *Advertiser*.

'Atom Rain Falls near Cloncurry' shouted the *Courier-Mail*.

Reporters with Beale at Woomera immediately pressed him on why he'd got it so wrong. Didn't he know what was going on? Did the British pull the wool over his eyes? Is Australia being taken for a ride? Beale dodged and weaved. He'd bungled it, and it was obvious to all he wasn't in command of what the British were doing. When reporters raced to the phones at Woomera

Airport to report the fiasco to their newspapers, they found all the phones were suddenly out of order. Beale's assistant had shut down the Woomera telephone exchange, cutting the reporters off from the outside world.

In Canberra the no-nonsense Country Party leader Arthur Fadden was acting prime minister as Menzies was overseas. Fadden received reports the G2 bomb was far bigger than expected and fallout was hitting the mainland. According to the radio operator on HMS *Narvik* at Monte Bello, a message arrived from the acting Australian Prime Minister: 'What the bloody hell is going on, the cloud is drifting over the mainland . . .'[12]

The radio operator, Bernard Perkins, told the Royal Commission he remembered the message very clearly as it was strong language. However, no written copy of this message has ever been found.

Fadden's message must have got through, as the next day, the safety committee sent a message to Beale assuring him the cloud was 160 kilometres out to sea and there was no danger to the mainland. Four days later Fadden issued a statement telling the public he had been satisfied by the safety committee that the whole operation went according to plan without risk to life or property on the Australian mainland.

A few days later Leslie Martin, chairman of the safety committee, filed a report to the government saying that while the cloud had gone out to sea, there had been 'some fallout of low-level activity in a restricted coastal region – and to a lesser degree in band reaching towards the centre of Australia.'[13]

The discrepancy left many politicians and commentators concerned. Were they being told the truth? Just what were the British keeping secret from Australians? Could the scientists be trusted – either British or Australian?

The safety committee was a farce. It depended completely on the British for information to make its safety assessments. It mounted no challenges to British actions. It was supposed to have the power to veto any explosion, but this power was never written down and it never vetoed anything the British wanted to do.

All the members of the safety committee had vested interests in the success of the nuclear tests and all of them, particularly Titterton, were ardent supporters of the project.

Titterton was unapologetic about his support for the British tests. Australian observers at the tests were 'totally incorporated with no holds barred into the entire operation' he later told the Royal Commission.

'No one on the safety committee was apprehensive about the fallout. They were apprehensive about the behaviour of the media and certain people with political objectives using the media in whatever way they could, even by misinformation, to stir up public opinion against the trials. That is what they were apprehensive about.'[14]

Stewart Stubbs was a mechanical engineer at the Comet goldmine near Marble Bar when he heard three distant explosions. He later learned he'd heard the sixty-kiloton atomic blast at Monte Bello about 400 kilometres away. A few hours later a light drizzle rain began falling on the windscreen of his vehicle. 'I realised that could be radioactive fallout from the bomb as the wind was coming from the west,' Stubbs told the Royal Commission.[15] 'There were some dark clouds, greyish-black clouds, coming from the west going faster than I could drive on the dirt road. I didn't think of it as fallout at the time. I was surprised when it did rain as they didn't look like rain clouds to me. They were very shallow, thin clouds, moving quite low.'

The drizzle continued for several hours. He suspected it might have something to do with the A-bomb so he got out a Geiger counter they used in uranium mining. He held it out in the drizzle and to the damp dust settling on the vehicles. He was staggered when the reading suddenly shot off the scale. He held the Geiger counter down to the boots of his son Maurice and again the Geiger counter clicked like crazy and the reading went off the scale.

Stubbs rang Port Hedland and got put through to a scientist he remembers as being Penney and told them what had happened. He asked whether there was any danger to people at the mine.

'I'm afraid I can't comment,' the scientist replied, and advised Stubbs to carry out procedures for breaking down contamination. Stubbs spoke to the matron at the Marble Bar hospital and heard some local people had come in complaining of feeling ill and vomiting. None of this talk got out of Marble Bar at the time. Stubbs kept it to himself, and advised the matron to do the same. He supported the atom bomb testing and didn't want bad news harming the project. He didn't speak out until the Royal Commission in 1984–5.

But those inside the atom bomb project knew fallout had reached the mainland. Contrary to assurance from the safety committee that all went well, the fallout on the mainland was far bigger than expected. Dangerous levels were found at Port Hedland and Derby on the north coast. Fallout was particularly high at Derby, well above safety levels for traditional Aboriginals who lived in the open.

As reports on the fallout came in from sources other than the scientists charged with running the atomic tests, the safety committee sought to justify its earlier assurances.

'We cannot over-emphasise the fact that the whole operation was carried out with no risk to life or property on the mainland or elsewhere,' it said.[16] But as news started reaching Canberra of fallout being detected on the north coast by monitor stations, the safety committee changed its tune, saying, 'some harmless deposition along north-west coast of Australia was always anticipated and measurements show that in those localities where there is some deposition it is completely harmless'.[17]

Put simply, the safety committee lied.

It didn't matter. The tests were to continue unabated on the Australian mainland. On 7 March 1956 Menzies signed a secret agreement handing over the Maralinga site to Britain for ten years, longer if both sides agreed. Use of the site was free from all rent and similar charges. Britain was responsible for ensuring the tests did not cause injury or damage to persons or property. Australia had to agree before any test was carried out, and Britain had to supply 'sufficient' information to enable selected Australian officials to determine whether safety provisions were adequate. Australia would set up and operate a chain of fallout-monitoring stations around Australia and provide the data to Britain. The UK undertook to indemnify Australia for all 'valid claims' arising from death or injury to persons or damage to property.[18]

No house owner would sign such an open lease for tenants, but Menzies did it for the whole country.

6

MARALINGA GUINEA PIGS

Leading Aircraftman Ric Johnstone was twenty-two in early 1956 and had been in the RAAF for twelve months when he was called to see his commanding officer at RAAF Base Lapstone west of Sydney.

'We need good mechanics at a place called Maralinga,' said the CO. 'It's top secret, so I can't tell you much, but here's your ticket for the train to Adelaide. Then catch the bus up to RAAF base Edinburgh. You'll be given further orders there.'

Johnstone was excited at the hush-hush mission. At Edinburgh base, just north of Adelaide, he joined about sixty servicemen waiting for orders. An officer told them to sign the Official Secrets Act. He threatened that if they talked to anybody about where they were going, took photos or made any sketches, they would be 'removed from society'.[1]

'They really tried to put the shit up us not to talk about this place we were going to,' Johnstone later recalled.

Johnstone and the other servicemen spent three days on a train chugging across the Nullarbor Plain until finally it stopped on a siding in the middle of nowhere. They were loaded into a convoy of military trucks and driven into the desert for more than an hour, to a large clearing.

'It was called Camp 43 because it was forty-three miles [sixty-nine kilometres] from the railway junction. A warrant officer told us we were there to establish the site for Britain to test its atomic weapons. I knew atom bombs had ended the war and forced the Japanese to surrender, but they told us nothing about radiation or the long-term effects of exposure.'

Johnstone's job was to drive into the desert to repair or salvage broken-down vehicles. He felt conditions at the camp 'worse than any jail'. Heat, dust, monotony and a lack of any entertainment made it a tough place. The worst thing about life in the camp was the secrecy.

'You couldn't talk to anyone about what you were doing or ask questions of others. You always feared other people were informants or spies put in the camp by security to see if you were talking. You couldn't relax with anybody in the camp. You couldn't trust them.'

Johnstone said many men at the camp did all they could to get out of the place, including inflicting injuries on themselves. He said there was at least one attempted suicide. And one simply loaded up a truck and headed off into the desert in the general direction of Sydney and was never heard from again.

Six months later Camp 43 was abandoned, as it was close to the base of the test tower where they were going to detonate the first atomic bomb. They moved south to the village of Maralinga, which had grown as thousands of servicemen and scientists moved in for the coming nuclear tests.

At the beginning of September 1956, just weeks before the first of four bombs in Operation Buffalo was to be exploded, Johnstone was assigned to the vehicles at the decontamination centre, well away from the village.

'It was run by the Radiation Detection Unit – mostly Canadian army engineers. They went in after the bombs went off to measure the radiation. Our job was to fix vehicles that broke down in the hot zone. We also decontaminated vehicles at the centre with high-pressure steam. We did this until the Geiger counter no longer clicked when it was waved over the vehicles. I always had a Geiger counter with me. We were supposed to leave the zone when it went past a certain point on the dial. That happened so often I wondered just how much radiation we were copping. We just didn't know.'

Like all the others at Maralinga, minutes before the bomb was exploded Johnstone was told to stand with his back to the blast, close his eyes and push the palms of his hands into his eye sockets. The flash of the blast was so bright Johnstone could see the bones of his hands. After thirty seconds or so they turned around and saw the mushroom cloud rising into the sky.

Johnstone often had to go into the radioactive hot zone shortly after the blast with scientists retrieving measuring instruments: this could be three times in the one day. They were given protective suits, but there were immediate problems with the desert heat.

'At first we wore protective masks and thick rubber gloves but it proved impossible to wear them in the forty-five-degree heat. You couldn't breathe through the rubber mask and it was so stinking hot you had to pull the mask open to let the sweat pour out. So we stopped wearing them. The gloves were so thick you couldn't work with them on. You had to take them off to work on the engines. The worst was the air cleaners that quickly filled up with fine dust. You had to turn a wing nut to open them and that was impossible with the gloves on. We knew it was full of radioactive dust but you had no choice. You had to take the gloves off to get the work done.'

When Johnstone went into the radioactive hot zone to repair vehicles after the blast, the sights he found were bizarre.

'The ground was covered in pellets of glass. The sand had been burned so hot it turned into glass. They planted lots of vehicles, tanks and planes, around ground zero to see how the blast would affect them. When I went in they were still burning.

I saw dummies in trenches and tied to frames to stand up to see what happened when the blast hit them. It was scary.'

When Johnstone got back from the hot zone he had to shower and scrub himself with coarse scrubbing brushes until the Geiger counter gave him the all clear.

'The biggest problem was fingernails. No matter how hard you scrubbed there was always something underneath the nails that set the Geiger counter off.'

One day Johnstone and another mechanic packed up their vehicles for a long trip north to try to find a man missing in the desert. What they found 240 kilometres to the north was staggering. It was marked on their map only as X200. It was the old camp at Emu Field, now a ghost town, abandoned as though everyone had left in a panic. Huts stood in the desert, their kitchens stocked with tinned food and cooking equipment left neatly in drawers and shelves. Some vehicles still had their keys in the ignition. They stayed two days in the abandoned camp, using it as a base while they carried on their search for the missing man. They didn't find him.

A short time after the tests at Maralinga began, Johnstone started getting bouts of nausea, diarrhea and vomiting. The medical orderly at the aid post told him it was just the food he'd been eating. Nothing was mentioned about the possibility of radiation sickness.

Once the atomic tests ended in October, Johnstone returned to New South Wales. He'd got married in Adelaide while on leave and his wife insisted he go to the military doctor as he was still suffering bouts of nausea and diarrhea.

'The air force doctor took blood tests and three days later I was ordered to report to the hospital. It was there I saw a form the doctor had filled in saying I had radiation sickness. I was there for a week and never saw that doctor again.'

Johnstone was kept in isolation and wasn't allowed to visit a mate from Maralinga he saw from the window.

'They told me he had a broken leg, but a couple of days later they told me he had died. What? From a broken leg? They said there were complications. I knew they were lying to me. Something stank and they were desperate to cover it up.'[2]

Johnstone was told he was suffering from an anxiety disorder. He asked if it was caused by his radiation exposure at Maralinga. The doctors replied he'd signed the Official Secrets Act and he'd better keep that to himself.

'I was given tablets and sent home. I didn't know what the pills were but I was walking around like a zombie. Finally I took the pills to a chemist and asked what they were.'

The pills proved to be chlorpromazine, a powerful anti-psychotic drug. Johnstone landed in hospital again, suffering severe bouts of nausea. Once again he was dosed up with high levels of drugs that left him weak and his memory shot.

Johnstone was discharged from the RAAF as medically unfit in 1958 – two years after his time at Maralinga.

He became the father of two boys – both born with genetically linked deformities. One never grew teeth or hair. The other had a cleft palate. By 1960 Johnstone was in a psychiatric clinic and stayed there for a year with 'emotional problems'. He went home and barely stepped outside the house for the next twelve years. But with time on his hands he set up the Australian Nuclear Veterans' Association. He became the focus for many ex-servicemen who had served during the British atomic tests. It was largely due to pressure from veterans groups like his that the Labor government in 1984 set up the Royal Commission. Johnstone died in 2011.

•

John Hutton joined the army on his seventeenth birthday. Two years later he was offered a secret assignment and leaped at it. He had to sign all sorts of Official Secrets papers but he was more interested in the money.

'They were offering seventeen shillings and sixpence a day at Maralinga and I was only on nine and six, so of course I said yes. They put me in a long military convoy from Sydney to the Nullarbor desert. I was shocked when we stopped at this one-horse stop called Watson. My boots disappeared in the bulldust and the flies were terrible. It was January and the heat was incredible.[3]

'We were told to drive up this track for miles. We got there at night. They had graded a big area. We slept in the truck, and the next day we started building Maralinga. The first tents they dropped off were for the air force, then the navy and finally us in the army. Till then we slept in the trucks. Typical.

'We still had no real clue why we were there. There were rumours it was for atom bombs, but I was nineteen and I didn't really care. I was working at One Tree – called that because there was only one tree there until they chopped it down. We took material in to build the 100-foot-high tower. We worked twelve hours a day, seven days a week. The food was bloody awful as everything went rotten in the heat. It was all canned food. We were hungry a lot of the time.'

Hutton said that before the tests, Aboriginals sometimes were escorted into the camp by police to sell things like spears, woomera sticks and carved bowls. But otherwise work was pretty dull and relentless.

'We got permission to shoot kangaroos for some fresh meat. One time we drove to Emu – it was quite a trek – and it was like the atom bomb had gone off just the day before. Everything was left where it was, including tins of peaches. We brought a lot of stuff back from there including eating and cooking equipment and sleeping gear. We knew nothing about radiation.'

Hutton left Maralinga just before the first Operation Buffalo tests, but returned in 1957 as a lance corporal and was there for the next series of tests in 1957, called Operation Antler.

•

Bruce Baker joined the RAAF aged just seventeen in 1955. Six months later he was told he was going to Maralinga. 'Where's that?' he asked. 'I don't know, just join the convoy,' he was told.[4]

Baker became the youngest person at the camp in early 1956. His job was to drive trucks from the railway siding at Watson to Camp 43, carting people and equipment.

'There was nothing there and we had to build a village in the desert. The dirt road from the rail to camp was graded every day and there was a constant stream of trucks going back and forth. There were always two of us in the trucks. They could be air force, army or navy. There didn't seem to be any order to it except trucks going to the camp had right of way as they were full. Going back to the railway you had to pull over the side and let them go by. It was incredibly dusty and hot, but I was young and didn't mind the work. We got two beers a night, which helped wash down the dust.'

Baker saw four atomic tests while he was at Maralinga. In each case they called the roll and had everyone turn their backs.

'We heard the countdown with our eyes closed and hands over our eyes. When you turned around it looked a boiling mass going up into the mushroom cloud. You'd think that looked pretty good but harmless and then the blast would hit you. It was a huge blast. Some of us had to take a step back. I wasn't worried by the bomb, as we thought they'd done their homework and it would blow away from us.

'I do remember we had to pick up live animals from the railway and take them in – goats and sheep. I don't know what they did with them.'

•

One of the more bizarre experiments done at Maralinga was to test the impact on humans of glass shattered by an atom bomb.

People in Hiroshima and Nagasaki were found shredded by glass shards, and the scientists wanted to know how far from the blast this 'casualty producing agent' would do its job.[5] Household glass windows were arranged at different distances from the blast and afterwards examined for their destructive capacity.

The biological subcommittee of the UK War Office included the smashed glass experiment in its field trials for the 1956 Buffalo series of atomic tests. The boffins were looking forward to using the tests to check the impact of atomic bombs on everything from humans to military equipment. It arranged for 120 dummies to be positioned in different poses – such as standing, kneeling, lying on the ground – inside vehicles such as trucks and tanks and at various distances from the blast zone. Dummies dressed in different uniforms were lined up to see which uniform faced up best to nuclear bombs. The dummies were to be fitted with blast-measuring devices 'in the appropriate cavities' such as head and stomach.

As the September deadline for the Buffalo tests at Maralinga approached, the War Office went even further, organising live human beings to be positioned in bunkers close to the blast area – mostly military officers from Britain and Australia, but also some from other Commonwealth nations including New Zealand, Fiji, India and Canada. They were to be called 'indoctrinees'.

•

Physicist Bill Hunter had been at Monte Bello and then saw all four tests carried out in 1956 at Maralinga.

'I was eight miles [12.8 kilometres] from the blasts in a caravan with measuring equipment. The third bomb was dropped from an aircraft and it flew right over my head. I was listening to the pilot on radio and when he said "Bombs away" I did a quick calculation and breathed a sigh of relief it wasn't going to land on our head. It was spectacular.[6]

'For the others I was inside the caravan working when it went off. One was in pitch-black night and when it went off the brilliant blue light lit up all the trees as far as you could see. It was the same colour as a lightning strike with a bluish tinge. After I had taken the measurements I decided to have a look outside to see what it looked like. I climbed on top of the jeep and the force of the blast wave knocked me right off the hood.'

•

Glynn Key reckons he has to be the only sailor who saw atomic bombs explode at both Monte Bello and Maralinga. He was on HMAS *Macquarie* about forty kilometres from the bomb blast, but he was much closer at Maralinga. Key was one of about twenty-four sailors assigned to provide water purification from bore water for the desert settlement.[7]

When it came time to explode the bomb in the special tower, Key and several other engineers had to stay with generators about fourteen kilometres from the blast site to make sure they kept going. A navy lieutenant kept an eye on them.

'We were close in case there was a power failure in the diesel generator which was needed to set off the bomb and the measuring instruments. There were two of us on each generator. The force of the bomb was like being slapped on the back of the head. We had no protective gear.

'After the explosion we were told to get back to Maralinga. The army took over then and they went into the blast zone to retrieve equipment.'

•

Neal Longden was in the RAAF based at Woomera airfield for three and a half years. 'I went out in a helicopter that had been told to measure radioactivity over the blast zones.'[8]

'We were at 8000 feet over the blast zone and the Geiger

counter went off. It was a very high reading. The reading was in the danger zone and we were at 8000 feet!'

Longden also made trips in the chopper to patrol for Aboriginals who might have strayed into the forbidden zone that spread for a hundred kilometres from the site.

'We did see five men in one group and we landed but we couldn't communicate with them. They didn't understand us. We just made it clear to them to walk away from the danger zone. They moved away.

'We did this patrol once a week and only saw Aborigines twice. In both cases they moved away.'

•

Tony Spruzen joined the army at sixteen in 1952 and was disappointed he was too young to be sent to the Korean War. But in 1956, aged twenty, he was excited to be sent to Maralinga.

'I thought if I was going to miss out on a war then an atomic bomb was pretty good.'[9]

Spruzen relished the work. He spent months constructing the Maralinga village. 'A lot of it was prefabricated so it was like putting together a giant Meccano set. The food was better than normal as we were on British rations and the kitchen was built for the scientists so it wasn't standard army food. That's important to a twenty-year-old who is always hungry.'

The camp ran on strict military lines. Majors and above had a separate mess. 'I've never seen so many red caps [senior officers]. Captains and lieutenants had their own mess as did the warrant officers, sergeants and so on. It wasn't an easy job to build there. It was sand for about a foot and then solid rock. We had to drill to insert pegs and foundations.'

Spruzen witnessed three bombs, each one about a week apart. The first was called One Tree, a fifteen-kiloton explosion high in a tower. The second, called Marcoo, was smaller, a 1.5 kiloton blast at ground level. The third, Kite, was a three-kiloton bomb dropped from an airplane.

Spruzen was assigned to drive a large group of senior officers to a site just a few miles from the One Tree blast. He saw dummies dressed in uniforms arranged at different distances from the tower. Tanks, airplanes, trucks and buildings made of differing materials were also laid out at certain distances. He tagged along and the officers didn't order him away as they lined up with their backs to the tower.

'They had a loudspeaker counting down saying thirty seconds, fifteen seconds – they told us to close our eyes – and then 10, 9, etc, down to 1.

'I could see everything through my eyelids, it was so bright, at least twice as strong as an arc light. I didn't hear anything at all at first. The loudspeaker counted to five and then we turned around. There was a boiling fireball deep inside the mushroom cloud. It lasted just a few seconds. This huge column of dirt and fire was going up into the air.

'It was miles away but it looked like it was just a hundred yards from us. I saw these rocket things going through the air in front of it. Then suddenly this huge bang hit us. It was a deafening crack rather than a roar, much louder than a thunder clap.

'Then the blast wave hit us. Then the wind. It was a blast, dirt flying into your face. I had to take a step backwards as we weren't prepared for it. Then we just stood in awe as this huge mushroom cloud grew and grew into the air. We stared at it for half an hour or more. Dust rained down on us. Everything in front of us had been flattened. Bushes, trees, everything gone.

'I turned to the bloke next to me and said, "That was incredible." He said he'd remember it for the rest of his life. I certainly have. I still see it like it just happened, it is so ingrained on my memory. I was in awe of it. The cloud floated away gently. It took time. The whole cloud moved on. It was a dirty grey mass.

'Nobody talked to us about it afterwards – we just went on with our work after saying how incredible it was. The next day or so we went back into the zone where all the dummies and tanks and buildings were. They were flattened and the top surface of the ground was shiny and felt like pellets of glass. The tank tread had blown off. Another tank had been turned around by the blast.'

Spruzen walked around in the dust not far from the blast zone but said at no point were they warned of radiation danger.

'The second blast was smaller but there was a lot more dust as it came from ground level. Again we weren't given any advice to shower or clean up afterwards. I believe there were some officers in a trench much closer to the blast. One of them told me it was very frightening as he thought the whole dirt wall would collapse on them. I later heard that within twelve months that officer had died from cancer.'

Spruzen left the army as a corporal in 1961. About a year later he received a questionnaire from the army asking about his health. Spruzen replied he had no health problems. But his wife certainly did. She had six miscarriages, including losing twins. Their first child developed a cyst on her pituitary gland. Their second daughter developed a back problem. Their grandson has Asperger's syndrome and their son developed acute myeloid leukemia at the age of forty-one – a rare condition brought on by exposure to chemicals, radiation and genetic problems. He recovered after his sister donated bone marrow for a transplant.

'The doctors never said it was due to my exposure to radiation at Maralinga, but I believe it was. It can't be proved either way.'

•

Alan Dennis and his brother Bobby served in the British army during the Second World War and joined the merchant navy after the war, ending up in Adelaide. They had a talent as vaudeville entertainers – song-and-dance men with a handy ability to impersonate famous people. Alan Dennis still has the flyers on his wall, and proudly says he was the first to call square dances where they had 3000 people whirling and twirling.

But times were tough in Adelaide in 1956 and the brothers needed paying jobs. They answered calls for jobs as stewards with the military. When they were asked if they would go into the desert on a special secret project they leaped at the chance. The money was good and there would be nowhere to spend it.

'We were assigned to the VIP mess and we served people like Penney and all the top scientists and generals who were at Maralinga.[10]

'When they were about to blow the bomb they got us to line up and face away from the blast. We saw the flash and turned around to see the trees bend from the shock wave and the rising mushroom cloud. The heat of the blast wave hit us. It was incredible. I was amazed. I couldn't believe the power of it. We were twenty-three kilometres away at Maralinga village.

'There was a big party for all the VIPs after the atom bomb. I was a waiter. The food was incredible considering we were in the middle of the desert. There were oysters specially flown in from Tasmania. I took the leftovers to the boys in the camp. The camp was buzzing with excitement and amazement at the size of the explosion.'

Alan Dennis developed bad feet after that, cut and split from the dust and heat. He was sent to Woomera and made a boiler attendant.

'I saw people washing down the planes dressed only in shirts and shorts when they came in to get their meals. I was surprised at that. It was pretty rough and ready.'

Eventually Dennis was sent back to Adelaide because of his split feet. He said goodbye to his brother Bob, who was staying on.

'Bobby said he was being sent to the five-mile post. That was close to the blast zone. He didn't say what he was doing there.

It was all top secret and we couldn't talk about those sort of things. I didn't see him again until two months later. He was all right for a while and then he started going out of his mind. Ten years after Maralinga, Bobby developed two tumours on the brain. He died in 1983. Bobby was the only one of eight siblings who developed a brain tumour. There was no history of it in the family. Bobby's two daughters are OK, which is good.

'I don't know how close he was to the atomic bomb or what he did there. He never talked about it. He was three months longer at Maralinga than me. There was no medical evidence the brain tumour was caused by what happened at Maralinga, but the family always had suspicions.'

•

In January 1956 Ken Meredith was a nineteen-year-old in the army engineers helping build Camp 43 and roads to the blast zones. After eight months of this hot work, Meredith was assigned to work close to the blast site.

Before the blast Meredith put sandbags into the doorways of bunkers. The engineers usually worked in a team of four. They were given orders at the base in the morning by a sergeant and then moved out with a plant operator and two or three field engineers, with Meredith as bulldozer driver. A corporal or lance corporal would be in charge of the team.

Just twelve hours after the first blast, Meredith drove into the zone to retrieve a bulldozer that had been left at a road junction closer to the blast site. He was in full radiation-protective gear and had been told to check his dosimeter every half hour. He was told if it reached a certain point he was to come back immediately. That happened once.

'It was high enough to scare me to make me come back,' he told the Royal Commission in 1985.[11]

When he got back to the supposedly safe distance of Roadside, the scientists simply gave him a new dosimeter and sent him back in again.

'They said the dosimeters couldn't be trusted and often played up.' He also wore a film badge around the village but it was never checked or reclaimed.

'I understood the film badges were to record how much radiation we were exposed to. But it was never examined.'

Meredith said the gas mask was impossible to wear in the heat and it was common practice by all the men to take them off.

'When you had them on, your head and face would perspire and the glass face of the gasmask would fog over and would fill with perspiration up to your chin level.'

He knew he shouldn't remove the mask and he would put it back on if officers or scientists drove up.

'Fine dust got in your throat and up nostrils, clogging your nose. It happened all the time.'

Back at the decontamination centre they would undress in one caravan and go through into another caravan where they were measured for radiation. He walked through an archway and somebody would be looking at instruments. 'Normally we had to shower more than once after being in the forward area. Specially the hands.'

No matter how clean Meredith became, the bulldozer he was driving remained in the blast area and was never cleaned. He never saw any attempt to check radiation levels on it.

Like others, Meredith made the trek to Emu Field to see the ghost town. He found a bulldozer that had been left behind. He told the Royal Commission the valuable heavy machine one day just 'walked out'.

Meredith admitted taking several tools left behind at Emu as there was no security – no gates, no barriers, no sign. He sent them home without knowing if they were contaminated. Many others souvenired material from Emu. Miniature cannons used by scientists to see what effect the bomb had on them were a much prized souvenir. One RAAF officer took an entire Land Rover jeep back to Laverton Air Base in Victoria. The word among the troops was that it was eventually confiscated and sold at auction, so some poor, unwitting civilian ended up getting a radioactive jeep.

Meredith later joined the Federal Police. He developed chest pains and depression. They were diagnosed as stemming from his police duties. He doesn't believe his time at Maralinga affected his health, but he does believe it affected others who received more exposure than him.

•

A large group of senior military officers, mostly majors, colonels and above, were brought in to Maralinga just before the first explosion. They were there for a very special and somewhat bizarre purpose. There were 283 of them – 178 British, 100 Australians and five New Zealanders.

They were called 'indoctrinees', so named because the idea from the UK Ministry of Defence was for them to be 'indoctrinated' into the experience of being close to an atom bomb going off. The most senior indoctrinees were a major general, a navy commander and an air commodore. Defence officials expected they would go back to their regiments, ships and squadrons to tell their men there was nothing to fear from atom bombs so long as you took the proper precautions. It was all part of a military strategy to build an acceptance among the armed forces that atom bombs could be used as strategic weapons on the battlefield.

The indoctrinees were kept apart from troops doing the donkey work of building the site and driving them around. They had separate sleeping quarters and generally ate on their own. They always dressed in full uniform while the troops were in shorts, many without shirts. The troops weren't told anything about the indoctrinees, so rumours circulated they weren't officers at all but mentally defective men dressed up for secret experiments. When you considered what they did in full uniform in the desert sun, maybe the troops had a point.

Most of the indoctrinees were placed eight kilometres up-wind from the One Tree tower. Some were much closer. Three Australian officers – named in a British document as Lt. Col. George Warfe, Lt. Col. William Ford and Major C.L.J. Ireland – were placed in shelters just 1600 metres from the blast.[12] When the fifteen-kiloton bomb was exploded, the indoctrinees in the open air turned their backs and then turned to face the bomb. They watched in awe as the boiling fire in the smoke built into a towering mushroom cloud. They were rocked back by the shock wave. They were not wearing any protective gear. The notion was to show them that soldiers could be near an atomic explosion yet still be ready for battle. Details of the indoctrinees' gamma ray exposures as measured on their dosimeters were recorded in what became known as the Blue Book – records kept by the UK Ministry of Defence but which are still not open to the public.

After the bomb went off a group of twenty-four 'volunteers' among the indoctrinees were dressed in different outfits – from battle uniform to cotton tropical wear. They were divided into three groups about 300 metres from the blast site. One group sat in the back of a truck as it raced around the blast area stirring up as much dust as possible, the second was ordered to march through the area and brush up against bushes and trees while the third was ordered to roll around the dust for fifty metres and crawl through the brush for another fifty. The aim was to see how much contamination got on the clothes. The report of the experiment said 'unfortunately' the level of contamination recorded on their dosimeters was too small to compare readings.[13] Scientists made no attempt to record how much contaminated dust the officers had ingested.

Other indoctrinees were taken into the blast zone wearing protective gear and respirators to see how the bomb blast had impacted tanks, airplanes and bunkers closer to ground zero.

A British Centurion tank, shipped specially to Australia for the test, was knocked a metre sideways. A handful of volunteer officers without protective gear were told to walk through areas with differing levels of contamination to see how much protection was given by regular military clothing.

Official reports said the indoctrinee officers were thrilled by the experience, and about half of them asked to stay on to see the next bomb go off in a week's time.

The next bomb, Marcoo, was to be much smaller but far dirtier. It was only 1.5 kilotons but when exploded at ground level it blew up a lot more dirt than the more powerful bombs. The indoctrinees were moved in close for the explosion. One group of two-dozen officers – including three Australians and one New Zealander – were put in covered trenches just two kilometres from the blast. Four tank officers were placed inside the Centurion tank next to the trenches to see how the blast affected them. Another hundred stood on open ground just three kilometres from the blast. The radiation badges they had been issued were far more sensitive than the badges issued to the lower ranks who had to go into the blast zone to retrieve instruments.

If ever proof was needed that these men were used as human guinea pigs the evidence came in an internal British government document uncovered at the Royal Commission. It detailed the reasons for the indoctrinee program and said: 'The army must discover the detailed effects of the various types of explosion on equipment, stores and men with and without various types of protection.'[14]

UK and Australian authorities both strenuously denied to the Royal Commission this meant indoctrinees were being used as guinea pigs. The Royal Commission in its report accepted assurances from the authorities that the 'men' this document was referring to were the dummies dressed up in differing uniforms to see how they withstood nuclear explosions rather than real human beings.

If that's the case, why didn't the document instead refer to 'differing uniforms' and 'dummies'? Several members of the indoctrinee force came forward to the Royal Commission to swear they weren't given protective gear when they were taken forward to the blast zone the day after the explosion. Several said they didn't even carry dosimeters.

One of the British indoctrinees, Colonel Peter Lowe, told the Royal Commission he retreated from the first bomb blast zone after his Geiger counter reached a dangerous level.

His dosimeter was 'ripped' from his protective gear by a 'burly Australian sergeant' and thrown into a bucket.[15] No reading was made of the dosimeter badge, but Lowe later saw his record and it showed he had experienced a maximum dose of 400 millirems during his time at Maralinga, a suspiciously low level. Lowe was mystified by this as he saw no evidence of records being kept of individuals' level of exposure.

The official records said the average exposure of the indoctrinees was 500 millirems. The highest was 2000 millirems, still well below the prescribed safety limits of the tests that had been set at 3000 millirems.

For the second test Lowe and two other officers were placed inside a Centurion tank about two kilometres from the blast. They were not wearing any protective gear. When the bomb went off Lowe was peering through a periscope and it instantly went blind from the flash and force of sand hitting the optics. The tank was thrown two metres sideways by the force of the shock wave. The men were shaken up. He couldn't start the engine or elevate the gun. About thirty minutes later they climbed out of the tank. The vehicle's sides were blistered and it was covered in dust. He was tested for contamination but continued to wear his uniform and wore it all the way home.

Lowe didn't like being called a test guinea pig, insisting he was a volunteer observer. He later developed a stomach tumour and had much of his stomach removed.

•

The 1956 explosions at Maralinga marked the first time media were allowed in to observe the British atomic tests on Australian soil. The *Canberra Times* carried a vivid front-page description:

> A Hiroshima-sized Atomic bomb exploded on a steel tower at Maralinga, on the edge of the Nullarbor Plains, at 5 p.m. (S.A. time) today, ending a 16-day wait for suitable weather. The bomb, much smaller than the Monte Bellos [sic] series, exploded with a blinding flash followed by a shattering blast which reached the Press observation post about seven miles [eleven kilometres] away 32 seconds after the detonation. The steel tower nestling the bomb was vapourised except for some red-hot fragments scattered over the range.
>
> The fireball, a white-hot mass, expanded into a gigantic bubble. All minerals and rock in the tower area were fused by the intense heat as the air heated to incandescence. A second or two after the explosion, the fireball shot upwards and as it lost its intensity it continued to expand with a brilliant orange glow.
>
> As the fireball swept upwards, explosive gases swirled up, forming the head of a mushroom, and earth sucked up by the fireball formed the stem of the mushroom.
>
> Ten seconds after the explosion the top of the cloud turned snow-white. A plume of radioactive dust fell from the cloud as it began to move up the mainland.
>
> A small number of animals, including sheep and rabbits, were in the vicinity of the target. About 250 officers and men of the three Australian defence services watched the explosion from about four miles [6.4 kilometres] from the tower.

A hundred monitoring stations throughout Australia and at Port Moresby will take samples of air and water. The radioactive cloud, constantly tracked by aircraft, is expected to clear the mainland within two days. Fine radioactive dust might travel three or four times around the world before falling. It might remain in the air for many months and even years.

Two hooded scientists covered by white protective clothing drove into the blast area and pegged out the boundaries of the dangerously contaminated area. This allowed other scientists to safely recover photographic and recording apparatus which measured the effects of the shock, heat and radioactivity.

The explosion set fire to tanks and trucks and obliterated steel framed buildings a mile from the bomb tower.

Pressmen viewed the damage from an aircraft which made several sweeps along the southern side of the target area. Canberra jet bombers flew through the atomic cloud to sample the radioactivity soon after the bomb exploded.

The sound of the explosion was heard more than 300 miles [482 kilometres] away at the town of Pimba, and people living at Penongy 170 miles [273 kilometres] south-south-east of Maralinga reported that the vibration caused windows and doors to rattle.[16]

The British press saw it all somewhat more poetically. The correspondent of *The Times* of London waxed lyrical:

Already starting to form the top of the fireball we saw a storming threshing cloud that seemed to seek in the heavens its peace from man's intrusion. The noise made the endless expanse of Australia's central desert feel for a moment like the enclosed and claustrophobic inside of a six inch gun turret. The blast wave was disappointing, no stronger than the wind from London's Underground that strikes one in the street. The black flies returned to our shoulders . . .[17]

The Minister for Supply, Howard Beale, told parliament everything had gone to plan and the test was a huge success. Labor leader 'Doc' Evatt wasn't easily convinced. He pointed out the wind had changed after the explosion. Beale replied that although there was a sudden change of wind after the firing of the bomb, it would not create any danger.

Behind the scenes, the Labor Opposition was deeply divided over the atomic tests. While the jurist Evatt was vocal in his opposition to the tests, his deputy, the gruff Arthur Calwell, a staunch Catholic anti-communist, was very much in favour of them continuing. In fact, when Beale came back at Evatt's question in parliament saying some members of the press were misleading the public, Calwell let out a 'Hear, hear' loud enough for both sides of the chamber to hear.[18]

Calwell later joined Beale for a guided tour of Maralinga by Sir William Penney for MPs along with carefully selected newspaper editors. Camp commander Richard Durance, a retired Australian army brigadier, later told the Royal Commission that, during the tour, Calwell said he fully agreed with what was going on at Maralinga, and that it was the best spot for the British to test their nuclear weapons. He heard Calwell tell Penney that the Labor Party privately supported the tests, but 'it is not what I am going to say on Thursday night in the House when I move a motion of censure against it'.[19]

Penney wrote to the British High Commissioner that after the Maralinga visit the Australian MPs were 'all purring on eight cylinders'. But the British were confused about the Labor Party's public versus private stance over the tests. The High Commission told the UK Foreign Office the Australian Labor Party was 'split from top to bottom over the atomic trials'.[20] To prove the point, a few days after Calwell's gushing private endorsement at Maralinga, left-wing Labor stalwart Eddie Ward told parliament something had gone wrong at the One Tree explosion and the

Menzies government was not telling Australians the true extent of dangers from the explosion.

While the bulk of public opinion in 1956 was still neutral or in favour of the tests going ahead, Sydney's *Daily Mirror* newspaper was a lone voice against the bomb. It was then owned by the colourful tabloid baron Ezra Norton, famed for once having a stand-up fist fight with Frank Packer at Randwick Racecourse. The *Mirror* questioned the constant assurances by Menzies that the bomb tests posed no threat to the health of Australians. Shortly before the first of the Buffalo series of tests at Maralinga, the *Mirror* called for all tests to be cancelled as it wasn't worth the risk of 'inflicting irreparable damage' to public health.[21] There were a handful of protests against the Maralinga tests in the capital cities, mostly attended by left-wing unionists. However, Menzies managed to brand any opposition to the atomic tests as subversive and communist inspired.

Well-known figures such as the philosopher Bertrand Russell and scientists Linus Pauling, Joseph Rotblat and Frederic Joliot-Curie spoke out against nuclear proliferation and formed the international movement Campaign for Nuclear Disarmament in 1957. Pressure was growing for the nuclear powers to cease their rapid expansion of nuclear testing, even to stop atmospheric testing altogether.

Penney was concerned at this growing opposition. Just before the Buffalo tests, Penney cabled London: 'Everything is going well. Greatest problem is to relieve public apprehension about radioactive fallout. Definite progress has been made but there are small hostile groups trying to make mischief. I am confident that we can handle these matters.'

Penney needn't have worried. The biggest story of the Buffalo trials came when the press were treated to a tour of the innocuous parts of Maralinga before the blasts began. Reporters were flown to Maralinga and were delighted when the shapely air hostess on board joined them for the tour. Nan Whitcomb was the first woman the thousands of men at the camp had seen in months – and she caused a huge stir as she walked around in her tight hostess uniform. The Sydney tabloid *The Sun* pulled out all the stops, splashing a huge picture of the beautiful green-eyed Whitcomb standing in the desert over a smaller picture of the atomic bomb mushroom cloud with the headline: 'She shook them . . . more than the explosion'.

'Bronzed bearded and lonely labourers stopped, stared and ran to tell their mates,' the reporter scribbled. The rival *Daily Telegraph* went one better, describing bearded men 'in the only womanless township in the world' staring in stunned silence at the first woman they had seen in six months.[22]

The UK media minders were overjoyed. The Foreign Office had been worried about notifying the Australian public that fallout tests would be done on animals in the upcoming blasts. They crafted a press release stressing the purpose was to learn how to protect the civilian population in the event of an enemy atomic attack. They advised the Australian government to put the press release out on the weekend and time it so that 'it will be lost in the weekend flood of sporting news'.[23]

7

'THE EARTH ITSELF LOOKED AS THOUGH IT WAS BOILING'

The British chose a macho name for the 1957 series of nuclear tests at Maralinga – Operation Volcano. Australian officials were aghast. Images of death and destruction, earthquakes and spewing lava, and a terrified fleeing populace weren't exactly ideal given there was growing public opposition to the nuclear tests.

An opinion poll had just found forty-nine per cent of Australians were against testing atomic bombs in Australia. Only thirty-seven per cent were in favour.[1] It was the first time public opinion had swung against the bomb, especially among women, where it was two to one against. Another poll found two-thirds of Australians wanted all nuclear bomb explosions in the world ended by an international agreement.[2] This was a dramatic reversal from when the first atom bomb exploded in 1952 at Monte Bello. Back then fifty-eight per cent were in favour of the test and only twenty-nine per cent against.[3]

Australian officials asked the British to change the code name to something less explosive warning Volcano could 'give rise to unfavourable public and press comment'.[4] Back came a new name – Operation Antler – still very male with images of virile stags.

This was just the start of the Australian government campaign to try to prevent public opinion swinging against the tests. Supply Minister Howard Beale recognised Penney was a good public speaker and came across sympathetically to the public, far more so than Titterton or himself. Beale demanded Penney be made available to the Australian public, give interviews and write newspaper articles to convince people the 1957 tests were necessary and posed no threat to health. It was arranged and Penney gave national radio talks on the promising peaceful use of nuclear energy. Titterton wrote newspaper columns with headlines like 'Our A-Bomb tests are a MUST – they can't harm us'.[5]

Menzies sought to allay mounting criticism that the British seemed to have complete freedom to do what they wanted at the nuclear testing grounds. Professor Leslie Martin, chairman of the Australian safety committee, warned his superiors that radioactive contamination of the atmosphere and the testing ground was becoming a vexed political issue that could impact on the tests. Martin advised there be a new body, independent of the safety committee, to advise the government on radiation levels detected around the country. This would leave the safety committee to concentrate on the actual testing procedures. This new body, the National Radiation Advisory Committee, was set up in May 1957, four months before the scheduled Antler series of tests at Maralinga.

With the British atomic tests becoming a seemingly permanent fixture in the Australian outback, Menzies decided Australia needed a more permanent role in the administration of Maralinga. This was by no means a challenge to British authority over the project. Rather, it was an attempt to demonstrate how closely Australia was involved in the project. The decidedly pro-British and pro-bomb Ernest Titterton replaced Martin as head of the safety committee. The new body established to handle administration of the test site was the Maralinga Board of

Management – a body under the control of the Australian Ministry of Supply with an Australian chairman and both British and Australian members.

The question that should have been asked by those protecting Australians' interests at this time was: why does Britain need to explode still more atomic bombs in the outback? After nine atomic bombs exploded on Australian soil, surely the scientists knew their bombs worked? But Menzies wasn't asking, and the British weren't telling. The official reason was British scientists were still perfecting their atomic weapons. The real reason didn't emerge until thirty years later when Penney told the Royal Commission: 'Scientific tests of the Antler series were needed to confirm understanding of the triggering mechanisms for the high yield thermonuclear explosions conducted at Christmas Island in the Pacific.'[6]

Britain planned for six atom bomb tests in 1957 at Maralinga, three from towers and three suspended higher in the air from balloons. Australia didn't say no to this number of tests, which was an increase on the four in 1956 (plus two at Monte Bello), but Canberra did express concerns they weren't being given enough information about what sort of tests were going to be carried out. Titterton was the only one being fully briefed on what the UK intended, and even though he was head of the safety committee, some officials in Canberra were starting to raise concerns that the government needed more than the say-so from such a pro-bomb supporter to make a well-informed decision whether to approve the tests.

The British pulled back before it came to the crunch, and scaled back the number of 1957 tests to three. The first bomb exploded on 14 September 1957 was called Tadje – a relatively small one-kiloton bomb detonated in a tower.

The British left nothing to chance. A file the author uncovered at the UK National Archives showed the British declared the test a success before it actually happened. A British Foreign Office press release dated 11 September 1957 – three days before the bomb detonated and marked to be released by the Australian Minister Howard Beale – said the test was 'highly successful and cloud behaviour was accurately forecast and in accordance with the requirements of the safety committee'.[7]

Eleven days later another tower bomb, called Biak, exploded with the force of six kilotons. The third, on 9 October, a 26.6-kiloton bomb called Taranaki, was suspended 300 metres above the ground by barrage balloons.

The tests were timed to explode at a period of the year when winds were thought best for the drift of the nuclear clouds. This proved to be very wrong.

•

Alan Batchelor was a young army lieutenant in a construction group when he was ordered to Maralinga in early 1957. Much later he learned four other officers had knocked the job back. By that time he knew why. His assignment was top secret and he had no idea what he was to do at Maralinga. He arrived the day before his birthday and it was only then he was told he would be involved in nuclear testing. On his first tour of the site he was shown the health physics decontamination area where people were examined for radiation exposure and showered till they did not register on the Geiger counter.

'It was my one and only visit to that section. I never went there again.'[8] Batchelor described health standards for Antler as being extremely slack. His job was to supervise troops building roads and platforms for ground zero.

'I was at Maralinga for six months. At no stage was I told of the dangers of exposure to radiation. I wasn't told to scrub and shower in case of radiation exposure. We weren't tested to see if we had radioactive dust on us. We had bush showers – just buckets tied up high on ropes. Under it was a shower head which we unscrewed to open the water.'

During six months at Maralinga, Batchelor saw all three Antler atom bombs detonated. The third was the second biggest ever exploded in Australia at 26.6 kilotons.

'We were eight miles [12.8 kilometres] from the blast and it was awe-inspiring. We were dressed just in shorts, shirts and boots. We turned away from the blast flash and there was this powerful white flash. It felt on my neck like someone just behind me had opened the door to a very hot oven. There wasn't much of a strong shock wave, certainly not enough to knock you over. I turned around and saw the fireball heading up into the sky. It was a boiling ball of red flame. The smoke ring went up and earth fell down the side of the cloud. The earth itself looked as though it was boiling. Then the mushroom cloud rose into the atmosphere.'

Batchelor and his men were at the edge of ground zero just thirty minutes after the blast.

'We had to pick up instruments used for the tests. They were in thirty-two shelters close to the blast zone. Half were so close to ground zero that sandbags covered the entrance door and they had two feet of concrete over the top. We weren't given any radiation equipment at all. The scientists with us had white coveralls but no helmet.'

Batchelor said people doing this close-in work were called 'immediate re-entrants'.

'It was hard work moving hundreds of sandbags. You can imagine how much radiation the men were exposed to as they did that. We were sweating and out in the open. We had a field badge on our clothes. It showed nothing to us, but they were sent away afterwards for readings.'

Batchelor wasn't involved in the Royal Commission inquiries and didn't start investigating what happened to him and his men at Maralinga until 1998.

'British documents showing readings taken from field badges do not include those re-entrants. We were excluded from official records because re-entrants had received higher dosages. People who later made a claim for radiation exposure were told their names aren't in the books, therefore they could not have received a dose.'

He said after the second Antler test there was a wide contaminated area because the winds kept shifting after the explosion.

'The area was covered in fine dust. We had to provide people to sweep the fallout to the edge of the work area. The health physics people told them to work up-wind as they swept but the dust was blowing up everywhere. They told them to take their masks and caps off and shower thoroughly. Once they finished, the site was classified as a red zone – that meant it was forbidden to eat in this zone. But on each occasion they served a meal while we worked there. They never tested us for inhaled material and that is the most dangerous of the lot. They knew about that, but they did nothing about it. If you don't test for contamination you can always argue there was no contamination.'

Twelve months before Batchelor went to Maralinga his wife gave birth to a healthy son. Twelve months after Batchelor's time at Maralinga his wife had a miscarriage. The foetus was badly deformed.

'I was sterile for the next nine years. They did tests on me and after that I was sent to survey remote parts of north Queensland. I think it was a deliberate move to get me away from the public. The troops I was with at Maralinga were broken up and sent to remote parts of the country so we couldn't compare notes.'

Batchelor stayed in the army for thirty years, reaching the rank of major. During that time his wife had test after test.

'My wife's doctor tried to find out from military doctors what I had been through at Maralinga and was told there was nothing wrong with me.'

•

Corporal Brian McCloskey was taken aback when the major sending him to Maralinga said he might come back sterile.

'That hit me as I was due to get married the next year. I tried to get out of it. I don't know if this major was joking, but he said I had to go as I had been nominated. I'd studied civil engineering and surveying so they picked me to "volunteer".'[9]

His job was to survey blast sites and roads being carved out of the scrub.

'We wore white overalls when we entered the zone where they had exploded atom bombs earlier. But we had no gloves or mask. We were working in dirt and dust for three to seven hours a day. We had a film badge but they didn't run a Geiger counter over us when we got back. We had to give the badge to the health physics people and they registered our name against it. We had a shower, but had no idea how much radiation we were exposed to. Dust got into everything, even back in our tents. We'd wake up with nose and mouth clogged with this fine dust.'

McCloskey was at the camp for the first two tests – Tadje and Biak. Like thousands of others who saw the bombs explode over the years, he was dressed in shorts and loose shirt. When the bomb flashed he could see the bones of his hands.

'Within a few hours of the bombs going off we were sent into the blast zone to recover instruments in bunkers four to five miles [eight kilometres] from the blast. We had to clear the sandbags for the boffins to go in and get their instruments.'

But for the third and biggest bomb – Taranaki – McCloskey was the last man closest to the bomb for the blast. He had to measure how high the bomb was hanging by the balloons above the ground and how vertical the three balloons were in the air.

'I was told to take a measurement twenty minutes before it exploded. I was pretty close to being right underneath it. I made my measurements and jumped in the jeep and got out as fast as I could.'

There wasn't much time for error. He had no back-up vehicle. It was twenty-four kilometres on a dirt road back to the camp. He floored it, and tore up the dirt road in a cloud of dust. He made it with just a few minutes to spare. He didn't notice anybody checking to make sure he was back. What if the jeep broke down? 'Well, then I'd be a bright spark,' he laughed.

Often the tests were cancelled at the last minute because of wind shifts. McCloskey said they had worked in forty-degree heat for hours, sandbagging the bunkers only to be told the blast was cancelled.

'We had to go out and shift all the sandbags, knowing we'd have to do it all again tomorrow. The blokes were getting pissed off at this happening day after day. We later learned the blast had been cancelled even before we did the work. That night the boys had a few grogs and decided to do some mischief. They sneaked some gelignite and drums of oil into a ditch out near the security watchtowers. Next morning while we were in the mess having breakfast they lit a fuse and it went off with a terrific bang that shook everything. It set off such a huge stink. Cables flew between Canberra and London. Security people questioned everybody. They thought it was sabotage.

'Some Aussie blokes confessed. One was a sergeant. The Brits wanted to put them in jail and strip their ranks. The Aussie officers stood up for them. They said nobody was hurt and it was in reaction to doing all the work with the sandbags when the command knew it wasn't needed. They ended up getting a slap on the wrist. Funnily enough we heard that same day a plane wandered over the forbidden area and had to be chased out. Cables were flying between Canberra and London.'

McCloskey married in 1958 as planned. They had children in 1960, '62 and '68. The first two girls had asthma. Four grand-children also have asthma. In 1972 McCloskey was diagnosed with glaucoma and diabetes. He believes it was caused by his exposure at Maralinga. One of the men he worked with, Sapper Harvey, died of cancer in the late 1960s.

•

RAAF motor mechanic John Bradley spent a lot of his time at Maralinga hosing down and cleaning vehicles used on the site. It was very muddy work. With others, Bradley was ordered to a spot about thirteen kilometres from ground zero to watch the third and largest atom bomb of 1957. He remembers the atom bomb blast as both amazing and frightening.

Bradley said a mere twenty minutes after the blast he led a convoy of trucks, caravans and water tankers to about 100 metres from ground zero. 'I was the closest to the actual epicenter of the blast.'[10] The few shrubs and trees that were still standing were on fire. Even thick wooden sleepers used as a base for the caravans were smouldering and Bradley had to shovel sand on them to put them out. During a break he sat in his truck eating an apple just 100 metres from the highly radioactive ground zero.

'One of the scientists ran a Geiger counter over me and said I was way over the safety limit and that I had to leave the area. But I was unable to do so until I had finishing setting up the caravan.'[11]

When he left the hot zone he handed in the radiation dosimeter attached to his shirt, but he was never told the result. A short time later his feet swelled up and a thick yellow pus started oozing from between his toes. A year later the same thing happened again. Doctors gave him no explanation and treated the problem with penicillin. In 1960 he had severe bouts of vomiting and was anaemic, a condition that lasted the next twenty years.

'I am convinced I suffered from radiation sickness. We were not given any instructions regarding safety precautions, nor issued with protective clothing. We wore our summer uniforms. The scientists were dressed in spaceman-type outfits and had showers equipped to clean off any radioactive dust. I consider we were used as guinea pigs at Maralinga – we were in a zone as dangerous as any war zone.'[12]

•

The use of protective clothing seems to have been haphazard at best. Navy rating Stewart Harrison worked on water purification at Maralinga for eleven months. It was difficult work – the bore water was much harder than seawater to purify and the machines had to be maintained constantly. He saw the explosions and the mushroom clouds. 'I wasn't worried about it at the time, you feel bulletproof at that age,' he said.[13]

'I got on well with the British soldiers I met around the camp and one of them, a sergeant, took me in to see where the bombs had blown up. I wasn't supposed to go there, but I was curious. They dressed me up in protective gear and I went through the decontamination process.'

Harrison later developed colon cancer, but he can't say whether it was because of that visit to ground zero.

•

Scientists wanted to know what impact there was on vital internal organs from walking into a contaminated zone. The only measurement of the men was the dosimeter on their shirts. The scientists made a wooden man, dressed him in standard protective clothing and attached dosimeters to parts of the body where the testicles would be, the ovaries, the spleen and the lungs. They then 'walked' the dummy over the contaminated ground on poles in front of vehicles.[14]

The military boffins had already made their mind up about how soon after an atom bomb troops could enter the blast zone. The British military's secret Nuclear Handbook for Instructors and Staff Officers, prepared in 1957, said it would kill a soldier if he walked across ground zero within one hour of an atom bomb exploding. Doing it three hours after the explosion would cause radiation sickness but he would recover. If he walked in six hours after detonation 'he should certainly arrive and remain fit for duty'.[15]

There was no mention of what might happen to him later.

•

Some servicemen working at Maralinga had hardly any contact with the contaminated sites or equipment. British RAF national serviceman Fred Stallard volunteered to go to Australia for a secret mission, thinking it would be a real adventure. It was a long trip in a Hastings troop carrier plane, stopping at north Africa, Iraq, Ceylon (Sri Lanka), Singapore, Borneo, Darwin and finally Maralinga.

'I then learned we were there for the atomic tests and my job was to look after planes at the airport, refuel, check oil, that sort of thing. We were in tents for the whole four months I was there and we saw the bombs go off from the airfield about fifteen miles [twenty-four kilometres] away. We turned our backs and I swear I could see the bones of my hand when the flash hit us.

'The only Aussies we saw at Maralinga were civilians building roads. They were a tough outfit, holding boxing matches for fun and a few bets. They invited us down on our first day – they were a tough mob.'[16]

Stallard was kept away from the planes that landed after flying through the atomic clouds. 'They were kept to one end of the field. Others were assigned to cleaning those planes.'

Stallard had a healthy life but two granddaughters had problems – one born with shallow hip joints and another with misshapen bones in her chest.

'I don't know if that was due to any exposure I got at Maralinga – I sure hope not. That would be terrible.'

•

John Hutton was on his second tour of Maralinga. He didn't see the bombs on his first tour when he was eighteen and doing roadwork. In 1957 he was nineteen and a lance corporal in charge of a small squad of soldiers preparing bunkers for the atomic blasts.

'We dug a long trench and put long tubes along it with one end up for taking measurements. We surrounded it with sandbags so it was level.'[17]

Hutton saw the late afternoon explosion from the camp, doing what others did – turning his back, closing eyes for the flash, then turning around to see the smoke and ball of fire boiling into the mushroom shape. He was awestruck. Then they were ordered to go back to the bunker to help the scientists retrieve instruments. The experience turned him from a happy-go-lucky teenager into a terrified young man with memories that haunted him for the rest of his life.

'We were one of the last to go into the blast zone and it was almost dusk. We topped the hill near the blast zone and saw everything was on fire: all the bushes were burning, flames were flying out of mulga trees like acetylene torches. Near ground zero, flames from the burning tree roots were coming out of the ground.

'We were in white protective outfits and had gas masks on. But as soon as you were out there it was so hot you couldn't see anything through the masks. You had to take them off to do the work. This was two hours after the bomb blast. We had to pull all these sandbags out to get to the instruments. That took about forty-five minutes in searing heat. We were about 150 yards [137 metres] from the concrete platform used for the blast. The instruments were buried about six feet under ground and we had to move hundreds of sandbags to get to the door of the bunker.

'There was an acrid stink. Your nose filled with dust and dirt. The scientist waited in the vehicle until we moved the sandbags and got the bunker door open. The scientist then went in and checked the instruments. He took the gear he needed and left, leaving us there. I realised then we were just slave labour. To me, what happened to the troops used for the British tests was the greatest miscarriage of justice of all time.'

•

RAF national serviceman David Farnell was an operations clerk at a bleak airfield in north Yorkshire when he saw a notice seeking volunteers for 'Atom trials in Australia'. He leaped at the chance to visit Down Under.

He found himself stuck in the Edinburgh base north of Adelaide handling paperwork. One day he saw a flight plan for a fully armed RAAF Lincoln to be on hand for an atom bomb explosion at Maralinga. The Lincoln was armed so it could shoot down balloons holding the bomb if they broke away and started carrying the atom bomb towards Adelaide. An Aussie pilot officer kindly managed to get Farnell on board the Lincoln as an observer. He was dressed in white overalls, white wellington boots, a dosimeter and an eye patch. 'The patch was so that if we saw the flash we wouldn't go blind in both eyes.'[18]

'Once we were out over the ocean they tested the guns and the delicious smell of cordite wafted through the plane. The gunners let me sit in the gunners' seats and swing the guns around. This was fantastic – I was only nineteen and this was heaven.'

The plane flew around and around the bomb site at some distance – after all they were only there if something went wrong with the balloons.

'At the allotted time the countdown started. The captain made sure no one was looking as time ticked down: 3, 2, 1 FLASH. The count went up again: 1, 2, 3. When the shock wave reached the Lincoln the plane was buffeted around the sky. After "3 LOOK" I craned up into the middle gun-turret to look. The cloud was soaring straight upwards until it topped the plane. The mushroom head was a turbulent ball of red fire. The crew went quiet. We did a couple more circuits and headed back to base. The cloud was by then sloping away to the east at about forty-five degrees. I went to finish off some of the chicken sandwiches provided for the flight but was advised against it. A bit mean, I thought at the time!'

When they landed back at Edinburgh base that night a scientist waved a Geiger counter over him and it chattered in beeps. Farnell was advised to go back to his billet and take a long shower and scrub hard. As he walked over the tarmac, he looked up at a sky full of stars and saw Sputnik 1, the Soviet satellite launched a few days earlier.

'It was a head-shaking moment – what incredible things mankind was doing! It wasn't until much later that I realised and felt some shame I had been part of the development of a weapon of mass destruction.'

•

When Farnell saw the mushroom cloud drift to the east, he could not have known it wasn't supposed to do that. In fact in not one of the three tests in the 1957 Antler series did the wind do what it was expected to do.

Preparations for monitoring the fallout as far afield as possible were far more extensive for Antler than they had been for the previous tests. Apart from aircraft flying through the mushroom cloud like they had from the first test at Monte Bello in 1952, for Antler there were mobile monitoring stations – essentially jeeps with sticky paper to catch contaminated dust – and eighty-five stationary mobile stations scattered around the nation.

The committee drew up a table showing safety levels for a radioactive cloud at varying times after the explosion. One hour after detonation the table had a maximum safety level of thirteen millicuries per square metre – up to this level there would be no observable effect on people living under 'civilised' conditions.

But for 'primitive' people (no footwear or clothes and sleeping in the open) the safe level was 4.6 millicuries per square metre. This number decreased the longer the time passed since the explosion. In Bourke twelve hours after the explosion, so-called civilised people were safe so long as the readings were less than forty-five millicuries per square metres – for 'primitive' people, the safe level was only up to 9.3 millicuries. But if millicuries reach 410 for 'civilised' people and 120 for 'primitive' people they could have 'temporary slight sickness' if they had a low threshold of sensitivity to radiation.[19] This was the safety committee's way of differentiating between whites and traditional Aboriginals for the Antler tests exposure safety levels.

The radioactive cloud from the first Antler bomb, the one-kiloton Tadje, drifted north when it was expected to head east. Radioactive fallout was detected as far away as Alice Springs. Parts of the cloud blew south-east, and detectable amounts of radioactive dust fell on Melbourne and Adelaide. Titterton's safety committee characterised the fallout on the major cities as 'trivial'.

Fallout from the second bomb, the six-kiloton Biak, headed north-west of the blast zone rather than the predicted north-east. The cloud rose to unexpected heights and then drifted east. Eight hours after the explosion the lower part of the cloud passed over the small town of Marree, 650 kilometres from Maralinga. Fallout was travelling much further than expected. It eventually crossed the east coast at Coffs Harbour. A higher part of the cloud drifted further north, passing out to sea near Queensland's Fraser Island. Another part of the cloud broke away and passed over Cairns.

The 26.6-kiloton bomb Taranaki, suspended by three huge balloons, didn't drop as much fallout over the test area because it had exploded 300 metres up in the air. The radioactive cloud drifted east. Twelve hours after the explosion the cloud sat over the New South Wales inland town of Bourke. It drifted on to Port Macquarie and out to sea. Ground stations showed fallout from Taranaki had spread over most of the eastern half of the continent. The highest level of fallout recorded was at Bourke, where 6.2 microcuries per square metre were registered the day after the Taranaki explosion. This was well below the safety level for 'civilised', clothed humans set by the safety committee, but was very close to the safety limit for 'primitive', unclothed humans, who live outdoors nearly all the time.

But the ground stations merely measured radioactive dust that settled on sticky paper at the monitoring station. It did not take into account dust that settles on roofs or dams and then ends up in drinking water. It did not take into account contaminated dust that is ingested, either through breathing or the digestive system through eating grass-eating animals such as sheep or cattle. During the Antler series, scientists also collected samples of soil, herbage and sheep thyroids at selected spots around the eastern half of the continent to see how much contamination penetrated the food chain. Official reports at the time said the thyroid tests showed there had been no detectable biological damage to sheep.

Fallout from Taranaki also reached Adelaide, Melbourne and Sydney. Levels detected in the cities were well below what the test safety authorities deemed harmful to humans.

But this wasn't the first time major cities and towns had received radioactive fallout from the atomic tests. The mining town of Coober Pedy copped a fallout level above the safety level for 'primitives' from the first test in the Buffalo series – One Tree – and fallout was detected from Coffs Harbour to Townsville as the broken-up cloud crossed the coast. The highest fallout recording was at Lismore in northern New South Wales, where it rained. A whole-body gamma dose of about 220 microsievert was recorded, double the strength of a dentist's X-ray; not harmful for short bursts, but the fallout was settling everywhere. Armidale, Tenterfield, Bourke and Marree also received fallout from One Tree.

It rained in the east when the radioactive cloud from the relatively small Marcoo test drifted over and fallout was distributed between Sydney and Bundaberg. A wind shift for the third Buffalo test blew the cloud south, right over Maralinga village. Fallout on the military men working on the tests was deemed 'negligible from a biological point of view'.[20] Part of the cloud continued south-east, dropping contamination over Adelaide, Hobart and much of Victoria, including Melbourne.

The fourth Buffalo test, Breakaway, a ten-kiloton bomb, sent a cloud north that went as far as Darwin, with the highest fallouts at Birdsville, Marree, Roma and Charleville. Part of the cloud drifted over Brisbane, where it met light rain. Contamination in the rainwater for Brisbane was the highest for the entire series.

Going further back, the second round of explosions at Monte Bello in 1956 – Operation Mosaic – had just twenty sampling stations on the north-west coast of Australia and one in each capital city. One would think for the biggest bomb the British exploded they would have had more monitoring stations. The British had certainly provided enough equipment for forty-eight sampling stations, but the safety committee (with Titterton as its central figure) thought it wasn't necessary. The wind changed direction after the first fifteen-kiloton bomb, depositing fallout over the north coast of Australia. The safety committee sent a message to the Australian government that conditions for safe firing and subsequent fallout were 'fully met'.

For the second bomb – the massive sixty-kiloton Mosaic G2 – the wind once again changed direction, bringing the cloud over the mainland. Fallout fell in totally unexpected places, including Broome and Port Hedland, passing safety levels set at that time in the remote town of Derby in the Kimberleys. More than half the population in Derby is Aboriginal, and the fallout would have had even more impact on them because of their lifestyle of living largely outdoors. Three years later, safety levels were tightened and the safe limit lowered.

'By later standards the doses estimated from the fallout at Port Hedland exceeded the levels for members of the general public,' the Royal Commission concluded.[21] Safe levels set for Aboriginals were exceeded in Broome and Nunkanbah.

The safety committee set up for the Monte Bello Mosaic tests lied to the Australian government. They covered up the fact that radioactive debris from the two bombs fell on the mainland. The Royal Commission was more polite, saying the safety committee's messages to the government after Mosaic were 'misleading'.[22]

Worse was to come.

8

'YOU NEVER SAW THOSE ABORIGINES, AND THAT'S AN ORDER!'

It was another routine incredibly hot day on 14 May 1957 at a radiation decontamination site called Pom Pom well to the north of Maralinga. Air Force engineer John Hutton just happened to glance out the dusty window of his mechanic workshop caravan. He was staggered to see a nearly naked Aboriginal man calmly walk over the little hill that lay between the camp and the nuclear test sites.

'Holy shit, that can't be possible,' he thought to himself.[1] He looked again. The figure shimmered in the heat. The man was tall and lean with a big bushy beard. He was dressed only in a loincloth and carried several spears in one hand and a billy can in the other. Hutton couldn't believe his eyes as the traditional desert Aboriginal man walked steadily towards the caravan.

'But there are no natives here. That's what they told us,' Hutton muttered to himself. 'Where the hell has he come from? Surely not from the restricted zone?'

The Aboriginal man walked right up to the caravan and tried to peer through the windows. Hutton knew the Aboriginal man couldn't see in because the windows were covered in a reflective plastic to keep out the heat. The man moved from the window and continued walking around the back of the caravan.

Hutton called out to army engineer Captain Rudi Marqueur, who was at the other end of the caravan.

'Sir, there's a darkie outside, er, an Aboriginal man, sir. He's just gone around the back.'

Captain Marqueur rushed over and peered out the caravan door. When he saw the tall Aboriginal man looking around he swore and his face dropped. Hutton had never seen a man so shocked.

'Quick, call security,' Marqueur shouted, his voice panicky.

Hutton picked up the phone and called Sergeant Frank Smith, who was in charge of security for the radiation detection team up at the Maralinga camp.

'Sarge, we have an Aboriginal in the camp.'

'What?'

'He just came in from the desert.'

'Oh crikey! I'm on my way.'

Hutton kept watching the Aboriginal man as he wandered out of the camp and leisurely strolled back in the direction he had come from. He was heading towards a site called Marcoo, where an atom bomb had exploded at ground level with a force of 1.5 kilotons seven months earlier. The area was highly radioactive.

Frank Smith raced up in his jeep in a cloud of dust. On his head was his usual big cowboy hat. He skidded to a halt and yelled out to Hutton: 'Where did he go?'

Hutton pointed in the direction of the hill and Smith roared off, the jeep bouncing around in the rough terrain as he tore up the hill looking for the Aboriginal man. After a while he saw a small family group of Aboriginals camped near the edge of the massive crater that the atomic test had left in the ground. They'd killed a kangaroo and cooked it the previous night. Smith couldn't see any evidence they had drunk from the pond of water in the base of the crater. He hoped they hadn't. He stopped the jeep some distance from them and got out slowly and calmly, not wanting to panic the group. He walked towards them, showing his hands were empty, and gestured in a friendly manner. When he reached them he tried talking to them but neither side understood a word of the other's language. With hand signs, Smith managed to convince them to follow him to the camp.[2]

Smith came back over the hill with the man, a woman and two young children – a boy and a girl. Four mangy dogs followed behind them. Smith was clearly shocked and concerned. Several scientists arrived from Maralinga, also looking shocked. Smith tried to ask the family where they'd come from and how long they'd been in the area. It was no use. They looked at each other confused and frustrated. The scientists said the family had to be taken to nearby decontamination showers in case they'd been exposed to radiation.

The desert Aboriginals had never seen showers before, let alone caravans and jeeps and trucks. They couldn't understand why these strange white men were pushing them to stand under the falling water and letting it just dribble away – water is precious in the desert and these crazy men wanted to let it just fall and soak into the sand.

The scientist in charge ordered Smith to force the Aboriginal family under the shower, but stopped short of having Smith lay his hands on to wash and scrub them. 'No, no, don't touch the woman or the girl,' the scientist ordered. He seemed to fear that any man touching the Aboriginal woman, especially to wash her groin area, might antagonise the man. Hutton thought the scientist also seemed to regard it as distasteful for any white man to touch the black woman's genital area, even if the purpose was to clean off any radioactive dirt.

The woman was clearly terrified. When she first went into the caravan she started talking to her reflection in a mirror. She had never seen a mirror before and thought it was another Aboriginal woman inside the caravan. She was asking the reflection what was going on.

After the washing, the family were bundled into a Land Rover and taken to Yalata, a former sheep station now operating as a government-sponsored Lutheran mission, 160 kilometres south of Maralinga. It was a long, dusty journey and Yalata was a terrible place of alcoholism and disconnected desert Aboriginals. It was far from the traditional tribal lands of the family.

Soon after the family had been taken away, Hutton and the other military men and scientists who had been present were ordered to assemble in the village parade ground.

Hutton couldn't believe his ears as a colonel in full uniform took the stand and yelled at them: 'You did not see any Aborigines in the camp today. They were never here. It did not happen. Is that clear? I said, is that clear?'

The assembled troops nodded and said: 'Yes, sir.'

The colonel continued: 'Now, the British and Australian governments have poured a lot of money into the atomic tests being conducted here and if word got out about what happened today it would reflect very badly on the program and on all of us. If I ever see stories in the press, or I hear any of you discussing this with anybody, there will be severe consequences. I will find out which one of you talked. I remind you all that you have signed the Official Secrets Act and if you breach that Act you can be shot or sent to jail for thirty years.'

Hutton was only nineteen, and the threat from the senior officer scared him. Many years later the Maralinga range commander at the time, Richard Durance, told the Royal Commission into the nuclear tests that he was undoubtedly the colonel who warned the men. He said he didn't remember the incident, but he confirmed it was an action he would have taken at the time.

'The whole range was a very secret affair. The less that was said about it the better. Any knowledge that started to seep out to the public, certainly an incident of that nature would, I think, have been very serious. It could have been an embarrassment to both [British and Australian] governments . . .'[3]

In other words, if the public found out that Aboriginals were moving around freely in the nuclear tests areas, it would be far worse for the authorities than whatever effect the exposure might have on the Aboriginals.

Worse was to happen to the family who wandered into the Pom Pom camp that day. Once at Yalata their distress grew when soldiers took their dogs away and killed them. They gave no reason. Not one they understood anyway. Their ordeal wasn't over. The true horror of their fate was not to emerge for another thirty years.

In April 1985 the legal team from the Royal Commission into the nuclear tests headed by Justice Jim McClelland travelled to Maralinga and sat down with the surviving members of the family to hear their account of what happened.

Through an interpreter, the commission learned their family name was Milpuddie. In 1957, they were father George, mother Edie, four-year-old daughter Rosie and little boy Henry. They had no idea they were in a restricted area. They had been travelling south right across the nuclear test site towards an old mission site called Ooldea, about forty kilometres south of Maralinga. They hoped to trade dingo pelts there for knives and axes. They didn't know Ooldea had been closed by the government five years earlier when the nuclear test site was set up. They had no concept of not being allowed to walk through their traditional lands.

George Milpuddie died in 1974 of pneumonia. Edie Milpuddie told the Royal Commission that after she stood under the shower the soldier held something near her that made a clicking noise. Recounting her story, sitting on the ground surrounded by other tribal women, Edie indicated there was something she wanted to say but didn't want to say it in front of the lawyers and journalists watching proceedings under the tarpaulin set up for the hearing.

McClelland and commissioner Jill Fitch walked away into the scrub with Edie along with her friends and the translator. Edie agreed the content of what she said could be recorded in the proceedings. In trembling voice, she told McClelland and Fitch she had been pregnant when they were found at the Marcoo crater. Shortly after they arrived at Yalata, she gave birth to a child that was dead. She buried the stillborn baby in the bush.

'She believes that fact is related to the Marcoo experience and to what they describe as the poison from the range,' counsel for the Aboriginals Geoff Eames told the commission hearing.[4] Her next baby, a boy called Allan, was born four years later. At age two he died of a brain tumour. A third baby, a girl, was very premature and weighed just one or two pounds (about 500–800 grams) at birth. Edie's daughter, Rosie, who was a four year old at the Marcoo crater, lost a baby in 1973. Edie's grandchildren have suffered extraordinary ill health and numerous deaths.

According to official records, however, the family had not been exposed to radiation. The Australian health physics representative at Maralinga, Harry Turner, went to Pom Pom when the Milpuddies were being showered. He took photos of them and later wrote in his report that the only reading above normal was on the boy's hair and around his buttocks, and that was just ten counts per second above background.

'None of the others had any detectable contamination on their bodies or clothing. There is no possibility that any of the family could have experienced any radiation injury,' Turner wrote.[5]

Interestingly, he wrote this report four days after the incident. He had reason to report everything was OK.

A file the author found in the UK National Archives shows that on 16 May, two days after the incident, the British commander at Maralinga sent a cable to head office in London informing them of the discovery of the family at a contaminated area near Marcoo. The cable says they were thoroughly washed and inspected before being sent to the mission.

'The count was practically negligible on all four and it is felt here that there will be no dangerous results. It is hoped to keep this incident from the press.'[6]

The cable says the Australian minister – Beale – has been informed 'in case there is any sudden publicity, but all possible steps are being taken here to prevent this'.

The cover up was ordered from the very top.

Durance told the Royal Commission that when Beale read the top secret account of the incident he asked Durance whether the dogs had been checked for radiation and what happened to them. When Beale was told they weren't checked and were still with the family at Yalata, he was furious. He ordered Durance to shoot the dogs immediately. Durance didn't know why Beale wanted the dogs shot, but it is probable Beale didn't want any chance of outsiders testing the dogs for radiation poisoning.

Frank Smith, the army sergeant who found the Milpuddies' camp near an atomic crater, told the Royal Commission he had previously seen signs of Aboriginals in the forbidden zone several times over the years he was there. But each time he reported it to the Maralinga authorities, they told him he was seeing things.

'They told me I was going troppo, that I had been up there too long; did I realise what sort of damage I would be doing by finding Aborigines where Aborigines could not be.'[7]

Smith said his reports about finding Aboriginals in the desert near the tests were met with 'hostility and absolute disbelief'.

•

From the very start of the atomic bomb tests the possibility of Aboriginals being within hundreds of kilometres of the blasts was discounted, ignored or deliberately covered up.

In the early 1950s there was hardly any data on the movements of desert Aboriginals in central Australia. There were no official figures. Aboriginals weren't counted in the national census. Sometimes they were listed along with farm stock. This didn't change until 1967 when a national referendum finally changed the constitution to count Aboriginals as citizens and allow them to vote.

Documents unearthed at the Royal Commission revealed that when the British first considered central Australia as the ideal place to blow up their atom bombs, their only source of information about the desert Aboriginals was *Encyclopaedia Britannica.* From the Australian authorities there were more statistics and scientific data concerning kangaroos, rabbits, cattle, birds and snakes in central Australia than there were about Aboriginals.

The treatment of the First Australians at the time was simply disgraceful – they could not vote, had no right to claim traditional lands, their children were stolen to be raised by white 'charities', they received little education and the health of many in white mission stations was deplorable. Alcohol and diseases brought in by whites had a devastating impact. Nothing much was being done to help the outback Aboriginals. Indeed, Australian government policy amounted to the slow and steady annihilation of traditional Aboriginal life. In 1952, Territories Minister Paul Hasluck told the Menzies cabinet: 'As more and more natives come into touch with mission stations or settlements and adopt European ways the need for large reserves as hunting grounds will decrease, and as the process of detribalisation continues the protection of their tribal grounds and ceremonial areas will become less important.'[8]

The British and Australian authorities planning the atomic tests had only one concern: to make sure no Aboriginal could get close enough to disrupt the tests.

For the first four years of the British tests at Emu Field and Maralinga, only one man was assigned to search for Aboriginals who might enter the no-go zone. The prohibited zone was a staggeringly huge area of one million square kilometres – five times the size of the United Kingdom; an area bigger than Germany, France, Belgium and Holland combined.

The man hired for this impossible task was a remarkable bush character called Walter MacDougall. A shy, lanky man with fiery red hair, MacDougall was the son of a Scottish Presbyterian Minister and went to the prestigious Melbourne school Scotch College. As a young man he liked rugged farm living and drove a team of nine horses. He headed to the outback as a missionary and got on well with desert Aboriginals, running the Ernabella mission in north-west South Australia, 200 kilometres north of Emu Field, and learning the Pitjantjatjara language.

MacDougall lost his right thumb and forefinger in a gun accident in 1938, and was knocked back when he volunteered for military service in the war. He kept on trying and was allowed to drive military trucks to Darwin. In 1947, he became native patrol officer for the new Woomera testing range, a job he found frustrating as it tied him to the office and he did not accept the bureaucratic dismissiveness towards Aboriginals. When he was reprimanded for using his vehicle to take sick Aboriginals living outside the range to hospital, he shot back that he would look after Aboriginals wherever they might be. It wasn't an easy fit. MacDougall was by far the best informed white person about Aboriginal life and culture in central Australia. Not only was he a skilled bushman, he was accepted by the traditional Aboriginals as *kuta*, a brother, and was given the rare honour of joining some of their sacred ceremonies.

In 1952 preparations started for Maralinga and all Aboriginals were to be moved out of the area. The nearby Ooldea mission was closed and the residents forcibly transported 120 kilometres south to a new mission set up by the South Australian government at Yalata near the Eyre Highway, the road running between east and west Australia. Lutheran missionaries ran Yalata and imposed harsh rules to stamp out traditional ways. The move was a disaster for the Aboriginals. They had been removed from their traditional land and cultural links. They had little to do. Resignation and apathy set in. At Yalata they came into contact with alcohol and disease brought by white men on the highway. MacDougall wrote about Yalata: 'Secret life significance has ended, mainly due to the lack of interest shown by young people and opposition to it by the missionaries.'

By this time MacDougall was promoted by the South Australian government to the post of Protector of Aborigines, and he strenuously protested at the atom bomb authorities building the new Giles meteorological station on an Aboriginal reserve close to the West Australian border. Scientists needed the weather station for the bomb tests. MacDougall warned the presence of white staff would adversely affect the Aboriginals' traditional way of life. Many desert Aboriginals had still never seen a white man.

MacDougall spent weeks travelling alone in the vast prohibited zone looking for signs of Aboriginals. He estimated there were between 1000 and 1500 Aboriginals in the million square kilometres of the test zone before Maralinga construction started in 1955. The Aboriginals' traditional paths between water holes and sacred sites took them hundreds of kilometres through the outback. MacDougall wrote numerous reports for the government, warning if traditional Aboriginals were removed by force from their traditional lands where they knew where to get food and water 'they were likely to die from homesickness'.[9]

MacDougall infuriated the test authorities when he wrote an article for an Adelaide newspaper in November 1955 warning that 2500 Indigenous people were in potential danger from central Australia being opened up by the atomic tests and miners: 'Whenever the white man finds something of value to him in any Aboriginal area the Aborigines are pushed aside. I believe that what is happening to these natives is contrary to the spirit of the declaration of human rights in the United Nations charter. If no check is possible they seem doomed to increase the number of displaced persons in the work world – to become prideless, homeless vagabonds living by begging, stealing and government handouts.'[10]

H. J. Brown, controller of the Woomera range, was furious. He tried to have the article suppressed before publication. When that failed, he hauled MacDougall over the coals, berating him that he had no right to speak to the public. MacDougall refused to buckle. He told Brown the government was breaking promises made to the Aboriginal people when Woomera was set up in 1947. Brown wrote to Alan Butement, the chief scientist in charge of Australia's contribution to the test program, warning him that MacDougall was out of control and might go public with his claim Australia had broken promises to the Aboriginals. Butement hit the roof. Determined to crush this lone voice against the tests, he wrote back to Brown that MacDougall had a 'lamentable lack of balance in his outlook in that he is apparently placing the affairs of a handful of natives above those of the British Commonwealth of Nations'.[11] Butement thundered MacDougall was 'out of step with current opinions and the sooner he realises his loyalty is to the department which employs him the sooner his state of mind will be clarified'. Butement told Brown to instruct MacDougall to stick to his 'sphere of activity and leave policy matters to those whose responsibility they are'.

Shortly after this clash, a second patrol officer, Robert Macaulay, was appointed to work alongside MacDougall. Macaulay was clearly out of his depth. Fresh from graduating in anthropology at the University of Sydney, he was a 23-year-old who hadn't been outside Sydney before. He came highly recommended by his professor, a pro-bomb conservative. It turned out, however, that Macaulay agreed with MacDougall that it was in the best interests of traditional Aboriginals to limit any contact with the white people working on the bomb. Macaulay mapped Aboriginal sites near the Giles weather station and barred the whites from going anywhere near them. They were forbidden to feed Aboriginals who came to the station and had to encourage them to move on.

Blocking traditional Aboriginals from their hunting and spiritual grounds had a crushing impact. In 1957, a West Australian parliamentary committee found Aboriginals on the border with South Australia were starving because they were denied access to hunting grounds by the prohibition zone. 'One thousand Aborigines are so beset with hunger and disease that they are living under the worst conditions in the world,' the MPs reported.[12] When this was recounted to the British Foreign Office they replied it was a matter for the Australians. The Australian Minister of Supply, Howard Beale, said starving Aboriginals had nothing to do with the atom bomb.

'No natives have been driven from Maralinga or Woomera area. The test area is uninhabited. No natives have been found there and therefore none have been interfered with,' Beale wrote.[13]

Macaulay joined MacDougall in the forlorn and hopeless patrolling of the vast stretches of the outback in their jeeps. They were woefully under-equipped for the task. Macaulay had to borrow a vehicle, and they patrolled in remote bushland hundreds of kilometres from the blast site along the South Australian–Northern Territory border. Neither patrolled close to the actual blast zone so there was no way of knowing whether any Aboriginals had got past them. With the vast distances involved, it was like searching in Paris and not seeing an Aboriginal family walk past on a dirt track in Munich. Macaulay couldn't search for Aboriginals before the Antler trials as there had been sudden floodwaters and he was stuck on a rocky outcrop for a week. If by chance they did come across an Aboriginal in the prohibited zone, neither had a radio to call the base to stop the test. Small wonder then that the Milpuddies could walk all the way into Maralinga without being spotted.

MacDougall died in 1976, before the Royal Commission. Macaulay told the commission Aboriginals were entering the prohibited area from Western Australia. With just two patrol officers it was highly unlikely they could be found. Macaulay said it was impossible to be sure there were no Aboriginals in the prohibited zone given the negligible resources they had. He said it would take at least ten people patrolling in vehicles and working closely with air patrols to check the zone properly. But with only two patrol officers there were enormous gaping holes in the totally inadequate efforts to keep Aboriginals out of the danger zone.

Alan Flannery was a security guard at the Emu Field site for the Totem tests and later at Maralinga for the Buffalo tests. He told the Royal Commission it was taken for granted there were no Aboriginals in the prohibited zone, so security guards at the camps didn't go out looking for them.[14] The guards put up signs in English around the blast zone that said to keep out as it was a prohibited zone, and that was about it.

The attitudes expressed by the senior officials in charge of the tests show the plight of Aboriginals did not rate on their scale of considerations. When the Milpuddie family strolled in it caused a huge panic and a deliberate cover-up.

Other more horrific stories were raised at the Royal Commission. Australian soldier Terry Toon told the commission he was driving on a rarely used track some distance from Maralinga in April or May 1956 when he found the corpses of two adults and four children in the dirt beside the track.

'They were all skin and bones and rags,' Toon told the commission.[15] He said five soldiers were with him but he refused to name them to the commission, saying it was up to them if they wanted to speak out. Toon said one of the soldiers later committed suicide. When he got back to the base he told his senior officer about it and the next morning they went out to inspect the spot. The officer marked the spot with a pile of rocks. Toon said senior people later went out with a bulldozer, but he never heard what happened.

British soldier Gordon Wilson from the Royal Engineers told

the Royal Commission and later interviewers from the Imperial War Museum that he was at Maralinga in 1957 for the Antler tests.[16] He often went hunting with a couple of Australian soldiers. One time they were about three kilometres from where the bombs were due to go off when he was stunned to see three men walk up to them out of the desert. 'One of the Aboriginal men asked me for a shirt. I gave mine to him and he gave me a boomerang. We were just being friendly.[17]

'He showed us his camp in the bush. It was a whole family, about seven of them with children. He showed us how to throw a twelve foot long spear with a woomera.'

Some time after the Tadje explosion, Wilson went looking for the Aboriginal family. He found them and one of them talked about seeing a bright light and a huge noise. Wilson said he saw them three times over the course of several months.

'Nobody told us they shouldn't have been there. I didn't tell anyone, such as an officer, we'd seen them, as it never occurred to me. I thought it was their country.'[18]

The widow of Royal Navy seaman Bill Grigsby claimed that before her husband died in 1977 he told her he'd seen Aboriginals camped in a Maralinga bomb crater in 1962. They were covered in sores.[19]

In 1984, before the Royal Commission was set up, former RAF officer John Burke made a dramatic death-bed claim that he'd found four dead Aboriginals in an atomic bomb crater in 1963 at Maralinga.[20]

Burke said when he reported what he'd found to his senior officers he was threatened with jail under the British Official Secrets Act if he ever talked about his discovery. He settled in Adelaide, and said he had received about a dozen anonymous phone calls over the years warning him never to reveal the dead bodies.

Speaking on TV the day before he died, Burke said he was breaking his twenty-year silence because it weighed on his conscience and he was dying of stomach cancer, probably caused by his exposure to radiation at Maralinga. Burke thought the four Aboriginals had died from radiation sickness after further explosions in 1963. He believed more Aboriginals may have died in the contaminated areas of Maralinga because nobody made any attempt to keep them out of the detonation zone. He also found about 200 dead galahs around the crater. He saw rabbits and kangaroos that were deformed with stunted limbs or extra features, like a third ear.

Eighteen-year-old British airman Patrick Connolly spent sixteen months at Maralinga in 1962–63. He also told the press he had seen four Aboriginal bodies in a crater there. The Royal Commission subpoenaed him to appear at the Royal Commission in 1985. By this time Connolly was living in Australia. He told the commission he saw groups of Aboriginals around Maralinga at least six times in the year he was at Maralinga. He said he never wrote up reports about seeing Aboriginal groups on the range, he just told them to head south to the railway rather than walk across the prohibited area.

'It was quite common to see them, everybody did. Everyone knew they were walking across the range, including senior officers.'[21]

Connolly said he was at the airfield when he heard Burke having a heated argument with another RAF officer over a problem with Aboriginals. Connolly said he drove Burke to pick up a senior RAF officer and a British army doctor and they drove to the range. He said the base commander, Australian Lieutenant Colonel William Henderson, followed in another vehicle. Connolly said Burke told him he had found remains of four Aboriginals in a restricted area and said: 'I told the fucking bastards something like this would happen. Now maybe they'll do something about it.'

Connolly said he stayed with the vehicle while Burke and the other officers walked up to the crater. Connolly said he could see four huddled shapes on the ground.

'They were four black people lying huddled together in a depression. I saw the officers talking for a while and the doctor bent down to examine them.'

He was told to drive Burke to the airport while the others stayed behind. Five or six weeks later Connolly went back to the spot and there was no sign of the bodies. Burke told him he couldn't say anything about it because of the Official Secrets Act. Later Connolly asked Burke what had happened. Burke told him to mind his own business and to shut up about it.

'He said if news about it got out, it would create one hell of a stink and not to mention it to anyone. There were rumours that many Aborigines had fallen sick from being in the radiation areas and that a radiation hospital had been set up at Yalata.'

Connolly said he was thirty to forty metres from the crater and had no doubt they were human bodies. Burke told him at the time they'd died from radiation exposure or were too close to the blast. Connolly said after he spoke to a Perth newspaper in the 1970s about radiation sickness at Maralinga, two men came to his home claiming they were from ASIO.

'They said I was rocking the boat and was breaching the Official Secrets Act by divulging anything I'd seen at Maralinga and they could send me back to Ireland if I talked publicly. I was told to keep my mouth shut.'

The Royal Commission rejected Burke's and Connolly's accounts after the other people, the two British airmen identified as being present at the crater, testified they had not seen any dead bodies.

Henderson, a general by the time he gave evidence, told the commission the incident never happened, that he was never told about any bodies being found on the range, and didn't remember Connolly serving at Maralinga while he was there. All records of what happened at the range were sent to Britain.[22]

9

MINOR, SECRET AND VERY DIRTY

Shortly after the explosions of Operation Antler, the Hollywood makers of the nuclear apocalypse film *On the Beach* asked the US Navy to lend them a nuclear submarine to make their film look more authentic. The US Defense Department refused, saying the movie and the Australian book it was based on had its facts wrong. Nevil Shute's 1957 novel, set two years after a nuclear war destroys all life in the northern hemisphere, tells the story of people in Melbourne preparing for the end as the deadly radioactive cloud rolls steadily towards them, extinguishing all life on the planet. US Navy chiefs said a nuclear war would not destroy all life on the planet. There would be survivors, they argued. They didn't want to assist a movie that was 'defeatist' and projected such a 'pessimistic and false notion of nuclear warfare'.[1]

The film's director, Stanley Kramer, asked how many people would be killed. The navy replied that only 500 million people would die in a nuclear war. Kramer shot back that the prospect of over 500 million fatalities should be an incentive for the US Navy to support a film that warned of the dangers of nuclear weapons. The US Navy didn't relent, wanting their ships used in more positive films.

But the Menzies government, drooling at the prospect of Hollywood stars Gregory Peck, Ava Gardner and Fred Astaire making a film Down Under regardless of the content, lent the Australian aircraft carrier HMAS *Melbourne* for the shoot.

Menzies probably regretted the decision. His fellow Melbournians weren't at all impressed when Ava Gardner reportedly said Melbourne was the perfect place to film the end of the world. (Decades later a Sydney reporter admitted he'd made up that quote, but it stuck.)[2] The film and Shute's novel had a huge impact on attitudes towards atomic testing and the terrifying prospect of nuclear warfare, and the anti-bomb movement grew.

In the mid 1950s to mid 1960s, the chances of the Americans and Soviets suddenly hurling nuclear missiles at each other was very real. In 1956 the Soviets brutally crushed a pro-democratic uprising in Hungary. In 1957 the US was shocked when the Soviets were first into space with the Sputnik satellite. The Cuban Revolution was followed by the CIA's failed Bay of Pigs invasion. Then the Berlin Wall went up, the Soviets shot down an American U2 spyplane, and the Cuban missile crisis brought the world to the brink of nuclear war.

John F. Kennedy read *On the Beach* and saw the film, and it may have influenced his thinking as his generals urged him to strike first during the 1962 Cuban missile crisis.

In 1958 Britain exploded a series of hydrogen bombs at Christmas Atoll in the centre of the Pacific Ocean, later renamed Kiritimati. The largest of the UK Grapple series bombs measured a powerful 3000 kilotons. The British had gleaned the knowledge to explode these hydrogen bombs from the bombs it had exploded in Australia.

Nuclear fever gripped the world's military and political leaders, and the thirst for bigger and bigger bombs continued. In 1958 a total of 116 nuclear bombs were exploded around the world: seventy-seven by the US, thirty-four by the Soviets and five by the UK. In 1961, the Soviets exploded Tsar Bomba, the most powerful nuclear bomb in history with a force of 50,000 kilotons. Over the next twelve months more atom bombs were exploded than in any other year – a record 178: ninety-six by the US, seventy-nine by the Soviets, two by Britain and one by new nuclear club member France.

The mood in Australia had turned against the British continuing to test their atom bombs on Australian soil. The reality was Britain no longer needed Australia as a place to explode its atom bombs. After the success of the British hydrogen bomb series on Christmas Atoll in the Pacific, the United States decided to join forces with its old ally and allow British scientists to resume work with the US nuclear program. Britain could explode its bombs at the American chief test site in Nevada and work with the Americans on Bikini Atoll.

But the British were keen to keep their hands on the Maralinga site. They still wanted to test firing mechanisms and explosive material used in nuclear warheads. They had been conducting secret experiments they called 'minor trials' in Australia since 1953, beginning at Emu Field and continuing at Maralinga in 1955. These tests were conducted in absolute secrecy.

For a while British scientists considered holding these minor trials at the northern tip of Scotland. They ruled it out because wet weather would lead to radioactive material leaking into rivers and lakes. Penney told the Royal Commission there was no chance of that happening in the dry scrubland of Maralinga.

The minor trials had to continue at Maralinga, the British said. The safety committee headed by Titterton fully agreed. Menzies accepted their recommendation without question, even though the minor trials were to be run on a 'need to know' basis. As far as the British were concerned, the Australians didn't need to know.

Australians were deliberately excluded from the so-called minor trials. Australian scientists weren't allowed anywhere near them. Australian military involvement was strictly limited to menial work such as laying roads and digging holes. Even the Australian safety committee was barred from attending the minor trials.

The British were anxious to avoid any attention on the minor trials. When Titterton asked the British in 1957 if he could publish a paper on the low level of fallout from the 1956 Mosaic tests, he was told there was no security objection. But they did express a concern that if fallout levels from Mosaic were made public, there might be pressure to release fallout levels from the later tests at Maralinga. Those levels could be higher than Mosaic and 'might cause alarm which could be exploited and tend to nullify the advantage of open publication'.[3]

Whitehall asked Canberra not to allow any publicity for the minor trials whatsoever. As usual, the Menzies government quickly acquiesced. With no huge mushroom clouds to see, few paid any attention to the minor trials anyway.

As far as the general Australian public knew, Britain's nuclear tests in the outback ended with the balloon-suspended 26.6 kiloton Taranaki bomb on 9 October 1957. The tests ended with a bang. Taranaki was the biggest atom bomb exploded on the Australian mainland. It's all over, the government let the public think. Menzies' Defence Minister, Athol Townley, told the Australian public any projects being carried out at Maralinga and Woomera were joint operations by the Australian and UK governments. He told parliament: 'We have access, of course, to everything in the nature of tests carried out at the two places.'[4] It was a bald-faced lie.

But some officials in Canberra worried these secret minor trials weren't quite so minor. The British gave them innocuous, even cute names such as Kittens, Tims, Rats and Vixen. Between 1953 and 1958 there were hundreds of these secret minor trials. Nobody in Canberra knew what the British were really up to out in the outback. Titterton, now chairman of the safety committee, kept on assuring the government that everything was fine, that it was all perfectly safe and no harm could come to the country.

One or two senior Canberra officials and ministers were asking how could Titterton be so sure all was fine if the British excluded him from the minor trials. When the minor tests picked up tempo again in 1959, the British wanted to include plutonium for the first time. Titterton assured the British there would be no problems from the Menzies government about plutonium. A British official in Canberra cabled London: 'A difficulty arose because the safety committee whose advice was sought had been given no information on the proposed trials. Fortunately Titterton took it upon himself to agree in principle even though he had no details.'[5]

Some senior Canberra officials, and one or two ministers, privately expressed doubts about the wisdom of allowing the British free reign in the outback. Menzies had such a strong hold on his government, however, that none dared go so far as to press cabinet to halt the minor trials. The Menzies government kept on approving the trials even though the British never specified the materials they were using in their tests. The British told Titterton 'radioactive and toxic materials' would be used, but he assured the British that the Australians didn't mind.[6] When the British mentioned there may be some long-term contamination on the Maralinga range from the trials, again Titterton said this was acceptable. By this time Titterton was virtually part of the furniture at Aldermaston, the centre of British nuclear research, with his frequent visits to Britain. He was lauded, flattered and feted by the British nuclear establishment. A knighthood was in the offing. Titterton loved being the centre of their attention, and he gave them everything they wanted.

The British were so thrilled by this meek acceptance of their trials, funnelled through Titterton, they decided not to mention any details of the trials to the Australian government. As one Whitehall mandarin wrote in an internal memo: 'I agree with

Titterton that we should avoid formal communications on these contentious experiments and propose that we proceed without going through the normal channels.'[7]

Proceed they did, right through 1959, 1960, 1961, 1962 and 1963, with hundreds of small explosions and other sorts of tests that involved extremely dangerous plutonium, uranium-235 and uranium-238, and beryllium. It is not known exactly how many minor trials the British secretly ran at Maralinga. Some estimates put it as high as 600. The British say it is around 300, but to this day are not providing more details, claiming the tests are still classified.

As the minor trials ground on, Defence Minister Townley did express some concern about the nature of the Maralinga minor trials. His question was whether the mysterious tests being conducted at Maralinga might breach the fragile international moratorium on nuclear tests which the US, Soviet Union and UK had agreed to in late 1959. It meant no atmospheric nuclear explosions were to be carried out while negotiations continued for a permanent nuclear test ban treaty. The pressure for a ban on atmospheric tests came after growing worldwide protests at the ever-increasing size of hydrogen bombs and the contamination of the Earth's atmosphere.

Despite it being arguable that Britain's plutonium tests at Maralinga broke the moratorium, Australia raised no questions about the minor trials and continued giving them the green light.

The superpowers had an easy way to get around the halt to atmospheric nuclear explosions – simply go underground. Britain considered moving its nuclear bombs under the Australian outback. Britain had been looking at a suitable site in Australia for an underground nuclear explosion as far back as 1958. They didn't want to be caught short if there was a sudden international atmospheric nuclear test ban. The ground within a few hundred kilometres of Maralinga was not suitable: it was too likely to break up and leak radiation. The most likely suitable place was under Mount Lindsay, 400 kilometres away, but that was inside an Aboriginal reserve. The British noted in a secret internal memo it would require a formal notice in the government gazette for drilling to be legal, and it would be difficult to devise a believable cover story.[8] The Menzies government never said no to the British blowing Australia up from underground as well as in the air. In the end it didn't become necessary, as the US allowed the British to join them at their underground test site at Nevada.

That didn't stop Menzies adopting the moral high ground in 1961 when the Soviets broke the test moratorium with a nuclear bomb. Summoning all his anti-communist bluster, the prime minister stood in parliament to berate the Reds for not wanting peace and having no respect for international agreements. He did not mention the fact Britain had continued its nuclear experiment program in the Australian outback right through the years of the international moratorium.

Despite more than five years' experience of the British exploding nuclear bombs on Australian soil, the Australian and British military men and civilian contractors sent to provide the manual work for the minor trials were treated more abominably than ever. They were used as virtual lab rats, sent into radioactive zones with no or minimal protection while scientists stood back in full protective gear taking their measurements.

•

Leading aircraftman Geoff Gates volunteered for twelve months at Maralinga in 1961. He knew what they were doing out there and he didn't worry about the tests. But the RAAF didn't tell him anything about the dangers of radiation. 'I was twenty-two and bulletproof,' he laughed.[9]

He was given top secret security clearance for twelve months, building platforms and pads elevated three metres in the air.

He helped build sixty tons of steel around the containers they were going to explode.

'When the trials were scheduled I was told to hang around with the Land Rover in case I was needed to drive scientists around. They all wore white overalls while I was dressed in just shorts and khaki shirt, boots and socks. We had dosimeters attached that showed how much radiation we'd been exposed to. It looked like a thick pen and you look down it and see the number. They wrote these readings in a book. It was 0.1, 0.2, all the way up to 1, then 1, 2, 3, 4, 5. It didn't go any higher. The safe level you were meant to be exposed to was a 0.2. I was a 0.5 most days.

'I'd watch the clerk read the dosimeter, mutter to himself that it was too high, say, "That can't be right", and write down a lower number. I looked at it myself and I could see the number.'

Gates is certain it was part of a deliberate cover-up of the levels of radiation service men like him were exposed to at Maralinga.

'I am sure the clerk was operating under orders to write down lower readings if they got too high.'

Other nuclear veterans tell the same story. Joseph Pasquini was an RAF navigator in a Canberra bomber taking measurements at 46,000 feet for the hydrogen bomb tests at Christmas Atoll in 1958. He insists the blast was easily three times the power of the official count of 3200 kilotons. He kept a record of the level of radiation the crew were exposed to in the plane's logbook. He later found the official recording of their exposure was far lower, even though they used the same film badges.[10]

During the minor trials, the British far outnumbered the Australians, but that didn't prevent Gates and his best mate at Maralinga, young RAAF airman Avon 'Rocky' Hudson, taking them on.

'I'd walk into the mess packed with Brits and say out loud to Rocky: "You won't believe this, Rock, there are Pommies out there actually queuing up to take a shower!" He'd reply, "Crikey, Geoff, that's incredible, and all in it together too!"'

But the more sinister side was that while the British scientists Gates and Hudson worked with did have showers after they'd been out on the range, Gates was never told to shower and scrub or warned of the risk of radiation. Gates said the British national servicemen he worked with weren't told to shower either. They didn't run Geiger counters over Gates after he'd been out setting up the platforms for the minor trial explosions. All he had was the dosimeter.

Gates left the RAAF six months after he finished his posting to Maralinga. Twelve months after Maralinga, his son was born with bipolar disorder. 'Some say it may have been caused by my exposure at Maralinga. His son is also bipolar. My family never had anything like this in our history. I got a pituitary tumour. The Department of Veterans' Affairs says it wasn't caused by the tests. We don't know, but so many Maralinga veterans have health problems there has to be a link.'

•

Avon Hudson joined the RAAF on his eighteenth birthday. Four years later he was ordered in to a room and two men in suits submitted him to a string of questions about his life, his family, his friends and his political thinking.

'What's this all about? Who are you?' Hudson asked, resenting this interrogation.[11]

'You don't ask questions here. You answer them,' the suits snapped back. Hudson later realised they were ASIO agents grilling him for security clearance for Maralinga. If ASIO had known at the time what a thorn in the side of the government Hudson would become, he would almost certainly have been barred from the test site.

Hudson expected it all to be a bit of a lark. An RAAF friend who'd been there the previous year urged him to go, as it was an easy job. 'Poor bloke didn't know it but he'd copped radiation and died of cancer a few years later,' Hudson said.

Hudson was surprised to find the desert camp a hive of activity. He worked six days a week for up to ten hours a day fixing machines and driving trucks delivering heavy cargo from the railway to the range. After a month or so on site he was assigned to British scientist Ken Taylor, to drive him around and work with him on building the platforms.

'Taylor was a decent chap. Most of the British boffins had an air of arrogance about them and treated us with disdain. I drove him every day to near the Taranaki site. I didn't know it had been used before in 1957. We were 200 metres from Taranaki's ground zero. We started building platforms for the Vixen series of tests.'

Hudson said neither he nor Taylor knew anything about the Vixen tests or what the minor trials were all about.

'We only got to know a little bit of the whole picture. Our job was just to build these sixty-ton platforms. We built about a dozen of them. I went in to have a look at one after they exploded it. We'd seen the explosion from the camp. The dirt and shit was blasted about 1000 metres into the air. At the site everything was blasted to pieces. Twisted and burned bits of steel and debris were lying everywhere.

'Security guys came up and very rudely ordered me out of the area. They took me back to the maintenance base. I was then reassigned to somewhere else. I couldn't see any logic to it as there was no secret in what I was seeing.'

Hudson was moved from one job to another, working on machinery and cranes, delivering fuel and water in special trucks.

'I was driving down a long dirt track when I saw three scientists in white coats working on a pad. They didn't hear or see me coming. I had to check a fuel tank nearby so I got out and walked to the tank. I saw it was full and I strolled over to the scientists to see what they were doing.

'Sitting on the pad was a nuclear weapon with all the bits pulled off it. It didn't have the nuclear fuel in it. It looked a bit like a radial engine with wires and pipes and all sorts of gadgetry. They were all concentrating on the weapon and didn't hear me coming in the soft dirt. I got right up behind them and said over their shoulder: "G'day, mate. How's it going?" Well, you should have seen them jump!'

The scientists were furious and demanded to know who this upstart Aussie was. Hudson was dressed only in his usual shorts and old shirt with no RAAF insignia. 'I looked like some kind of urchin. I told them I was checking the fuel. Two of them grabbed a canvas sheet and threw it over their bomb.'

'You are not supposed to be here. You are supposed to ask permission to come in here,' one of the scientists blustered.

'There was no bastard to ask,' Hudson replied. 'I just walked up this track to check on fuel for the generator, which is my job. I could see you through the bush but you didn't look up from whatever you're looking at.'

'You don't do that, you know.'

'Righto, mate, I'll see ya later.'

One of the scientists followed Hudson all the way back to the fuel tanker to make sure he was leaving. Hudson never heard anything about it but he knows the scientists would have filed a report. Hudson didn't tell anyone about seeing the weapon as there were informants among his own people, agents planted by base security.

'They ruled by fear. You didn't say anything to anyone about what you saw around the camp. I was in a fairly unique position as I moved around doing lots of different jobs. You didn't trust anyone as they could be a plant.'

By this time Hudson was suspicious of what was going on at Maralinga. He'd never been formally warned about the dangers of radiation and contamination, but he'd learned a lot from talking with Taylor and a few other friendly scientists.

Hudson took Taylor out for a bit of bush-bashing in the Land Rover, racing over sand dunes and exploring. Taylor liked the outback. Hudson showed him scorpions, snakes and poisonous spiders in return for a bit of scientific knowledge.

'I realised they'd never told us the truth of the dangers we were being exposed to. I suspected we were facing a far bigger risk from contamination. One time I went up to Emu to pick up some things they wanted and I was stunned. The place had been abandoned really quickly. You had to ask why. Taylor didn't know anything about it. The scientists were just like us – they just did their job and weren't told anything more than they needed to do their work.'

Hudson secretly decided to disclose what was going on at Maralinga once he got out. He couldn't openly ask questions, but he kept his ears and eyes open, taking a mental note of everything he saw. He was walking a thin line if anyone spotted what he was doing. Nothing could be written down. No notes, diary entries, maps or diagrams. That was far too dangerous. It would be a serious breach of the Official Secrets Act and he could be charged with spying. But sometimes things just slip out. One night Hudson was in the mess having a few drinks with British squaddies and, after a few good-natured jesting digs at each other, tempers started rising. Hudson resented the way the Brits were always looking down on the Aussies. One squaddie taunted that if it wasn't for the Brits, the Aussies couldn't even feed themselves. It was silly, but things got heated. The booze helped.

'I tell you, mate, Australia is like a red rosy apple and you Poms are like an old rotting apple that fell on the ground with all the other shit,' snarled Hudson.

One shot back: 'Well, mate, we have got things you colonial bastards will never have.'

'Yeah, like a queen,' said Hudson, a committed republican.

'She's your queen too, mate.'

'But she doesn't bloody live here, does she?'

'Hah, we got weapons you wouldn't bloody dream of. We have nuclear bombs and we'll drop them on any bugger we like,' said the Brit soldier.

With that a warrant officer stepped in and grabbed the loud-mouthed Brit and dragged him out of the mess.

'That was the last we ever saw of him,' said Hudson. 'It set me to thinking about what he had said about nuclear bombs and using them on anybody. I knew that's what the experiments were all about at Maralinga and I was very uncomfortable being part of it.'

Even though the Brit soldier was jumped on quickly after uttering the forbidden N-bomb word, security was generally pretty lax in the camp. Hudson kept on moving freely around the range in his roving job of delivering fuel and water. One of the places he went to regularly was a hangar at the airport isolated from all the rest. It was surrounded by a high wire fence with a locked gate. Hudson had to deliver water to the tank outside the building.

'You had to enter the house to get them to open the locked gate so I could drive in. One day the entry door was open. It was usually closed and you had to knock and wait till they came to open it and check you out. One time I knocked and it took them twenty minutes to open the door. So I couldn't believe that this time the door was wide open. I went in looking for someone to open the gate. It opened to a small room with nothing in it, like an air-lock or a waiting room. Another door led to the main building. I opened it and went into a hall about thirty metres long and fifteen metres wide. It was one of the biggest buildings at Maralinga, stuck way out on its own. Planes could come right up to the bay at the far end of the hangar.

'I couldn't believe what I was looking at. There were rows of bombs; well, you couldn't see they were bombs as they were all in a silver cylinder cocoon lying on trolleys. They were about two metres long and a metre high. I immediately thought they were nuclear weapons. I reckon there were ten to twelve of them all lined up. A door led off on the other side of the hall into another room and I saw the Poms were all in there with music going. Nobody was in the hall with the bombs.

'I walked over and hammered on the door. An RAF sergeant turned around shocked, and shouted: "What the bloody hell are you doing here?"

'"I've come to deliver water and I need you to open the gate."'

Hudson said the men inside were all British RAF and they looked alarmed and embarrassed that he'd walked right through the hall where the bombs were lined up. Years later Hudson saw photos of similar cylinders and learned they were filled with nitrogen to control the environment of the weapons inside. Hudson delivered the water, and he's certain the RAF men were roasted for leaving the guard post at the front door.

Hudson's resolve to expose what was going on at Maralinga was strengthened when he witnessed an arrogant British army officer's treatment of some raw conscripts who'd just arrived at the range. Hudson was delivering two-metre-high hydrogen cylinders to the site called Wewak, used for the Vixen B tests. He didn't know it at the time, but Vixen was the most dangerous and contaminating program of the minor trials. Hudson arrived at the checkpoint in his truck and the health physics officer said he had to wait as the area hadn't been cleared yet. This was quite normal and Hudson settled down to wait.

'Then this very plummy Pommie captain arrived with a squad of young British conscripts. He even had a baton stuck under his arm – in the middle of the bloody desert. I ignored him and just leaned in the shade of my truck. I watched as the captain argued with the health physics officer about the delay even though on the range a health officer outranked an army captain.

'This captain wanted to be back in the camp by twelve thirty and insisted he go down there now with these eighteen- and nineteen-year-old pale-faced kids just arrived from England. The health officer explained the dirt road had to be watered to get the dust down. Well, this bloody captain ordered his men back into the truck and defied the health officer, driving right past him.

'The health officer was left floundering. I often think what happened to those poor young blokes after they went down there with all this dust flying around contaminated by plutonium just because this arrogant bastard of a captain wanted to get back to the mess in time for his midday gin and tonic.'

Hudson waited until the water truck came and watered down the dust on the road. Its mudguards and bonnet were painted yellow, meaning it was used in highly contaminated areas. Yellow vehicles were kept in isolated compounds. They were later buried because they were too contaminated.

In the last few months that Hudson was at Maralinga, he found he was being sent less and less to sensitive areas.

'I have no doubt suspicion fell on me after seeing those bomb canisters in the hangar and wandering up to those scientists working on the nuclear bomb. It could be because I had reached my limit of exposure, or it might be they thought I was too nosy. When my time came to an end I was glad to be out of there.'

Hudson was promised a promotion if he stayed on in the RAAF, but when his six-year stint was up he left the force.

'I told them that, after what I saw at Maralinga, I wouldn't sign up again. I said we were handed over to the British who treated us with arrogance and disdain, and the Australian air force couldn't care less about us.'

Hudson was to live up to his promise to expose what he'd seen, and more.

•

The minor trials did not always go smoothly. For the Vixen B tests in 1960, eight barrage balloons, like those used in the Taranaki blast in 1957, were attached to measuring and sampling equipment. They were tethered by cables at different distances from the blast point. A sudden squall hit the site the night before the test, and seven balloons broke away. Five were found within a few kilometres from the range, but one blew 1400 kilometres east, all the way to the New South Wales country town of Cobar. Another blew to Hungerford, way up on the New South Wales/ Queensland border. It was extremely embarrassing for both British and Australian authorities as it led to questions whether a nuclear bomb could also break away and drift across Australia. There were huge concerns in Canberra that the British were bungling the tests.

Two senior British nuclear officials, Roy Pilgrim and L.T. Williams, were given the task of going to Canberra to issue grovelling apologies. They reported back to their London bosses that the Menzies government wasn't so much worried about the safety aspect of the balloons escaping, but were far more concerned with the political embarrassment it could cause them. They reported that Australian government ministers were very concerned about their slim majority of just one seat in parliament, and how any kind of incident at Maralinga might affect the voting public. In their cables to London the officials said Labor under Arthur Calwell would probably allow the current arrangement at Maralinga to continue, but a Liberal government without Menzies as leader might insist on more information being provided. Pilgrim said from his talks in Canberra, he believed the Liberals without Menzies might push for Australia to have a nuclear capability of its own and join the nuclear weapon club.[12]

Wayward balloons were the least of the bad news headaches being left by the minor trials. Some tests were designed to find out what would happen if plutonium, the most dangerous element on the planet, was burned in an accident. Plutonium was exposed to intense heat in controlled explosions. As a result, highly radioactive plutonium was scattered across the range after the Tims and Vixens trials as dust or tiny pebbles. Precisely how much wasn't clear as British record-keeping was surprisingly slack for an element that has a radioactive half-life of 24,000 years. Plutonium is most dangerous when inhaled as dust, causing damage to DNA and boosting the chances of cancer. Just a dozen milligrams of ingested plutonium are lethal for a human. A speck the size of a grain of sand lodged in the lung would be enough to cause cancer.

It wasn't until the Royal Commission in 1984 that the British finally came up with the figure of 24.4 kilograms of plutonium that had to be lying around the Maralinga range or under the first few centimetres of soil. About 900 grams had been found and taken back to Britain by this time. That still left 23.5 kilograms lying around.

Britain admitted that around 100 kilograms of beryllium – not as deadly as plutonium but a very toxic material – was also splattered around the Maralinga site. Oh, and there were more than eight tons of uranium-238, which has a half-life of four billion years. Last, but not least, there was 22.4 kilograms of uranium-235 with a half-life of 703 million years.

UK Prime Minister Sir Winston Churchill with Australian Prime Minister Robert Menzies in London, 31 January 1955. Menzies gave the UK all it wanted in testing its nuclear bombs in Australia. (*Newspix*)

ir Ernest Titterton – should he have faced harges of criminal negligence over the ests? (*photo by Peter Luck/National Library of ustralia ref. nla.pic-vn3158619-v*)

Nuclear bomb blast at Taranaki test site at Maralinga, 9 October 1957. (*Newspix*)

Sir William Penney, the UK scientific director in charge of the nuclear tests, watches through binoculars as the mushroom cloud builds after the first test at Monte Bello on 3 October 1952. With him on the aircraft carrier HMS Campania is Rear Admiral A.D. Torlesse, Commander of Naval Forces at the test. *(Imperial War Musuem GOV 5636)*

Christmas, Maralinga, 1960. From left: Avon Hudson, Bill Blight, 'Blue' Fisher Nev Laird, Ern Mace. *(Photo courtesy Avon Hudson)*

Fourth atom bomb test at Maralinga, Operation Buffalo, 22 October 1956. (*Newspix*)

Dummies in vehicle after test detonation, Operation Antler, 1957. (*UK National Archives, WO 320/3*)

The Advertiser

Woomera Atomic Explosion "Great Success"

U.K. MAY HAVE SMALLER BOMB

Second Blast Within Few Days

SIT-DOWN STRIKE BY CHINESE P.O.W.

Capitulation Forced By Indian Guards

Australian Security Effective

Mrs. Grills Unmoved At Sentence Of Death

"Distant Thunder Roll" Heard In North

Britain "Ahead Of World" With Atomic Weapon

The Adelaide *Advertiser* marks the first atom bomb exploded on the Australian mainland, 16 October 1953. (*Newspix*)

Avon Hudson at the Taranaki blast site, Maralinga, 2011. (*Photo by Jessie Boylan*)

Caretaker Robin Matthews holds clumps of melted and fused sand from the heat of the atomic blasts.

Sand melted into green glass by the heat of th atomic blasts still litters the ground at Maralinga

Signs mark the huge site of buried radioactive waste at Maralinga.

Lance Edwards holds his flight logbook from the time of the tests.

Bench in Adelaide commemorating those affected by the atomic tests.

Left: Edward Cheney holds his flight logbook from the time of the tests.

Below: Avon Hudson holds nuclear medal made by the veterans; they were never given an official medal.

The Advertiser

Adelaide, Wednesday, May 7, 2003 | State Edition | www.theadvertiser.com.au | Phone (08) 8206 2000 | $1.00* including GST

EIGHT GREAT FOOTY NAMES

AFL CARD COLLECTION - TOKEN, PAGE 117

Mystery of how 68 Woomera babies died

SECRET SITES

EXCLUSIVE

By COLIN JAMES

ANDREW Patrick Smith lived only one day after being born in Woomera in the early 1960s.

He was not the only baby to suffer such a fate during the British nuclear tests in South Australia between 1952 and 1963.

The Woomera Cemetery contains the gravesites of 68 children, including 22 stillborn babies and 34 newborns, who died when they were only hours or days old.

Now, 50 years later, new questions about their deaths have arisen in the wake of fears the nuclear tests caused widespread genetic defects and multiple cancers.

Answers to why the babies died so young are not easy to find, with official secrecy shrouding the small township where British missiles were fired into the desert.

Defence Department records from the Woomera Hospital have been sealed by the National Australian Archives with instructions they are not to be publicly inspected.

These include the hospital's outpatient cards and birth records.

Several former Woomera families have privately expressed concerns about whether the deaths of their children – particularly stillborn or young babies – were linked to radiation exposure.

Full Report: Pages 12-13

Campaign to force Hollingworth out

By Chief Political Reporter PAUL STARICK in Canberra

SENIOR Federal Government ministers are waging a public campaign to oust embattled Governor-General Peter Hollingworth.

During what they hope will be Dr Hollingworth's last days in office, Government leaders are speaking out in a bid to convince him to quit.

They believe Dr Hollingworth's position is untenable since an independent report last week revealed he, when Anglican archbishop of Brisbane in 1993, allowed a pedophile priest to remain in the ministry.

Foreign Affairs Minister Alexander Downer yesterday stepped up the pressure on Dr Hollingworth to consider his future, already conveyed by Acting Prime Minister John Anderson and Treasurer Peter Costello.

It is understood some of the senior ministers have been speaking on the issue with Prime Minister John Howard during his visit to the US.

Mr Howard has ruled out dismissing Dr Hollingworth, because the conduct happened before he took office in 2001. Senior ministers, however, are trying to prevent long-term political damage by forcing Dr Hollingworth's hand.

None is believed to have spoken to the Governor-General.

One prospect being considered, however, is asking a confidante to urge him to quit.

Liberal senator and former ACT chief minister Gary Humphries predicted Dr Hollingworth would resign because the pressure was becoming intolerable.

"It's quite likely, at the end of the day, he will resign on the basis that there is too much damage done to the position of the office of the Governor-General by him staying in his position," he said.

Continued Page 6

 | Metro forecast: Fine, 23° | Index: Page 2

The mystery of the baby graves at Woomera is one of the many unexplained legacies of the British nuclear tests in Australia. Adelaide *Advertiser* front page, 7 May 2003. (*Newspix*)

Yami Lester, Wallatinna Station, South Australia, 2006. *(Photo by Jessie Boylan)*

The sign and locked gate at the entrance to the Maralinga test site.

10
WHISTLEBLOWER HEROES

There are heroes in the sorry saga of Maralinga, heroic individuals who discovered what was really going on and stood up against powerful forces to try to bring out the truth. They risked their jobs, their careers and their finances. They withstood threats of being charged with breaking the Official Secrets Act and being thrown into jail or thrown out of the country. Some were hit with anonymous threats to their lives. But they would not be silenced.

Without these heroes much of what we know today about government lies and cover-ups in the British nuclear tests would still be buried beneath the red dirt of Maralinga and under the blue waters of the lagoon at the Monte Bello Islands.

•

Doug Rickard was just eighteen years old in 1957 when he answered an advertisement for a job as a technical assistant with the Australian government. No details were given, just that knowledge of electronics would be a help. He'd left school at Year 10 so was thrilled when he got the job and was sent to Melbourne for training. He joined fifteen others at a Melbourne office. They were told only that the job was in a remote location. They were questioned about their families and told to sign secrecy documents by men in suits who didn't give their name or organisation. Naturally Rickard and his new colleagues were curious, but when they were sent to the Commonwealth X-Ray and Radium Laboratories for two weeks' training with radiation equipment and decontamination procedures their excitement grew. They'd seen pictures of the atom bomb mushroom clouds in the papers and guessed they were being sent to Maralinga. For an eighteen-year-old it was an incredible adventure.

Rickard was told he'd be monitoring fallout after an atomic bomb. He was sent on a long journey to remote Mount Clarence Station in the north of South Australia, a homestead 180 kilometres from the Maralinga blast site. The vital importance of secrecy was again stressed to him and the others. Rickard was puzzled when a black car arrived in the middle of the night. He heard men get out and come into the house. There was a hurried discussion in the living room, then one of his team was escorted to the car and it drove away. The man was never seen again. Rickard thought he'd said something to a friend or family or perhaps the security people had discovered something in his past that ruled him out for the top secret work. Rickard never found out.

As the time for the test approached Rickard and the others were told to fan out in the path of the expected fallout and take measurements. The fallout went right over them and a fine dust fell on their clothes and head. Rickard had to cut off all his hair as he couldn't get the radioactive dust out of the Brylcreem he used to slick down his hair in the fashion of the day.

'That did the trick,' he later wrote.[1] 'After a final shave of my scalp and a washing at last the fallout was all gone. However I have often wondered if the amount of fallout on our clothes and skin was sufficient to create problems, and just how much we inhaled?'

Rickard was then moved to Maralinga where he was told to measure radiation levels on the ground around the blast zones of the bombs exploded in 1957. As a nineteen-year-old assistant he was about as low on the hierarchy at Maralinga as one could get. His first job was washing radioactive clothing.

'I had to salute the cleaners,' he later told the Royal Commission.[2] Nine months after the Tadje bomb he was told to take readings of the ground of the blast site in a set grid pattern. He said the white overalls he was given to wear while in the radioactive zone 'gave about as much protection as a piece of tissue paper'. Rickard noticed when he strayed outside the official grid he got far higher readings in specific spots. He turned over some of the dirt with his boot, and his Alpha particle measuring instrument went off the scale. He looked closely and saw several metallic-looking particles. When he waved his instrument over the particles it literally fried. He put thirty or so particles in a tobacco tin, shoved it into the back of the Land Rover and drove forty-eight kilometres to the health physics laboratory. As soon as he pulled up in his vehicle, his colleagues raced out of the building waving their arms and telling him to back off. Instruments inside the building had gone haywire as Rickard approached. They demanded to know what the hell Rickard had brought with him. When he showed them the pellets in the tobacco tin they reeled back as their instruments screamed at the power of the particles.

They used a gamma ray–measuring instrument to check one of the pellets. They were stunned when the radiation being emitted from the tiny particle overloaded the machine. Eventually they had to move the pellet to a wooden chair about ten metres away outside the building and got a reading of thirty millicuries. Just half that amount can cause injuries and even death if a person is exposed to it for an hour.

The material was Cobalt-60 – a by-product of the nuclear bomb tests with a half-life of 5.2 years. Harry Turner, head of the Australian health physics team, reported the discovery to the test authorities at Aldermaston in England. That's when the proverbial hit the fan.

'Immediately a heavy security blanket went into effect,' Rickard later told the Royal Commission. 'I was interviewed by a security officer and it was impressed upon me not to speak to anyone about this at all, particularly any Australians, no matter what their position at Maralinga. As the person who actually discovered the particles, and was involved in their recovery, I was under the distinct impression that the British authorities did not want the Australian government to know anything at all about what happened.'

Rickard was told not to even speak to his boss Harry Turner about it, only to British scientists. The British wanted as much of the Cobalt-60 collected as possible. The health physics team had all gone way past their safe level of exposure, so the British got a group of freshly arrived Australian soldiers who were on a training course to do the dirty work. Rickard said the young Australian servicemen could not be told what they were working with because of the security ban. They were given scoops made from used jam tins hammered on to the end of wooden broom handles and sent out to pick up the Cobalt-60 particles. Some pellets were so small they had to be picked up with tweezers. The troops' fingers turned red from the close contact. The pellets were then placed into heavy lead containers and flown to the UK.

The British were keen on keeping Rickard under close wraps. While at Maralinga he did a correspondence course to get his school matriculation certificate. When Rickard went to Adelaide to do the exam, two Federal Police officers went with him and stood beside him as he did his paper. 'The other people doing the exam in the hall must have thought I was on release from jail.'[3]

The British didn't want the teenager anywhere near people to whom he might reveal his experience, so they offered him a job in England at Aldermaston. Rickard naturally leaped at it. Much later he realised they were just keeping him under supervision and silent. 'This would have been a political bombshell if ever the Australian government were to find out about it.'[4]

Meanwhile Harry Turner told Titterton, the head of the safety committee, that Cobalt-60 had been found on the range by Rickard. Turner complained that the Australian health physics team and countless servicemen had walked over that range for nine months since the Tadje explosion without knowing the danger. Turner said Titterton replied he'd known about the Cobalt-60 all along.

'Titterton told me he had been told prior to the test that Cobalt-60 would be involved but they didn't tell me because they knew that I would find out anyway.'[5]

Turner told the Royal Commission he suspected Titterton was lying. When asked if the purpose of the tests was for the British to use Australia as a laboratory for scientific tests, Turner had no doubt: 'Yes, yes, I should imagine that is the situation.'

Turner said he was 'a little bit unhappy' the British kept the presence of Cobalt-60 secret from the people who would have to work in the contaminated area.

When questioned about this by the Royal Commission, Titterton said the health physics people could get lax over the long boring months of repetitive sampling in the outback, and keeping the Cobalt-60 secret would be a good test to see how alert they were.

'It was possible by this curious circumstance to give Harry and his workers a bit of a test, quite a small test, because the radioactivity of the cobalt was quite trivial compared to the radioactivity in the weapon.'[6]

Titterton denied a suggestion from the lawyer Greg James QC, who was representing nuclear veterans at the Royal Commission, that Cobalt-60 was deliberately concealed from the Maralinga workers.

'No, it was absolutely a guaranteed situation that Turner and his group would find it. It was interesting to us, who were responsible for this operation, to see how quickly they found it. They came out of it with flying colours, actually. They did the job really well.'

James suggested to Titterton that his claim he withheld information about Cobalt-60 as a 'little test' was nonsense.

Titterton angrily snapped: 'Are you calling me a liar?'

'Yes, Sir Ernest, I am calling you a liar.'

Puffed with outrage, Titterton floundered: 'I find that whenever people lose arguments that they cannot win logically they resort to shouting outrageous things at the person that they were unable to beat. That is all I wish to say.'[7]

It was a weak reply. Titterton had been exposed for what he was. He was lucky he wasn't charged with criminal neglect.

There was nothing trivial in the consequences of this 'little test' for the teenager who found the Cobalt-60. Rickard fell ill within a few years of his experience at Maralinga. He started to feel extreme pain in his right foot, the same foot he'd used to turn over the ground to find the pellets. He was feverish, with aches throughout his body. Doctors compared it to malaria, but could find nothing wrong. Despite the pain, Rickard studied and became a space engineer at the Woomera Deep Space Station. He was a popular speaker about outer space and his talks were recorded by the ABC.

In 1980, the Fraser government set up its AIRAC inquiry into allegations about fallout from the British atomic tests. Rickard tried to tell the inquiry his story of cobalt exposure. 'It was the most farcical meeting I ever had in my life,' Rickard told the Royal Commission four years later.[8] He said the AIRAC officials asked 'stupid' questions for exactly one hour, then dismissed him without getting to the Cobalt-60 issue.

By this time Rickard's health was deteriorating rapidly with severe stomach pain. He was diagnosed with myelofibrosis and underwent many operations. Climbing stairs left him winded. Doctors said his health problems were caused by his exposure to radiation as a young man. Rickard's bone marrow disintegrated and he was on morphine full time to dull the pain. When he sought his medical records, government health authorities said they were 'lost' and there was no record of him working at Maralinga. When he pressed his case the government authorities suddenly 'found' his medical files but they showed no unsafe exposure to radiation at Maralinga. After a long fight the compensation commission did eventually recognise his claim and held the Australian government liable.

The law could have gone a lot further and charges of criminal neglect could have been brought against Titterton and others for not warning of the presence of Cobalt-60.

The penalty for criminal negligence under the South Australian Criminal Law Consolidation Act 1935 is five years jail if the victim is seriously harmed, fifteen years if they die.

After many years of pain and agony stemming from his exposure to Cobalt-60 at Maralinga, Doug Rickard died in 2002 aged 63.

•

Biochemist Hedley Marston was a domineering and vindictive snob. He cultivated an air of superiority, revelled in displaying his superior knowledge of fine wine and food, and turned on the charm for those who could advance him.

By the time of the nuclear test in the 1950s, Marston was regarded as the doyen of public servant scientists at the fledgling Commonwealth Scientific and Industrial Research Organisation (CSIRO). He'd gained considerable respect in agricultural science circles for discovering that small amounts of cobalt in the feed brought sheep back to health from a diet deficiency. Scientist Roger Cross, author of a book on Marston, *Fallout*, says Marston was skilled at taking credit for the work of junior researchers.[9]

But Marston, an anti-hero to some, was the scientist whistleblower who stood up to British and Australian nuclear test authorities, as well as governments, for their lies about nuclear fallout. While the governments repeatedly assured the public there was no fallout outside the Maralinga test site, Marston persisted with research that clearly showed fallout was reaching capital cities like Adelaide, and he fought against efforts to silence him.

Marston's involvement began in 1956 when he was chosen to conduct a biological survey to determine the level of fission products in the fallout from the nuclear tests. It was one of the few scientific collaborations between Britain and Australia during the entire test series. ASIO had its suspicions about Marston as he'd received a favourable profile in a communist newspaper.[10] ASIO agents interviewed Marston's friends and colleagues only to find he was a strong supporter of Queen and Empire. He got his security clearance.

From the start Marston was highly critical of the methods used by the British to test fallout levels. The British method was to place boxes of growing grass in the fallout area close to Maralinga then feed it to sheep to see how much radiation they absorbed in the thyroid. Researchers cut out the animals' thyroid glands because they readily showed the uptake of Iodine-131, one of dozens of radioactive isotopes in nuclear fallout. Thyroid glands were easy to extract from the animals' throats and send to the lab in a jar for testing. Marston was to test sheep and cattle a few hundred kilometres from the blast zone to see what happened further downwind of the nuclear tests.

Marston decided it was pointless only to check a few hundred kilometres from the blast. If the aim of the sampling was to find how far fallout stretched, it would be necessary to take thyroid samples right across the continent. He decided to do the job as he thought it should be done. He'd show those Pommie so-called experts.

Marston never told farmers what the thyroid samples were needed for. The whole operation was kept as quiet as possible with staff sworn to secrecy. By the May 1956 tests at Monte Bello, he'd set up thirty-four monitoring stations across northern Australia with sticky paper to collect any radioactive dust. Marston was ready to take dozens of spot checks across the eastern half of Australia.

•

After the second 1956 test at Monte Bello – the massive sixty-kiloton blast on 19 June – old outback prospector Jack Tunny was the first whistleblower to get word out to the public about the fallout hitting Australia. Tunny got word to newspapers that his Geiger counter had gone off the scale when he held it against rainwater falling on his camp near Mount Isa. The report hit the front pages of newspapers around Australia and sent the government into a feverish effort to hose down the story. They said there was no reason for alarm as it was an insignificant level.

In Brisbane that night, electronics technician Luke Van Houdt was working late to finish calibrating a Geiger counter for the RAAF. He was puzzled as the device was registering higher levels of background radioactivity than it should.

'I walked around with the thing in my hand wondering what it could be, where had I gone wrong,' Van Houdt told Peter Butt for his 2008 documentary *Silent Storm.* He went to the window and suddenly the clicks of the counter rose. He couldn't work out where the radioactivity was coming from. He thought it must be something lying around the workshop. But when he ran it around the windowsill it shot up even higher.

'It was raining heavily outside. I stuck it out the window and the counter went off its rocker. Obviously we had radioactive rain.'

Van Houdt rang his boss to tell him what he'd found, but the young technician never got the chance to be a whistleblower. Within an hour a car turned up and silent men in overcoats and hats took everything away. Van Houdt's boss told him never to say anything as they were now subject to the Official Secrets

Act and they could go to jail if they discussed radioactive rain with anybody.

The government was in a huge cover-up mode. The safety committee and the Australian government repeatedly assured the public fallout from the huge atomic blast had drifted harmlessly out to sea. The minister with responsibility for the tests, Howard Beale, later wrote in his memoirs that the public revelations of fallout over Queensland and Brisbane was a massive problem for the government and could have cost him his job.[11]

•

Within a few days fresh animal thyroids were arriving at Marston's lab in Adelaide and he was staggered at what they revealed. The results were hot. Samples from across the country, from Alice Springs to Rockhampton in Queensland's north, showed thyroid iodine levels were 4000 times higher than expected.

The atomic safety committee didn't want to hear it. The British insisted the levels were within the safety limit and there was no danger to the public. The safety committee continued to feed that line to the Australian government.

Marston was furious at the reaction from the safety committee. He suspected he would not get a positive response when he rang Leslie Martin, at that time chairman of the safety committee, and took the extraordinary step of secretly recording his side of the phone call. Marston accused the safety committee and the government of lying to the Australian people.

'Les, this is beyond a damn joke. Have things got away from you? We took it on faith that there was no fallout on the continent. The government said at the time there is no possible harm to anybody. It is the most disgusting thing I have ever seen, and that will make every scientist indignant and I should imagine stir up the socialists. We just lack confidence in anybody now.'[12]

Marston wrote to his friend Mark Oliphant, distinguished nuclear physicist and opponent of nuclear weapons testing, calling the Maralinga tests a 'quasi scientific pantomime under cloak of secrecy and evasive lying by government authorities about the hazard of fallout. Apparently the people of Whitehall and Canberra think the people of northern Australia to be expendable.'[13]

Marston decided he could not trust the safety committee to tell the truth about fallout from Maralinga. He secretly set up his own rooftop monitors to measure the air over Adelaide. The third test, Kite, in the Operation Buffalo series at Maralinga exploded on 11 October 1956. It was smaller than previous blasts, but it was far more politically explosive. Within minutes of the three-kiloton explosion, the wind shifted towards the south-east, carrying the radioactive cloud towards Adelaide.

Farmers hundreds of kilometres north of Adelaide in rich orchard country saw a strange streaky reddish-brown cloud rolling towards them.

'It didn't look normal,' remembered farmer Rex Penna.[14]

Marston checked the air measurements on the roof of his building and was shocked to find radiation material levels of 96,000 when twenty was normal. The thyroid results came in again and they were 5000 times higher than normal.

But still the safety committee was assuring the public no radioactivity from the blast had spread outside the Maralinga testing zone. No news of the fallout was carried in the media.

Marston was furious. His anger wasn't just at the lies to the public, but that scientists could ignore facts and involve themselves so deeply in a political cover-up. He wrote to Oliphant two weeks later that Martin had admitted to him that the bomb had been let off in haste. Marston said he had decided to make his findings public. It would breach the Official Secrets Act, but he felt a higher duty to the public and to scientific truth. His anger grew even stronger when he learned Leslie Martin received a knighthood in the Queen's New Years honours list and Titterton the chivalric award Companion to the Order of

St Michael and St George, the CMG, dubbed by wits as 'Call Me God'. Marston felt if anyone deserved a gong it was himself.

Marston wasn't one to be discreet in his anger. ASIO quickly got wind of his threats to go public and marked his file 'scientist of counter espionage interest'.[15] Marston believed he was being followed, his correspondence monitored, his phone tapped, assessed for who he met and what he said. He was a marked man in a very dangerous game. At stake was the continuation of the British atomic test program and the future of the Australian government.

Marston wrote a report accusing the safety committee of lying to the Australian people. In it he warned the nuclear tests would result in increased cases of thyroid cancer in humans as Iodine-131 would enter the food chain through farm animals, and produce Strontium-90, particularly in children through drinking milk. He warned Strontium-90 would collect in children's bones quickly while they were growing and it would stay all their life. At the time there was a national campaign to provide children free milk in school to build stronger bones.

'There is a very serious likelihood that internal radiation from Strontium-90 may after a number of years result in many painful deaths from cancer of the bone.'[16]

He said his thyroid tests proved that extensive areas of Australia had been contaminated and that rain falling in heavily populated areas 2400 kilometres from Maralinga contained nuclear fallout. He said his air tests proved the third Buffalo bomb had contaminated Adelaide and surrounding countryside.

If the report was published it could put an end to future atomic tests. Titterton, who had taken over chairmanship of the safety committee, insisted Marston delete all references in his report to the safety committee and to Strontium-90. Titterton noted Marston hadn't tested for Strontium-90 and said, despite Marston's claims, international results showed Strontium-90 fallout in Australia was among the lowest in the world. Titterton said the evidence was the British tests hadn't had any impact on Australia.

Marston acknowledged he hadn't tested for Strontium-90, but said the proof would be found in the bones of toddlers and children. He sought to get his report published in the respected *Australian Journal of Biological Sciences.* But the publication cowered under Titterton's protests and refused to publish it. The row caused a furore in scientific circles, but the public was locked out of the revelations the report contained.

Sir William Penney warned there could be 'political grounds' in Australia to justify a restricted circulation of Marston's report.[17]

Sir Macfarlane Burnett, chairman of the National Radiation Advisory Committee and editorial board member of the journal, told Titterton he was worried the press might see the row as an attempt by government to interfere with scientific integrity, or as an attempt by 'left wing scientists' to interfere with defence preparations.[18] Marston was branded a Red Commie by his fellow scientists in a concerted effort to discredit him personally. It's standard operating procedure to silence whistleblowers and troublemakers: if you can't discredit what a person says, then discredit and disgrace the person saying it.

But Marston wasn't alone. Leading scientists around the world were starting to register alarm about the impact of nuclear-weapon testing on the human population of the entire planet. In Britain, the newly formed Association of Atomic Scientists, chaired by Professor Joseph Rotblat, warned that even a small dose of radiation fallout could increase the chance of contracting cancer.

Mark Oliphant attended a major scientific anti-bomb conference in Pugwash, Canada, in 1957 that concluded Strontium-90 from nuclear fallout could irreversibly harm the human race. Nobel prize winner Linus Pauling warned 15,000 children around the world were sacrificed for every nuclear bomb exploded in the atmosphere.

Pro-bomb scientists like Edward Teller, so-called father of the hydrogen bomb and model for the mad scientist in the 1964 movie *Dr. Strangelove*, argued small amounts of radiation could actually be good for you.

But a growing number of physicists were questioning whether there really was a 'safe' level of exposure to radiation, saying the science had not been proven either way. This issue divided scientists for decades, and still does today.

In 1958 Marston's report was eventually published in the *Australian Journal of Biological Sciences*, but it was edited to remove some of the contentious matters Titterton had objected to. The long delay in publishing the report benefited the British enormously. They had ended atmospheric nuclear tests in Australia. With no big mushroom clouds in the outback to photograph, the focus on British nuclear weapon tests shifted elsewhere. The dirty minor trials would continue for five more years, but they got little attention.

Marston's report sank like a stone. Only a small farmer's periodical, *Stock and Land*, picked up the explosive evidence.

'Vast areas of Australia's sheep and cattle pastures were heavily contaminated by radioactive fallout following the Monte Bello and Maralinga atomic weapons tests in 1956,' the normally staid rural affairs paper blared in its national scoop.[19] In an editorial, the paper that normally backed Menzies to the hilt called for all atomic bomb tests to end. It said Marston's report was a 'devastating document of profound significance not only to this country but to the world'.

Perhaps Marston, a hero to many farmers for his earlier agricultural work, had tipped off a friendly rural editor to his research being published in an obscure scientific journal. Mystifyingly, the small farming journal's national scoop remained just that, a one-off story – the national media failed to pick up the story. Marston couldn't understand why the big city media weren't interested. He suspected the government managed to get it suppressed. Certainly the government struck back with Athol Townley, Beale's replacement as Minister for Supply, getting a letter published in the next edition of *Stock and Land* headlined, 'No Danger in Fallout from Atom Tests – Minister's View'.

Even though Marston received academic accolades before he died just two days after he retired in 1965, he was a bitterly disappointed man still seething at the lies from the nuclear bomb scientists. Marston accurately predicted that some day there would be a major judicial inquiry into the lies and cover-ups of the British nuclear tests in Australia and the government's willing complicity in those lies.

'When this happens some of the boys will qualify for a hangman's noose,' he wrote to Oliphant.[20]

•

Marston may not have got his message about fallout and exposing the lies of the nuclear test authorities as widely to the public as he wished. But in parliament rumblings against the British tests were growing. In 1957 South Australian Labor MP Clyde Cameron pressed the Menzies government hard on the effects of fallout and launched a scathing attack on the British and Titterton:

> It is all very well for English scientists to come over here, 12,000 miles from Great Britain, to conduct their tests close to Australia's shores and to expose the Australian people to the ill-effects of those tests. English scientists like Professor Titterton have the cheek to come out to this country, accept our hospitality and tell us that there will be no ill-effects from nuclear radiation as a result of those tests conducted in Australia for the benefit of the Conservative government of Great Britain. That is something that should not be tolerated by the Australian government . . . The greatest scientists today are contradicting the views of the English scientists who, to suit

> their own purposes, are persuading us that there is nothing to fear from carrying on these dangerous tests in Australia.[21]

Cameron said the British government was complaining about strontium levels in sheep in Wales found to be 100 times higher than normal due to fallout from Soviet nuclear tests. Labor leader 'Doc' Evatt stood up to denounce Titterton and Martin over their public assurances no Strontium-90 was found in Australia. Evatt wondered what the situation would be under the rules of negligence in civil law if they were proved wrong.

It may well be that behind the scenes, Marston or Oliphant had briefed the Labor MPs. We don't know. But that 1957 debate put Menzies on notice that the tide was turning against him on nuclear testing.

•

It wasn't until 1972, nine years after the last British test in the minor trials, that the first nuclear veteran went public with stories of what happened at Maralinga.

RAAF leading aircraftman Avon Hudson had kept his eyes open at Maralinga, collecting knowledge on what was happening the entire time he was there. He was still seething with anger at feeling like he'd been used as a guinea pig. When he left the military, he took a driver's job at Woomera rocket range for two years then worked at the space projects at Tidbinbilla and Honeysuckle Creek near Canberra. In 1972 he heard there were plans to hand Maralinga back to the Aboriginal traditional owners. He went to see Labor's deputy leader, Lance Barnard. It was four months before the election that returned Labor to government after twenty-three long years in opposition.

'I told them everything about my time at Maralinga and contamination of the site. I said the site had to be cleaned up before they gave it back to the Aborigines. Lance asked questions in parliament about the radioactive stuff buried out there, but the Libs trotted out the usual lies about there being no risk as the contamination had gone over time.[22]

'I thought, bullshit, as this stuff has a life of quarter of a million years. I was really furious that they were continuing to lie to the people.'

Labor's Whitlam government didn't get to the decontamination issue in its three tumultuous years in office. When Whitlam was sacked by the Governor-General John Kerr in 1975, Hudson felt he had no choice but to act himself. He feared retribution for breaking the Official Secrets Act, but saw no alternative. Hudson spoke to anti-nuclear activist Dr Helen Caldicott and Dr John Coulter, a conservationist who later became a South Australian senator for the Australian Democrats. They said the risk of being arrested was low, and the more he spoke out, the safer he would be.

Coulter paved the way, talking on ABC Radio about Hudson's revelations of contamination. In December 1976 Hudson spoke live in Adelaide on the ABC current affairs program *This Day Tonight.* It was a sensational story. Hudson told of buried contaminated tanks and jeeps, and radioactive material lying on the surface that could kill anyone allowed into the area.

Newspapers and radio picked up the story. The Adelaide *Advertiser* headline screamed 'Nuclear waste dump in SA: ex-RAAF man'.[23] The paper reported Hudson broke fifteen years of silence to reveal he had helped bury twenty-six boxes of radioactive plutonium waste at Maralinga under just three metres of sand.

'There is a lot of stuff buried out there, and I mean a lot,' Hudson told the paper. 'My reason for speaking out is one of conscience. It has had a marked effect on my life, knowing there are dangerous elements out there – elements that I now know are the most dangerous things in the world.'[24]

At 2.15 am Hudson got a phone call from journalist John Gilbert at the then relatively new Channel 10. Gilbert wanted to fly Hudson to Maralinga the very next day to film the buried plutonium.

'They picked me up at a local airstrip and we flew 600 miles [1000 kilometres] to Maralinga. Dr Coulter came too. It's not that easy to find as everything was bulldozed flat. We followed the railway, then up the old dirt road. It was a speck in the scrub. We landed at the old Maralinga airstrip and got out. The caretaker ran up demanding to know what we were doing there. He couldn't do anything to stop us with the TV crew.[25]

'I led the walk to the dump where the contaminated gear was buried. There was nothing to show anything was there. When I was working at Maralinga there was a big fence with a radiation sign, but when I went with the TV crew there was nothing. The fence was gone. The Poms had cleaned up the area in Operation Brumby. They'd put everything into a hole and covered it up – debris, trucks, jeeps, drums of waste, everything.' (Operation Brumby was the first attempt to clean up the Maralinga site. More about this in Chapter 14.)

Hudson showed the TV crew where the earth had subsided half a metre or so and said to the camera, 'This is the contamination dump.'

He dug around a bit and found fence posts just below the surface. The uncovering made good TV. Hudson told how Australian servicemen had been forced to work in contaminated areas and he revealed the health problems among veterans.

It was a sensational story. For the first time Australians sitting in their homes could see what had happened in the very centre of their country and the effect the British nuclear tests were still having on veterans.

'It caused a massive reaction. I got hundreds of calls over the next weeks. Widows told of men who'd died of cancer after being at Maralinga, dying aged thirty-five or forty. All young men. It was the start of the veterans getting together and comparing notes. Angry widows who'd lost their men in terrible deaths at a young age.'

Several veterans contacted Hudson and they decided to form the Australian Nuclear Veterans' Association – South Australia. Similar groups set up in New South Wales and Queensland.

'We were fighting against impossible odds. I had to listen to all these people contacting me, telling me shocking things that had happened to veterans and their families. I felt totally inadequate and helpless. There was nothing I could do for them. On top of that was the frustration that the government was still covering it up. I always believed that one day, next time, next week, something will happen and we'll get what we want, that they'll admit their guilt in what they did to us and their failure to help us or do anything about it. Maybe they will apologise. That is what drove me on. It's like climbing a mountain. You keep going because you hope, you believe you'll get to the top one day.'

The story caused an uproar in Canberra and put the Liberal government on the ropes. Within days of Hudson's public revelations, Labor frontbencher Tom Uren, a nuggety fighter and survivor of the horrific Japanese POW Burma–Thailand railway, rose in parliament to demand a royal commission to uncover the truth of what happened at Maralinga and whether the British buried plutonium in the outback.

'There is one certain thing which can be said about Maralinga – this parliament and the Australian public have not been told the whole story – instead a succession of Liberal–National Country party ministers have made misleading and contradictory statements to the parliament and outside the parliament about Maralinga. Public concern has been answered with a series of untruths and half-truths about what testing took place at Maralinga, and about the waste which now remains, and the hazards at present.'[26]

Uren continued the blistering attack, accusing Defence Minister James Killen of not only misleading parliament but also deceiving the public. Uren said the whole Maralinga story was one of 'negligence, dishonesty and secrecy' by successive conservative governments. He said the dirty secrets of Maralinga would never have come to light if it weren't for the courage of a few nuclear veterans, brave public servants who spoke out, and tireless investigators who uncovered the truth.

Killen admitted the government didn't know what was buried at Maralinga, and said he was ordering an urgent inquiry.

There were consequences for Hudson. He was called a traitor for speaking out.

'One day this bloke I'd never seen before stopped me in the street in Adelaide and called me a bastard. He was well dressed in a suit. "You are a traitor," he said. I said, "Fuck you", and he punched me in the gizzard. I have no idea who he was. He didn't look like a military veteran. He said I was full of bullshit and kicked me in the leg as he went away.'[27]

Other strange things happened. Hudson felt he was being followed even in the small rural town outside Adelaide where he lived. A car followed him whenever he went to the city. When he got there the same person would follow him on foot. Hudson played spy and watched them in the reflection of shop windows. It was the same person for weeks on end.

'It had to be ASIO as who else would be bothered? I knew I'd upset the government going public. There was one man who regularly followed me. He waited outside while I visited Dr Coulter. I told Coulter about it and he helped me get out a back door into Adelaide Hospital. I went back right past this bastard who was waiting for me to come out the front door and he never saw me.

'Another time it was pouring rain and I went into Coulter's building and this man was watching as I left my black umbrella at the front door. We could see him watching the doorway from the trees outside. Coulter lent me his wife's big pink umbrella. I went out the back as before and as I walked past him under the pink umbrella I whistled to him and waved. He saw me, and he looked really red faced. I never saw him again. He might have been replaced, but I don't know.'

•

The government of Prime Minister Malcolm Fraser was extremely embarrassed by the sudden rush of media stories with revelations about the dirty secrets buried at Maralinga. A new generation was running Menzies' Liberal Party, and they feared the hidden mess their icon had left them. The Fraser government ordered an inquiry by the Australian Ionising Radiation Advisory Council (AIRAC).

The government only had to look in its own classified files to find out what was buried at Maralinga. The report by British scientist Noah Pearce on the 1967 clean-up had been gathering dust in Canberra and London ever since. It stated plutonium and other radioactive and toxic materials were buried on the site. After Hudson's publicity about plutonium, somebody dug up the eleven-year-old Pearce report and brought it to the attention of Defence Minister Jim Killen. The old Cold War warrior immediately envisaged communist terrorists digging up the plutonium and blowing up a major city. Killen submitted to cabinet the plutonium either be reburied in Woomera where security was tighter, or ask Britain to take it back.

Investigative journalist Brian Toohey knew his way around the back rooms and watering holes of Canberra. He had been working in Lance Barnard's office in 1971 when Avon Hudson came in to spill the beans on what he'd seen at Maralinga. In 1978 Toohey was writing for the *Australian Financial Review* when Killen's submission to cabinet on the plutonium terrorist threat mysteriously landed in his lap. Toohey's story, headlined, 'Killen warns on plutonium pile', caused Killen to hit the roof.[28] He virtually accused Toohey and the paper of treason for endangering the nation by publishing secret cabinet papers and alerting terrorists to the presence of unprotected buried plutonium.

'It is a day for regret when a journalist and a newspaper, aided by a criminal act, have published a story which is against the interests of the nation and its people,' Killen thundered.[29]

But Toohey's article forced the government to act. The next day the Fraser government asked Britain if it could come and collect the leftover plutonium and other toxic and radioactive material buried at Maralinga.

Titterton, now working at the Australian National University, immediately wrote to Killen and Fraser saying there wasn't enough buried plutonium to be useful to terrorists. But he did concede there was a half kilogram chunk 'about the size of a hen's egg . . . This is hardly a cause for hysteria or fears.'[30]

Britain agreed to take the waste from Maralinga – but Australia had to cover the cost: about $162,000 – that's $700,000 in today's money. The removal was done in strictest secrecy in February 1979. Australian military and British scientists returned to the old bomb sites with a bulldozer, cement mixers and radiation-measuring equipment. The retrieval was carried out in the worst possible conditions in summer temperatures of forty to fifty degrees Celsius and winds of 120 kilometres per hour. Dressed in stifling protective suits, which made the workers sweat so much it puddled in their boots, men lost four kilos within a few days. Over twelve days the team dug up the drums containing the plutonium from the pit near Maralinga airstrip. The drums had rusted badly and had to be put into new containers. The entire waste weighed 12,000 kilograms when it was flown out of Maralinga to Edinburgh RAAF base near Adelaide. There it was put into an RAF VC10 and flown to Britain.

The operation wasn't announced publicly until March, when the plutonium was already in Britain. Once again Australia had to sign an agreement that this was the last request that could be made of Britain over the tests, and that Britain had no further responsibility.

It didn't work out that way. More pesky troublemakers would soon force the governments to reveal even more of the dirty deeds done in the outback.

11

DIAMOND JIM TAKES ON THE POMS

Bob Hawke, a knockabout rogue who as a Rhodes scholar held the Guinness speed record for beer drinking, was elected prime minister in a Labor landslide in March 1983. This ended seven years of patrician rule under the Liberal Malcolm Fraser. It was a major turning point for those who sought the truth about Maralinga and the British tests.

Two months before the election, Fraser had sought to put to rest the growing clamour for answers to media reports of what had happened at the nuclear test sites. Fraser released the AIRAC 9 report, commissioned three years earlier. It gave the British nuclear tests and the situation at Maralinga a glowing report – pun intended. The government-appointed council found there was no radioactivity problem, minimal impact of the bomb tests, no possibility of a 'black mist', and no illnesses or early deaths caused to Aboriginals or anyone else.

Few believed AIRAC had done the job properly. Its panel of scientists were seen by many as being far too close to the nuclear industry. As 1983 rolled on, advocates like Tom Uren, who'd called for a royal commission five years earlier, became increasingly frustrated. The Hawke government approved new uranium mining contracts, and refused to gain more Australian control over US satellite-listening bases in remote sites such as Pine Gap, near Alice Springs, and North West Cape.

It was the press that finally pushed Hawke into action on Maralinga. In May 1984 journalist Brian Toohey wrote in the *National Times* that plutonium contamination continued at Maralinga. His story was based on a leaked copy of the complete 1967 Pearce Report, about the clean-up after the minor trials ended, and Marston's scientific paper published in 1958.

Several politicians were also demanding action on a series of hard-hitting stories in the Adelaide *Advertiser* about Maralinga and the radioactive cloud that drifted over the city from the 1956 tests. The stories focused on the high level of radioactive material still in the ground at Maralinga.

More and more nuclear veterans were coming forward with harrowing stories of what they had seen and done during the atomic tests. Grieving families were finally heard telling horrific stories of veterans dying of cancer and other afflictions they attributed to being used as guinea pigs at the nuclear tests. Demands for action grew.

Hawke's minister for resources and energy, Peter Walsh, responded by setting up a committee to review all records of fallout from the nuclear tests. Chaired by Professor Charles Kerr of the University of Sydney, it had to report back within just two weeks. Kerr had a respected team of experts on the committee, but two weeks was a tough ask. Nevertheless, Kerr's findings completely demolished the Fraser government's AIRAC 9 report. Kerr said AIRAC set out to provide the most 'comfortable picture' of the British tests.[1] Kerr recommended a full public inquiry into what happened at Maralinga. South Australia's Labor Premier John Bannon demanded a royal commission.

AIRAC's chairman, geneticist Professor Maxwell Clark, protested at the questioning of the organisation's independence, but the Hawke government had already decided to dump AIRAC and launch a full royal commission. It was a big step. It was by no means certain to what extent the British government would cooperate. A royal commission is not a court of law and has no power to charge or convict. They have the power to subpoena witnesses, and its lawyers have considerable power to grill witnesses as though they are in a murder trial. A royal commission can compel people to give evidence or produce documents. The commission can jail those who fail to comply for up to six months. People cannot refuse to answer a question, but it cannot then be presented as evidence against them in a subsequent trial. Giving false evidence or concealing a document can lead to five years jail.

British Prime Minister Margaret Thatcher pledged full cooperation, but it was unclear what this meant. The British could deny access to nuclear documents and prevent its nuclear experts answering questions under the catch-all excuse of national security.

The Royal Commission started hearing witnesses without a single document released from Britain or by the Australian government. Most of the early witnesses were nuclear veterans and Aboriginals who had personal stories to tell. The UK government didn't even send a lawyer to represent it at the commission hearings for the first four months. Normally lawyers representing the various vested interests involved in a royal commission stay with the inquiry for the one to two years it takes to pursue the inquiry.

A royal commissioner is usually a judge who sits relatively silent above the fray in the hearing room, leaving the questioning to senior barristers acting for the commission. But the judge the Hawke government chose to appoint as Royal Commissioner into British nuclear tests in Australia was no stiff wig.

James 'Diamond Jim' McClelland got the moniker not because he was hard, but because of the snappy way he liked to dress despite his working-class upbringing and left-wing sentiments. He was a colourful raconteur with a sparkling wit and a devastatingly sharp tongue. He was in the RAAF during the Second World War, became a solicitor specialising in industrial law in 1951 and was elected to the senate for the Labor Party in 1971. During the Whitlam government he was minister for manufacturing industry, then held the portfolio of labour and immigration. He resigned from parliament in 1978, still furious that Labor-appointed – and former personal friend – Governor-General Sir John Kerr, had sacked the Whitlam government. McClelland became a judge in the industrial court and it was from there that Hawke appointed him president of the Royal Commission. McClelland had a deep distrust of power and authority and an ingrained determination to right wrongs. If anybody could get to the truth of what happened at Maralinga it would be Diamond Jim McClelland.

Counsel assisting the Royal Commission was 37-year-old Sydney barrister Peter McClellan, a persistent, methodical lawyer with an eye for detail. His task was to question witnesses and keep the commission focused, a role needed by the more flamboyant and impatient McClelland. (The similarity in their names caused confusion throughout their legal careers. McClelland died in 1999. McClellan became a royal commissioner himself in 2013/14, investigating institutional responses to child sexual abuse.)

Criminal lawyer Greg James QC appeared at the commission for two of the larger Australian nuclear veterans' groups. The various veterans' groups had splintered with internal wrangling over tactics, money and personality clashes as they pursued compensation for members.

Aboriginals were represented by two South Australian barristers – Geoff Eames and Andrew Collett. Both had experience in fighting for Aboriginals in a legal system which most often went against them. Eames was a tough, penetrating and uncompromising inquisitor and handled most of the questioning for his clients. Collett's detective work was crucial, ploughing through thousands of government documents dumped on the commission. He uncovered an innocuous-looking scientific paper that proved

British scientists had exploded the bomb that released the black mist in weather conditions they knew would most likely spread radiation.

When the Royal Commission moved to London on 3 January 1985, the British government assigned distinguished English barrister Robin Auld QC to represent their interests at the inquiry. Initially Auld came across as polite, friendly and helpful. But as the months of the inquiry rolled on, the Australian legal teams realised Auld and his sizeable support team of British government lawyers were there to protect their Whitehall masters.

Peter McClellan and the legal team flew to London in advance of hearings in December. Despite promises of cooperation from Thatcher, the Australian investigators spent the miserable, cold weeks before Christmas being shuffled from one dank government reception room to another, but no promised files were forthcoming.

British defence and nuclear officials gave their most patronising reception to the colonial upstarts. Over cups of tea in leather armchairs, the public service mandarins assured the Australians they could inspect the index of all the files relating to the nuclear tests stored at Aldermaston, but it was all rather pointless and a dreadful waste of time.

When McClelland arrived after Christmas the legal team still had nothing. He decided a bit of brash Aussie bravado was needed to stir the pot. Even if the British government and its lofty public servants felt the inquiry was tiresome and annoying, media interest was enormous. British veterans had been clamouring loudly for justice and compensation for years, and they fully backed the Australian inquiry to get to the hidden truth. On the first day of the hearing, the public gallery was spilling over and the media section overflowing. McClelland knew it was time to let rip.

'It is only in recent weeks that the British government has

decided to be represented before the commission,' McClelland said to the packed hearing room.[2]

'There are grounds for believing that this decision was taken reluctantly and only after the commission had publicly suggested the British government was dragging its feet. The nuclear tests were carried out by the British and the evidence which has already been adduced suggests to us that they told the Australian authorities almost nothing about what they were doing in Australia during the tests. Since the British know so much more than we do about what they did in our country at that time, cooperation now, if it is to mean anything, involves not simply telling us we are free to delve into the mountains of documents which are in British hands, but positive assistance in bringing to light anything of relevance which those documents may disclose. Secrecy in the national interest has always been a convenient alibi for failure of disclosure. But today it is hard to believe that Britain is in possession of any atomic secrets unknown to the great nuclear powers. We're not here to poke our noses into British technical secrets, but there is a certain minimum of information to which, as the host country to nuclear tests, we feel entitled to have access.'

This stinging rebuke of the mother country from the upstart colonial Royal Commissioner produced an explosion of its own in the British media. The harangue led the BBC and ITN news and was on the front pages of most British newspapers the next morning. McClelland had sure stirred the possums, as he liked to say and titled his 1988 autobiography. Inside Whitehall word came down from the government to change tactics. Panicky phone calls were made, levers pulled and buttons pressed. Within days an avalanche of newly unclassified files and documents suddenly landed in the Royal Commission's London office. It grew over the next two weeks until the paperwork totalled an incredible thirty-eight tons. The civil servants obviously thought if they couldn't get rid of the Australians by brushing them off, they would drown them in so much paperwork they wouldn't possibly be able to make any sense out of it.

In the end, the mountain of paper almost did overwhelm the staff of the Royal Commission. Much of it was useless – staff logs, requisition orders, technical papers and the like. But buried in the avalanche were some very revealing documents with correspondence between the British and Australian governments. They clearly showed the British had expected more questions about safety and exactly what they were up to in the desert from the Australian government. The British had prepared briefs for their officials to dodge or explain matters that might be raised by the Menzies government. They needn't have worried. What was staggering in the documents was the absolute subservience displayed by Menzies to his British masters. It was a disgraceful abrogation of his duty to look after the people who had elected him to power. He virtually said to the British, do whatever you like to this country and its people.

More than forty witnesses appeared before the Royal Commission in London, the most notable being Lord Penney.

Penney's evidence to the Royal Commission was the only time he spoke publicly about the type of nuclear tests he was in charge of in Australia. He conceded the public was 'kept in the dark' about the size of the bombs, and how fallout forecasts were 'drastically off course'.[3] Penney said he never wanted to take part in the trials, but felt the only way to prevent a global nuclear war was to have a balance between East and West. 'I really wanted to be a professor,' he said.

Penney died from liver cancer in 1991 aged 82. As part of the UK *Daily Mirror*'s campaign for compensation for nuclear veterans, the paper reported Penney's exposure to fallout may have eventually killed him.[4]

The Royal Commission was hampered in the UK by not having power to subpoena witnesses. While many British nuclear veterans were only too happy to tell their stories, the commission could not summon those senior public servants, military and government scientists from the 1950s and 60s who could have shed more light on the management of the tests.

The Royal Commission returned to Australia armed with thousands of British documents. The legal team had made giant steps forward in uncovering the secret story of Maralinga. But when hearings resumed, the seemingly friendly lawyer representing the British government, Robin Auld QC, stunned the commission with an unexpected blistering attack on McClelland and the commission. With surprising bitterness, Auld blasted the commission for concentrating on British documents, while lagging in investigating and declassifying Australian documents. Auld nailed Peter McClellan for failing to get the Australian documents released at the same time the commission complained about the British lack of cooperation.

Auld had grounds for complaint. Almost 3000 files from the Australian government were not tendered in evidence until just days before the Royal Commission ended its hearings in July 1985. Auld attacked the way the Royal Commission had been administered from the start, saying it was normal to question witnesses after examining the relevant documents. This royal commission, Auld said, had gone about it the opposite way.

'That is the evil that cannot be undone,' Auld thundered.[5] The British lawyer might have been positioning his client, the UK government, for a defence against the commission's inevitable anti-British finding by saying the inquiry was badly administered and biased. It was ugly and personal.

The return fire came from an unexpected quarter: the usually staid Peter McClellan, who accused Auld of being a 'whingeing Pom'.

'I wondered how long I would get through this inquiry without somebody calling me that,' Auld shot back.[6]

It had been a long and tiring investigation, but it was an

extraordinary outburst. Once the commission was over the two men never talked to each again.[7]

Auld's final 700-page argument to the commission putting the British government's position suggested it was all a big, unnecessary fuss about very little.

'The wider ranging and detailed investigations of the royal commission do not show that the health of anyone in Australia has been harmed by the nuclear tests or minor trials. The commission has found no evidence upon which it could conclude that any Aborigine has suffered harm from any of the tests or minor trials including Operation Totem One at which the "black mist" occurred. The weight of the evidence is that the low levels of ionising radiation to which people may have been exposed as a result of the nuclear tests or trials have not exposed them to any greater risk of harm than that to which the general population is subject.'[8]

Despite all the statements and evidence amassed by the commission, the British government was sticking to the same line it had given thirty years earlier – there was no fallout and nobody was hurt.

The Royal Commission took evidence from 311 witnesses over 118 days of hearings in London, five major cities in Australia and three remote outback settlements. The transcripts ran to more than 10,000 pages and it received in evidence more than 10,000 documents that had been kept top secret for thirty years in Australia and Britain.

It was a remarkable achievement. When the Royal Commission released its two-volume, 615-page report, 201 conclusions and seven recommendations on 20 November 1985, the country was stunned at the revelations of what had happened during the British tests and the extent of the betrayal of the nation by Sir Robert Menzies.

The commission recommended compensation be paid to Aboriginals, military and civilian veterans exposed during the tests. Maralinga and Emu Field should be properly cleaned up to the point the traditional Aboriginal owners could enjoy unrestricted habitation of their land. Monte Bello should be cleaned so that it was safe for people to be there. Britain should meet all costs of the clean-up. Traditional owners of the land should be compensated for loss of their lands since the tests.

Clearly identified as the chief villain in the whole story was Sir Ernest Titterton. The clash between Titterton and McClelland during the hearings was personal and hostile. The commission pushed Titterton on whether he was really working for the British the whole time he was supposed to be looking after the safety of Australians. He was still on a British passport and had only been in Australia six months when he was appointed by Menzies as Australia's chief representative at the first test at Monte Bello.

When Titterton was questioned over several days at the Royal Commission in May 1985, relations with the commission president 'Diamond Jim' McClelland were immediately tetchy. Titterton said he loved living in Canberra, McClelland shot back he couldn't stand the place. Titterton used scientific terms to explain fallout and McClelland interrupted him and told him to use simpler language so 'lay' people like himself could understand. McClelland stepped in to question Titterton himself on whether he still claimed thirty-three years after the tests that no harm was done to any human during the tests. Titterton dodged and weaved, saying that was the conclusion reached by the safety committee, AIRAC and the Kerr committee. Three times McClelland came back at Titterton, trying to pin him down.

At last McClelland got the answer from Titterton: 'We know positively that the fallout over Australia of all the British tests can have had no effect on the Australian population.'[9]

McClelland thanked him. 'I just wanted to know what you say.'

McClelland had what he wanted. He had Titterton on the record.

Despite Titterton's rather arrogant dismissal of stories of the black mist, the commission concluded there was a black mist as described by the Aboriginals, but there wasn't enough evidence to establish whether it killed people or blinded key witness Yami Lester.

When the commission caught Titterton out on exactly when he was first approached to be involved in the British tests, it was McClelland who again stepped in to nail the scientist. Titterton had said the first he knew of being asked to join the tests was when he was approached by Menzies to represent Australia. But documentation unearthed in London showed Titterton had been approached by the British to be part of the tests several months before he left for Australia to take up a position at the Australian National University. McClelland pressed him on why he could not see a conflict of interest. Titterton lamely replied that 'gentlemen are gentlemen' and suggested McClelland was prejudiced by having a large number of political friends.[10]

'That is an unwarranted remark, Sir Ernest,' shot back McClelland. Again he pressed Titterton on whether he now saw he had a conflict of interest. Titterton refused to bend, saying he saw no conflict of duty and still didn't. Titterton was clearly exasperated with the questioning, insisting he had already answered questions, and showed his frustration that the lawyers seemed incapable of understanding a respected senior scientist like himself. Titterton talked to the commission lawyers as though they were children, further aggravating the growing animosity in the room. The bad feeling was mutual, and McClelland had the last say, writing in the commission's report: 'It is inconceivable, especially in the light of Titterton's cavalier treatment of the truth throughout his evidence, that he did not know he had been planted on Menzies . . .'[11]

The commission concluded Titterton regarded himself as a member of the British 'team' rather than the custodian of the safety of Australian citizens.

When the commission told Titterton that Penney had told them that, in hindsight, the Totem One bomb at Emu Field should not have been exploded that day because of the weather, Titterton snapped that when Penney said that he must have been tired and exhausted and trying to get away from questioning by the commission. Pressed for his reaction to Penney's thoughts, Titterton said simply that Penney was wrong. Titterton repeatedly compared the notion of the risk of being affected by fallout from an atom bomb as the same sort of risk everyone faces when they cross a city street – the risk is always there but there are degrees of risk and you calculate them and still cross the street. It was an analogy that really annoyed McClelland, who repeatedly told him to move on.

Titterton did have to acknowledge he ignored recommendations from weather experts that conditions before the Totem One blast were such that the explosion should be called off.

Titterton insisted it wasn't possible for there to be a black mist from an atomic bomb and that it was impossible for Aboriginals 160 kilometres away from the blast to have died from such a mist.

Titterton's second day in the witness chair began just as confrontationally. He twisted and turned under a barrage of questions about why he, as Australia's safety officer, didn't try to stop the explosion when there were warnings from the meteorological team that fallout might land on populated sites.

Titterton rather pompously said it was 'never in the British temperament to do irresponsible things', that anything they did was always going to be meticulously planned and tested before the event.[12] McClelland couldn't resist.

'Like the charge of the Light Brigade?'

'Might be a few who disagree about ANZAC too,' added McClellan.

Titterton fumed. He later accused the commission of threatening him. But what the commission was doing was no threat. They had pinned him as working for the British rather than the Australians in getting an ongoing green light for the nuclear tests. When Titterton said he had not told anyone about the Cobalt-60 left on the ground because it would make a good test for the troops to find it, he was called a liar by Greg James QC, who was representing nuclear veterans.

In their final report the Royal Commission stated: 'Titterton played a political as well as a safety role in the testing program, especially in the minor trials. He was prepared to conceal information from the Australian government and his fellow committee members if he believed to do so would suit the interests of the United Kingdom government and the testing program.'[13]

The Royal Commission found the safety committee 'failed to carry out many of its tasks in a proper manner. At times it was deceitful and allowed unsafe firing to occur. It deviated from its charter by assuming responsibilities which properly belonged to the Australian government.'[14]

•

In the end many people were disappointed in the Royal Commission's conclusions. It failed to produce the smoking gun: evidence that British nuclear tests had caused deaths and illness to Australians who were used as guinea pigs by the British to test its nuclear weapons.

Many of the more dramatic claims made to the commission were struck out as they could not be substantiated. Claims such as dead Aboriginals found in a bomb crater, mental patients being secretly hidden in a bunker to be used as human guinea pigs, and servicemen being ordered to bury atom bombs in the desert were all dismissed.

The commission found there was no evidence of an 'emergency evacuation' of Emu Field after the Totem series as the material left was low priority. The servicemen who found abandoned vehicles, food, tools and equipment would disagree.

Even though the commission said the safety committee's report that all went well at the Mosaic series of tests at Monte Bello was 'grossly misleading and irresponsible', the commission concluded safety precautions for servicemen at Mosaic were 'generally adequate'.[15]

The commission disappointed anti-nuclear campaigners, nuclear veterans and their families, as well as Aboriginal groups, by finding research had not indicated any increased risk of mortality nor increased genetic or heritable effects from the tests.

'The Royal Commission has been unable to quantify the probable increase in the risk of cancer among the participants in the trial program or among the Australian population in general,' it concluded.[16]

The commission said divers and navy crew at Monte Bello were exposed to the risk of ingesting contaminated sea water, but safety regulations of exposure for navy crews were not breached.

Air force veterans were disappointed at the finding of 'negligence' for their lack of protective equipment. The finding could have been much harsher given the detailed evidence provided to the commission by air and ground crews.

Titterton got off lightly over withholding information about the Cobalt-60 contamination. The evidence was there for Titterton to be charged with criminal negligence.

The commission also failed to condemn the safety committee for insisting Marston delete figures relating to fallout over Adelaide in his paper. It said only that Marston was treated in a 'high handed manner'.[17]

The struggle to expose the real impact of the British nuclear tests on Australians and the nation was far from over.

12

THE BABY BODY SNATCHERS

The chilling list is long and goes on and on:

- The tiny femur of a male foetus from Adelaide's Children's Hospital.
- A three-week-old baby girl's rib from Melbourne's Royal Children's Hospital.
- A 33-hour-old baby girl's femur from Adelaide's Children's Hospital.
- A six-month-old baby boy's tibia from Sydney's Royal Alexandra Hospital for Children.
- The vertebrae of an eighteen-year-old woman from Brisbane's Institute of Forensic Pathology.
- The vertebrae of a six-year-old boy from Sydney's Royal Prince Alfred Hospital.
- The skull of a 36-month-old girl from Brisbane's State Health Laboratory.
- The lumbar spine of a fourteen-year-old boy from Sydney Morgue.
- A six-month-old baby girl's femur from Adelaide's Children's Hospital.

- A two-year-old girl's femur from Perth's Princess Margaret Hospital for Children.
- The spine of a thirteen-year-old boy from Royal Perth Hospital.
- The vertebrae and ribs of a stillborn baby from Sydney's Royal Women's Hospital.

All neatly catalogued and documented like something out of a horror movie or mad scientist's experiment – thousands upon thousands of dead babies, toddlers, children and adults who secretly had their bones cut out and sent to a laboratory to see how much fallout from nuclear tests had penetrated their bodies.

Each was given their own code number linking to their age at death and where they came from. Many had a code number linked to their real name.

It was one of the longest ongoing scientific experiments on humans in nuclear history. For twenty-one years from the days of the Maralinga nuclear tests, the covert bone sampling collected a staggering 22,000 bones of Australians aged from zero to middle age. The most sought-after bones were from stillborns, babies and toddlers: they had the best bones to reveal what the nuclear scientists were looking for. Next best were little kids of pre-school age, then kindergarteners and young kids. Pre-teens were good too. Even teenagers were sought after. After that, young adults and people up to their forties, but definitely not older. The middle-aged and elderly were not wanted at all. They could go to their graves with their bones intact.

Grieving parents weren't told what was happening to the bodies of their loved ones. The overwhelming majority of families were not asked whether the bodies of their children could be used for science. The little bodies were simply taken away to the mortuary where attendants and pathologists secretly cut out the bones and sent them off to a lab in Melbourne. They did this out of a perverse duty, and for the few quid or bucks quietly slipped their way. It was one of the longest and most surreptitious scientific experiments ever carried out in Australia.

The disturbing experiment began in 1957, just before Operation Antler, the last series of three atomic bomb tests held at Maralinga. At the time Hedley Marston was threatening to reveal the level of fallout that was spreading across Australia and was warning that radioactive fallout had to be entering the food chain in the form of Strontium-90. Titterton, leading the atomic safety committee, was insisting this was impossible as there was no nuclear fallout beyond a few hundred kilometres from the blast zone. Titterton, however, did see Marston's warning as a tremendous opportunity to find out just what effect there would be on a vast area like Australia from an atomic bomb explosion.

It had long been on the agenda of nuclear scientists to determine the effect of nuclear radiation exposure on humans. Prime Minister Churchill had asked the UK Medical Research Council to appoint an independent committee in March 1955 to 'report on the medical aspects of nuclear radiation'. A year later the council reported back there was too much they didn't know. In the UK parliament in July 1956, debating the report, Labor MP Dr Edith Summerskill said there were 'many large and serious gaps in our knowledge of the medical and biological effects of ionising radiation'.[1] She said the importance of finding out this effect transcended all others 'because only through controlling nuclear radiation could plans for the future have any significance at all'.

In 1957 nuclear authorities in England started secretly examining corpses of nuclear industry workers to see if exposure to radiation had anything to do with their death. To the public they announced radiation exposure couldn't have killed them and that they had died of natural causes. But some radiation scientists were concerned what they might find if they looked too closely and tested sick people. A file at the UK National Archives shows scientist D. Newton at the UK Atomic Energy

Research Institute's Whole Body Monitoring Department refusing a request from a general practice doctor A.J. Fairfax to test his patient for Strontium-90 and radiation. Newton said it 'had no medical purpose' and could have 'possible legal implications' and would lead to an avalanche of requests.[2]

In spring 1957, Titterton was visiting the Atomic Energy Research Establishment (AERE) at Harwell and there was already considerable pressure to find what effect radiation had on humans. The team was already working on exploding a full-scale hydrogen bomb the next year and they needed to know how fallout from atomic bombs could work its way into the food chain far from the area destroyed in an atomic bomb attack. Could Britain survive if atom bombs were dropped on its major cities? Could people continue to grow food in country areas after a nuclear attack? How long before people could return to the devastated cities? Could the human race survive? Would children be able to grow into adults after a nuclear war? What happens to the human body exposed to nuclear fallout? How long can they live with certain doses of radioactive ingestion?

Titterton and his fellow scientists and military planners needed answers to these questions. At the time a nuclear war with the Soviet Union seemed a very real possibility. The upcoming series of tests at Maralinga would provide the opportunity to find some of the answers.

The meeting at Harwell on 24 May 1957 decided to sample soil taken from spots around Australia in August every year. They would also take samples of vegetation and the ashes of specially planted cabbage. Milk from cows around the country would be taken, dried and tested for the presence of Strontium-90. Sheep from farms near the east coast capital cities would be slaughtered and a leg bone crushed and burnt to ash and sent to England for testing.

These measures still didn't go far enough for Titterton. Even though he was appointed by the Australian government to ensure the safety of Australians during the British tests, Titterton was very much batting for the Brits. He was thrilled to be at the centre of this group discussion with the top British nuclear officials. He was back in the land of his birth, and he was the key to Britain's drive to become the West's second nuclear power.

The British group was aware that the United States had started a program a few years earlier collecting very young human cadavers from the US and South America to see how much Strontium-90 was being absorbed into the bones from fallout from atmospheric nuclear-bomb testing. The Americans gave it the pleasantly innocuous name Project Sunshine. They lied to the medical staff who supplied the bodies, saying they were measuring natural radiation, not fallout from nuclear bombs. The project had received legal advice that what they were doing was legally very suspect; they kept it hush-hush. Within a few years they were struggling to find enough bodies – particularly the bodies of children, which were most desired as growing bones best absorb Strontium-90. US Atomic Energy Commission chief Willard Libby lamented in 1955: 'Human samples are of prime importance and if anybody knows how to do a good job of body snatching, they will really be serving their country.'[3] The Americans spread the net for bodies even wider. They approached Britain, Australia, Canada, Japan and India, in some cases offering money for bodies. They focused on Houston, Texas, as it was an impoverished area and had a plentiful supply of dead babies and children. The British knew they were in competition for the best young corpses.

Titterton turned to his British colleagues at Harwell and told them that to do the fallout sampling job properly they would have to take human bone samples from Australians. He said it would be tough to get enough baby cadavers in Australia, and that it might not be received well by the public if word got out. But they had to try. The group agreed. They set down the sample requirements – twenty to fifty grams of wet bone that would be burned down to two grams of ash and sent to the UK for testing. The date of birth, age at death and home location of the body would need to be recorded. Titterton said he would get the safety committee to organise the collection.

They got straight to work. In November 1957 the secretary of the safety committee, John Moroney, wrote to pathologists in each of Australia's mainland capital cities asking them to supply human bones, particularly of children under five years old, to gauge the impact of fallout on the human population. Although not officially classified secret, it was certainly a clandestine operation.

'You may have perhaps considered it possible that the question of sampling and radiochemical assaying of bones would not be regarded kindly by the general public. Consequently I would be most grateful if in the future you could treat this matter and its related correspondence as either confidential or personal, as you wish.'[4] Moroney said he hoped for ten samples from each capital city every six months from four separate age groups: under two years old, between two and five, between five and twenty and over twenty. He wanted vertebrae, ribs, femurs, skulls and sternums. But the Australian project ran into immediate problems. Several pathologists replied they already had agreements to supply body parts for the American global study Project Sunshine.

Moroney and Titterton needn't have worried about the ethical qualms of pathologists. It turned out it wasn't too hard to get enough bone samples. A Department of Supply clerk in Adelaide, Peter Ryan, was overwhelmed as packages of bones taken from little kids suddenly poured into his clearing office. He asked his workmates: 'What the bloody hell is going on here?'[5]

Over the next twelve months, 441 bone samples were collected from pathologists in Sydney, Brisbane, Melbourne, Adelaide and Perth. In England the bone analysts complained they were being inundated with work. The UK Atomic Energy Authority's F.J. Bryant protested to Dr Dawson they had agreed on testing seventy samples a year but it was already passing eighty. Bryant said they would have to choose between human bones or sheep bones.[6] More money was allotted to the testing. The bone collecting rapidly accelerated – 1096 in 1959, 1200 in 1960, 1149 in 1961. Enthusiasm waned for the study in 1962 and the number of samples sent in fell to 839. It stayed at about this level until 1968.

After ten years of collecting bones Moroney was concerned that it was 'becoming difficult to maintain the active interest and cooperation of some pathologists and their technicians'.[7] A bit of pocket money might assist their interest, Moroney decided, and he offered fifty dollars to each pathology office to keep sending samples. He extended the offer to Darwin and Papua New Guinea. Moroney was aware that paying for body parts had 'unfortunate overtones' and may have problems in law.[8] He suggested the money be listed as 'pathology services'. In 1970, the scientists running the program had the equipment to do the Strontium-90 testing in Australia and no longer sent the ashed bones to Britain. In 1973, control of the program passed from Titterton's Atomic Weapons Tests Safety Committee to the Australian Ionising Radiation Advisory Committee. Both reported to the Department of Supply.

By 1977 the number of samples coming in had once again fallen and the payment was increased to $100. It was sent out in early December when it could help pay for the staff Christmas party.

In December 1978, the nice little earner was over – the Australian sampling program was shut down. Australia had kept its strontium-testing program going for six years longer than Britain. The Australian program, still operating under the influence of Titterton, kept gathering data from dead babies and dutifully sending the information on to Britain. The British had an ongoing interest in the figures.

The British nuclear industry had another covert body sampling program going. Between 1960 and 1991, organs were secretly taken from seventy-six dead people who either worked at UK nuclear power plants or lived nearby. Once again families were never asked. The secret corpse stripping was finally exposed when a wife at the funeral found her dead husband's leg had been replaced with a broom handle. The body snatchers had tried to make the body appear untouched. The uproar forced the UK government to apologise in 2010 to families of the dead nuclear workers.

No such shock revelations or apology came in Australia. For twenty-one long years the covert body snatching had successfully run without the public becoming aware of it. Grieving parents weren't told where the remains of their children and babies were going. Some were handed back bodies after autopsies, unaware bones had been removed to test for residue left by nuclear fallout. In one Sydney hospital, plastic tubes were inserted to mask where the bone had been removed. Many parents never learned that the bodies had been dumped into mass graves after they had been sliced open for their bones.

As far as the scientists were concerned the operation had been very successful. The decades long project had quietly collected the bodies of 688 stillborns, 244 a few hours old, 1147 a few days old, 530 a few weeks old, 2162 a few months old and 11,246 measured in years. There was no age recorded for 5803 bodies. The most cooperative state was Queensland followed by New South Wales, Victoria, South Australia and Western Australia. Papua New Guinea supplied 171 bodies and Darwin thirty-nine.[9]

Strontium-90 was found in the bones of babies across the country. Levels in babies and children were five times higher than the adults. Analysts found Strontium-90 levels suddenly shot up in 1959, increasing by fifty per cent. This was while the dirty minor trials were continuing and two years after the last atomic blasts at Maralinga. In 1958 there had been a large increase of hydrogen-bomb testing around the world, a total of 116 atom bombs exploded, including the massive British Grapple series in the Pacific. A temporary freeze in atmospheric testing in 1959 saw Strontium-90 levels in bones fall the next year. It took off rapidly again in 1961 as soon as atmospheric testing resumed. In 1962, a record 178 nuclear bombs were exploded around the world. The highest recordings of Strontium-90 were in 1965, after which levels fell. The UK Medical Research Council examined the figures and concluded everything was fine – even the highest levels of Strontium-90 found were no cause for concern.

Scientists around the world warned fallout from the increasing number and power of nuclear bombs was poisoning the world to the point it could cause permanent harm to the entire human race.[10] In the US, where scientific studies of fallout were less secretive than Australia, it was discovered Strontium-90 levels found in baby teeth in 1962 were fifty times higher than baby teeth tested in 1950. The study assisted in prompting President John F. Kennedy to sign the Partial Nuclear Test Ban Treaty with Britain and the Soviet Union in 1963.

In a landmark speech announcing the nuclear test ban, Kennedy said:

> Every inhabitant of this planet must consider the day when this planet may no longer be habitable. Weapons of war must be abolished before they abolish us . . . Continued unrestricted testing by the nuclear powers, joined in time by other nations which may be less adept in limiting pollution, will increasingly contaminate the air that all of us must breathe. Even then the number of children and grandchildren with cancer in their bones, with leukemia in their blood or with poison in their lungs might seem statistically small to some in comparison with natural health hazards. But this is not a natural health hazard – and it is not a statistical issue. The loss of even one human life or the malformation of even one baby – who may be born long after all of us are gone – should be of concern to us all. Our children and grandchildren are

> not merely statistics toward which we can be indifferent . . . these tests befoul the air of all men.[11]

Titterton wasn't convinced. He remained one of the few pro-nuclear voices insisting Strontium-90 levels were still low and couldn't cause any harm. Whenever the issue came up, he told the Australian government Strontium-90 levels were much higher in the northern hemisphere. In a memo sent to Menzies in 1959 after a story about Strontium-90 appeared in the UK *Daily Mirror*, Titterton said, 'nobody is clear that there is even a dangerous level of Strontium-90'.[12] He said it had not been clearly established that exposure to Strontium-90 resulted in leukemia. In 1985, Titterton told the Royal Commission there was no problem with strontium in Australia. He denied there was anything clandestine about his strontium-testing program. He said the project was well known, at least in medical circles, and he published findings of the test every year in an academic paper.

'All the parents who provided this facility were consulted by the medicos involved. They saw it as a way of helping the country in which they were born,' Titterton haughtily told the commission.[13]

How wrong he was. In 2001 there was a sudden media frenzy over stories from overseas that bodies of stillborn babies and dead toddlers had been secretly shipped to the US Project Sunshine from around the world in the 1950s and 60s, possibly including Australia. In just one consignment from Britain there were twenty-seven cadavers. In all, about 1500 cadavers had been sent to the US, where they were burned and the ashes examined for Strontium-90. Horror stories emerged including a British mother who was not allowed to dress her dead baby for her funeral because authorities didn't want her to find out the baby's legs had been removed for strontium tests.

'I wanted to put her christening robe on her as she hadn't been christened and that upset me enormously,' Jean Prichard told a BBC TV interviewer.[14]

The then Australian Health Minister, Dr Michael Wooldridge, ordered an inquiry into Australia's role in the Strontium-90 tests. The 21-year project was revealed publicly for the first time in a 2001 report by the Australian Radiation Protection and Nuclear Safety Agency (ARPANSA).[15]

It was shocking news. 'Australian babies' bones used in nuclear tests' reported the international news agency Reuters.[16] 'Secret atomic child files opened' headlined the Adelaide *Advertiser*.[17] The South Australian government checked and found almost 1000 child and adult specimens, including 284 baby hearts, were stored in a basement at Adelaide's Women's and Children's Hospital. 'Corridor of Shame' screamed the front page of *The Advertiser* when its intrepid reporters discovered the blue steel door to a vault at the end of a basement corridor that held the body parts.[18] The South Australian government said ten families had immediately contacted them saying they thought their stillborn baby had been buried or cremated, but had now discovered parts of the body were removed for Strontium-90 testing without their permission. Pauline Allman, whose son Ben died shorty after birth in 1985, was angry it had taken so long for the information to come out. 'I feel for all the many parents out there who are wondering: did this happen to my baby?' she told the paper.[19]

The Adelaide families weren't alone. Across the country thousands of parents and siblings wondered if their loved ones who died between 1957 and 1978 could have been one of those grabbed by the nuclear body snatchers, as the press dubbed the scientists. ARPANSA said, as far as the records showed, no whole bodies had been sent to the US for testing, but human bones may have been sent. The safety committee had kept detailed records that, in many cases, included the identity of the stolen bones.

The Australian Health Ethics Committee, chaired by Melbourne University professor of moral philosophy Dr Christopher Cordner, recommended to Wooldridge that families who believed the body of their loved one may have been caught in the program could find out by contacting health authorities. The ARPANSA report said permission was not sought from families to take these bones. The legality of the sampling program was 'uncertain'.[20]

During his investigation Cordner was shocked to find 3452 samples of ashed bones from the program still lying in storage in Melbourne at a government lab.[21] Cordner said many families may have felt taking the bones without asking was a disrespectful violation of the body. Wooldridge announced that, where it was possible, the remains would be returned to families who requested them. Those samples not returned after three years would eventually be disposed of respectfully and not left in a nondescript storage room.

There was an outpouring of grief and bewilderment, as well as strong feelings of betrayal. In South Australia 1200 families asked if the ashed remains of their loved ones were among the stored samples. A total of 900 samples from dead babies, toddlers and young children were returned from the Melbourne warehouse to Adelaide. Around 300 South Australian mothers found where the bodies of their dead babies had been buried by the nuclear authorities after their bones had been removed for testing.

'There has been a mix of emotions from extreme anger and betrayal to relief that finally some answers have been given about what happened,' a health spokeswoman told the *Advertiser*.[22]

Dr John Loy, head of ARPANSA, said the Strontium-90 tests did have a positive effect despite the improper way the samples were gathered. 'The [strontium] tests probably played a role in decisions to end atmospheric nuclear tests. It's clear the samples weren't as we would want them to be these days. If we were doing such a thing these days you would want people to give their consent.'[23]

That is little comfort for the families who still suffer the pain of feeling their baby was stolen from them by nuclear scientists. Marian Napier-Winch of Perth never saw or held the baby girl she gave birth to on 17 August 1968. She had carried the baby to full term but everyone was shocked when the baby was stillborn at the Salvation Army maternity hospital in Fremantle. She called the baby Laurie. Doctors told her it would be too painful for her to see her little daughter. But the pain of losing a child never goes away.

For four decades Marian and her husband John never stopped thinking of their baby Laurie. Then came the news in 2001 that bodies of 22,000 Australians, mostly babies and toddlers, had been used in the strontium tests. Baby Laurie died while those tests were being conducted. Almost 3000 bodies had come from their state of Western Australia. The couple tried to find out from health officials if their baby Laurie had been one of them.

It took eight long years before they got an answer. ARPANSA wrote to them in 2010 and said they had found an entry in the test records for a baby with the surname Winch who had died on the same day as Laurie. The tiny baby's femur had been used in the testing and there were no remains. The couple, who had another three children, were devastated by the news.

'At no time was our permission sought for our baby girl to be used for experimentation,' Marian told the *West Australian* newspaper.[24] 'We never would have agreed to it.'

At the time she had agreed to have Laurie's body put in an unmarked mass grave at Fremantle Cemetery. Now she questions whether her baby really was buried there. She wonders what else could have been done to her baby's body.

'Because there was so much dishonesty who is to say it is definitely Laurie in that grave?'

13

'WHAT DID THE BASTARDS DO TO US?'[1]

Ernest Titterton and the other scientists involved in the decades-long testing of thousands of baby and child cadavers for residues of nuclear fallout should have looked in their own back yard.

Six hundred kilometres east of the Maralinga test site is Woomera, the top secret Australian Defence Force weapons testing base. Around 7000 defence people and their families lived there in the 1950s and 60s, when it was the busiest military firing range in the world after Cape Canaveral. Many of the planes monitoring the nuclear bomb clouds used Woomera airfield.

In the flat, windswept stony Woomera Cemetery, a fifty-year-old mystery lies unsolved. In the cemetery are the graves of sixty-eight children, including twenty-two stillborn babies and thirty-four newborns who lived just a few hours or days. Twelve gravesites hold children who died between the ages of one and seven.

The stillborn baby gravesites are chillingly identical, lined up in martial uniformity. They all have the same-sized metal plaque stamped 'Baby', then the family surname, underneath which is written 'Died', below that is the date of death and at the bottom just one word: 'Stillborn'. No personal words from grieving parents, no name for a baby who didn't have a moment of life. It has the stiff bearing of a military gravesite.

The babies all died during the years of the nuclear tests at Maralinga or within a few years of the tests ending. There is no clue as to which government agency is responsible for the macabre memorial. Despite decades of questions over whether these deaths could possibly be linked to nuclear fallout drifting east from Maralinga to Woomera, no investigation was ever carried out, or at least not one that was made public.

Colin James, a reporter on the Adelaide *Advertiser*, tried to get answers in 2003 but ran into a brick wall of government secrecy and sealed hospital files. Staff and grieving families were too afraid to talk, citing the Officials Secrets Act and privacy. 'Eleven years later it is still a mystery. Despite promises of investigations, nothing has come out,' James said.[2]

Families in Woomera were told the deaths had been attributed to the desert heat. Health experts said heat couldn't have caused the deaths. Besides, many died in winter. Woomera is a defence facility and had a well-equipped hospital with experienced doctors and nurses.

One mother told the *Advertiser* everyone knew they were close to the atom bomb tests. 'We now know the mushroom clouds came over Woomera, so what is there to say we weren't exposed to radiation?'[3]

Another former resident said that during the British tests families from Woomera drove west for hundreds of kilometres to sit down and have picnics while enjoying the spectacle of atom bombs exploding.

One grieving mother told James she was still wondering fifty years later whether the nuclear tests could have had something to do with the deaths of so many babies in one place.[4]

Pauline Lester lived in Woomera in the late 1950s with her two young children and husband, who was a junior doctor at the Woomera hospital. She told the *Advertiser* her family got out of Woomera when people started 'dying like flies' from cancer.[5] She said wives of Woomera servicemen also started having large numbers of miscarriages and stillbirths.

'All of my friends were having miscarriages at the time,' Mrs Lester said.[6] 'We knew they [government officials] were blaming the heat but we knew it wasn't the heat. But we couldn't do anything about it. We either stayed there or got out and so we got out. We kept saying to each other that if you want to have children, don't have them at Woomera because they will die. It was really sad. Everyone seemed to die.'

The Howard government responded to the Woomera babies story by promising to investigate. In 2010 Western Australian Greens Senator Scott Ludlum asked Defence in a senate committee hearing what the investigation had found. Defence later replied in writing they could find no evidence they were ever asked to investigate the claims made in the *Advertiser*.[7] Defence also said there was no evidence to suggest any government agency conducted post mortems on the Woomera babies, or that there was a file on the babies marked 'Never to be Released'.

Birth and death records of the Woomera Hospital between 1951 and 1965, held in the Australian National Archives and released to the author in 2014, show that no reason was given for the twenty-two stillborn babies in the years of the atom bomb testing. In every case, the cause of death was curiously left blank.[8]

British lawyers setting up a class action against the British government on behalf of nuclear test victims were approached by several Australian families of the babies who died at Woomera.

One mother of a girl stillborn in March 1963 is still not satisfied with the reasons given for the death. Edith Hiskins' husband John was a serviceman at Woomera when she lost her baby due to what officials later said was 'mild toxemia'. She only found out that cause of death years later, after they had pushed the authorities for a death certificate. At the time, the baby was taken without Edith seeing the body and was buried in the cemetery the next day.

'As far as I know her records were sealed. It was years before we even got a death certificate,' Mrs Hiskins told the *Advertiser*.[9]

The team from the London law firm Hickman and Rose that was seeking to bring a class action on behalf of nuclear test victims was headed by Cherie Booth, the wife of former British Prime Minister Tony Blair.

Coincidentally Blair may be a childhood victim of the nuclear tests. In 1956 he was three years old and living with his family in Adelaide where his father Leo was a law lecturer at the University of Adelaide. As Hedley Marston discovered in his readings, a radioactive cloud from the third Operation Buffalo bomb on 11 October 1956, drifted over Adelaide, dropping fallout and contaminating the food chain, in particular milk.

British medical researcher and toxicologist Dick van Steenis said the death of Blair's mother Hazel nineteen years later, after a long battle with thyroid cancer, could have been caused by the fallout.[10] Van Steenis said there was a good chance Tony Blair absorbed Strontium-90 in his bones after drinking local milk and would be at risk of bone cancer. When Blair was eleven, his father had a stroke and couldn't talk for three years. Soon after, Blair's sister Sarah was diagnosed with rheumatoid arthritis and hospitalised for two years.

Blair's spokesman dismissed the news story when it appeared in 2004, but van Steenis said Blair had never denied fallout caused his mother's death.

'He won't acknowledge it because to do so would strengthen the legal case against his government for the compensation entitlements of British and Australian servicemen involved in the British atomic testing program,' van Steenis said.[11]

The news about Blair prompted many other families to come forward to tell quite horrific stories. They all hoped that by going public, the attention would pressure the government to finally take some action to assist them, or at least acknowledge what happened.

•

Some nuclear veterans tried to get compensation only to be met with a bureaucratic brick wall. In October 1953 army tank driver Warrant Officer Bill Jones parked Centurion tank, serial number 169041, just 500 metres from ground zero at Emu Field. Army commanders wanted to see what effect a nuclear bomb blast would have on the powerful brand-new tank. Centurions were designed by Britain during the Second World War but arrived too late to join the fighting. They were used with distinction by the British forces in the Korean War and in 1950 Australia bought 150 of them. Jones parked the tank facing the spot where the atom bomb would go off. It was filled with sensors and dummies to see if humans could survive inside a tank so close to an atom bomb. The dummy at the controls was given the name Cecil.

Sixty minutes after the blast, scientists and tank experts went in to see what was left. They were surprised to find the tank still upright but pushed back two metres and to the left by the force of the explosion. The heavy metal side plates were torn off and dumped 200 metres away. The opticals were all fried. Metal facing the blast was sandblasted. Aerials and light equipment attached to the tank had been carried away.

Jones was ordered to start up the tank and drive it around. He climbed into the tank and moved poor battered Cecil aside. The tank wouldn't start. He got out, examined the engine and discovered he needed to replace several parts that had been fried in the extreme heat of the blast. Like a good soldier, Jones waited by his tank for three hours while somebody fetched the parts. He was never told of the risk of radiation. He replaced the parts, got the engine going, climbed into the tank and drove it around while senior officers cheered.

Within weeks Jones fell ill. He vomited every morning for years, getting weaker and weaker. Doctors drilled holes in his chest and scraped skin off his arms, sending samples to the US for testing.

Twelve years after the tests, Bill Jones was discharged from the army as medically unfit. He went to a local doctor and was told he had six weeks to live. He tried to get compensation for his exposure at Emu Field, but the army said he was never exposed to radiation. Nobody was allowed to give evidence. Nine months later, he died of cancer. It was a long and agonising death. Bill Jones was just thirty-nine years old, leaving his wife, Peggy, and four children to fend for themselves.

'When he did die, he died a terrible death,' she said. 'I am only sorry the army officers weren't there to see what he went through.'[12]

Peggy applied to the army for compensation as she believed being ordered to fix and drive a radiation-contaminated tank an hour after an atomic bomb would have caused his cancer. For eight long years, she battled Defence bureaucracy but the government refused to admit it was in any way responsible. In 1974 the Commissioner for Employees' Compensation finally conceded Jones died from metastatic carcinoma of the bone, a disease contracted due to the nature of his employment in the army. They awarded just $8600 to the Jones family. For three more years the army continued to haggle over how much they should pay for Bill Jones' medical bills. The amount was clearly inadequate, but it was the first time any of the victims of contamination had received any compensation from a government that was still insisting there was no impact on humans from the nuclear tests.

In 1980 Labor MP Tom Uren, who eventually called for the Royal Commission, raised the Jones case in parliament. He accused the Fraser government of refusing to carry out or follow up any health studies of the Australians who served at Monte Bello, Maralinga and Emu Field.

'How many other people who worked on the weapons tests have cancer?' asked Uren. He detailed cases of six Commonwealth police officers who had died or were dying of cancer. Their families had difficulty verifying their duties at the nuclear sites as all their colleagues were sworn to secrecy.[13]

•

Some families came forward with horrific stories in a desperate effort to get the government to do something. Robert Williamson was in the RAAF at the time of the Monte Bello test in 1952. He died aged forty-five from lymphoma and his damaged DNA has left a horrific trail of illness and death. The TV current affairs program *60 Minutes* detailed the family's tragic history in 2011.[14] Williamson's son Alan was chronically sick all his life and died at twenty-one. Son Jeffrey had liver and bowel cancer and died at thirty-six. Another son, Graham, died of brain tumours, aged eight. Granddaughter Natalie died of brain tumours at eleven months. Grandson Matthew died of brain tumours aged sixteen. Robert Williamson had six children but only three – Susan, Jennifer and Ken – were alive in 2011 when they were interviewed by reporter Liam Bartlett. Ken developed prostate cancer and melanoma. Susan fought three bouts of breast cancer. She had a bilateral mastectomy at age twenty-eight. The cancer came back seventeen years later. The family can't prove their terrible health problems were caused by their father's exposure at the Monte Bello nuclear test. Robert Williamson never talked about what he had seen and done, and his service records provide no clue to the extent of his exposure. He is included among RAAF personnel in the Nominal Role of Australian participants in the British atomic tests by the Department of Veterans' Affairs in 2001.

'I reckon it stinks,' Ken Williamson said in 2011. 'Nobody is willing to say "Yes, this is what happened. This is what we did. We took sons, brothers, fathers, uncles and put them in front of this new technology just to see what happened." Well it's happening.'[15]

British nuclear scientist Dr Chris Busby told *60 Minutes* people at the tests in Australia would have received more exposure to radiation fallout than someone at Nagasaki. 'We found a ninefold excess of congenital heritable disease in the offspring of test veterans compared with controls.'[16]

Leading Australian geneticist Professor Grant Sutherland said in an earlier news report on the Williamson family, however, that nuclear tests could not be blamed for the birth defects and serious medical conditions of nuclear veterans' families.[17] Sutherland was an adviser to the government on a study into the deaths of an estimated 10,000 of the 17,000 Australian nuclear veterans and civilians in the twenty years since the tests ended. He said there was no medical research to support widespread claims the tests caused genetic defects or multiple cancers. Sutherland believes the Williamson family was carrying a mutated gene, but not one caused by exposure to radiation.

While the scientists continue to argue, firing statistics and experimental findings at each other, the British and Australian governments continue to stay mute, sticking to the old line established by Titterton that safety standards at the tests were so good, nobody was exposed to unsafe levels of radiation.

•

In Britain it's the same story. Hundreds of cases were highlighted in the media of people with health problems who were among the 25,000 British servicemen who'd served at the British tests.

British nuclear authorities had secretly been testing bones of dead nuclear veterans since 1958. Two servicemen who died within months of the hydrogen bomb that was exploded at Christmas Atoll in 1958 were tested for Strontium-90. The femurs were removed from the bodies and examined. The results found the level of Strontium-90 wasn't above what is normal for the general population in either case. In one case an open verdict was returned. In the other, death was put down to natural causes.[18] As a result, the men's families' claim for a pension was denied as their death was deemed to have had nothing to do with their military service. It was to be a line repeated over and over in the decades to come as Defence officials sought to block every claim that suggested the atom bomb tests caused deaths among servicemen.

In Britain a 2010 inquiry into the use of human tissue analysis by UK nuclear facilities discovered fifteen nuclear veterans secretly had organs removed at post mortems for radiochemical analysis. The tests by Atomic Weapons Establishment nuclear authority scientists were carried out for the UK Ministry of Defence to determine the likelihood of the individual being exposed to harmful radiation during the test explosions. In nearly every case, relatives had no idea organs were being removed. In half the cases, official records stated no tests were done on the organs, possibly because of the cost involved. Conveniently, it was deemed that in all cases the veterans' involvement in the nuclear tests had nothing to do with their deaths.[19]

•

Reports of links between nuclear veterans and health problems of descendants were growing. RAF aircraftman Stanley Macdonald from Edinburgh, Scotland, watched three atom bombs explode at Maralinga. Within ten years he developed a string of illnesses and by his seventies had two very rare brain conditions – multiple system atrophy and progressive supranuclear palsy. His grandson was diagnosed with arteriovenous malformation that caused a knot of blood vessels in his brain.[20]

Jeff Liddiatt of Bristol was nineteen and had been in the RAF just two years when he was sent for the minor trials in 1959 and 1960. 'I wondered what on earth I was doing there,' he recalled on landing at Maralinga.[21] 'It was a diabolical place.

But there were some good things – we were fed well and beer was sixpence a pint.

'They didn't tell us anything. Planes landed with equipment painted with the radiation sign, but it meant nothing to me. When I learned what the signs stood for it was the first time I realised I was involved in exploding an atomic bomb.'

Liddiatt didn't see many Australians when he was at Maralinga and didn't see any dramatic atomic mushroom clouds. 'I learned later these minor trials were the dirtiest bombs of all. They set fire to lumps of uranium and plutonium just to see what would happen. We had to have been exposed. We had weekends off and went exploring in Land Rovers. We drove all over the blast zones left by the previous tests and had a look around. Nobody told us not to go to certain places. We had a barbecue at one spot and learned later it was right next to one of the ground zeros.'

Liddiatt later developed a degenerative spine, which he is convinced is due to his exposure to radiation at Maralinga. His three children all have genetic illnesses that he believes could only have been passed on from his damaged genes. His daughter had cancer at twenty-three, his eldest son has a low sperm count and his youngest son suffers from shoulder bones growing at unusual places.

'He has to go to hospital every so often to have them shaved off. Doctors refused to write it down, but they said verbally it was probably due to my exposure to radiation.

'What did the bastards do to us? I looked at my medical records and all it said was I had an eye test and was given glasses. If they just said they didn't know at the time and apologise, it would be all over. But they won't even admit something went wrong. I think they're worried if they did admit they got it wrong, they'd look stupid and that scares them more than anything. There is no doubt they looked down on us. We are like ghosts. We shout in the dark but they don't see us, they don't hear us. They just pretend we're not there. We are just working-class squaddies so we didn't count. The senior officers and scientists were all given awards and medals and made knights and lords, but we in the ranks got nothing. The only thing we got was the legacy of it in our blood and genes. They hope those still remaining will die sooner rather than later. That way there'll be no one left to bother them.'

It seems the British Government knew all along that testing atom bombs could cause damage for many generations. In 1956 the UK Medical Research Council sent a secret report to the UK government warning serious genetic damage could be caused to the population if nuclear testing continued. On 31 July 1956 the UK Ministry of Defence sent an internal telex urging officials to turn the report's conclusion on its head and publicly state the opposite. It said: 'We do not want you to release any statement on genetic effects of radiation. If you have to, a safer interpretation of the MRC report would be "has not shown an increase" rather than "shows an increase".'[22]

The US Government has been far more open. A 2002 US Department of Health and Human Services report to Congress estimated radioactive fallout from the world's nuclear weapons tests during the Cold War killed 11,000 Americans through cancer. Many thousands more people were killed around the world from the 390 nuclear bombs exploded above ground worldwide between 1951 and 1963. The US figures did not include internal radiation exposure caused by inhaling or swallowing of radioactive particles. If those are included, as many as 17,000 Americans and more people worldwide died because of the atmospheric tests.[23]

•

More nuclear veterans went public with their shocking stories as they saw their children and grandchildren born with deformation. Neville Howard was a young airman at Amberley RAAF base near Brisbane given the job of cleaning contaminated planes used to fly in and out of the radioactive clouds. By this time a special concrete chamber had been built where dismantled parts of the planes would be brought in for cleaning. All the waste water was specially siphoned off into a holding tank.

'We used to hose them all down and just keep hosing them down and hosing them down until such time as they were clean of radioactivity.'[24]

'My son was conceived when I was working in that chamber. He had twisted feet that he had to have special shoes [for], which he wears today.'

•

In 1999 the incessant public pressure from the heartbreaking stories of families suffering health problems from what they believed was the atomic tests eventually forced the Howard government to announce there would be a cancer and mortality study of Australian nuclear participants. It was run by the Department of Veterans' Affairs with a panel of hand-picked scientific experts. The aim was to determine whether there was an increased rate of early death and cancer among the men involved in the nuclear tests compared to the general Australian community. The study took a long time as first they had to compile a list of servicemen and civilians who had been present at the tests. The list of 16,716 men did not include people involved in the subsequent clean-ups of the site. The list was completed in 2001. The cancer and mortality study, led by Rear Admiral C. S. Harrington, took another five years and was made public in June 2006.[25]

Its official finding was that the overall death rate in test participants was similar to that of the general population – an unbelievable conclusion.

The study found cancer death rates among nuclear veterans were eighteen per cent higher than the general population. It dismissed this figure by saying cancers were balanced out by death rates from other causes, such as heart attacks, which were lower than the general population.

It counted 4233 deaths among the 11,000 veterans examined – the general population had 4150 deaths.

The study found that compared to the general population:

- Deaths from cancers of the lip, mouth and pharynx were fifty per cent higher.
- Lung cancer deaths were twenty per cent higher.
- Colorectal cancer deaths were twenty-four per cent higher.
- Prostate cancer deaths were twenty-six per cent higher.

Nuclear participants had a far higher rate of getting cancer compared to the general population:

- Forty-three per cent higher for all leukemias.
- Sixty-one per cent higher for leukemias, except for chronic lymphatic leukemia.
- Forty per cent higher for melanoma.
- Forty-eight per cent higher for oesophageal cancer.
- And 180 per cent higher for mesothelioma.

RAAF personnel had nearly double the expected number of deaths from melanoma, and cases of contracting melanoma were increased by sixty-six per cent.

Navy personnel had the highest death rate from cancers. Of the twenty-six participants dying from mesothelioma, sixteen were in the navy.

Despite these facts, the report still managed to come up with an official conclusion that the tests didn't cause a higher death rate. Its twists and tumbles in logic would make a circus performer envious.

'The increases in cancer rates do not appear to have been caused by exposure to radiation. No relationship could be found between overall cancer incidence or mortality and exposure to radiation. None of the above cancers occurring in excess showed any association with radiation exposure in this study. In particular there was no link between radiation exposure and leukemia, excluding chronic lymphatic leukemia that is commonly found to be increased in groups exposed to radiation. These findings are consistent with the low levels of radiation exposure found in this study. Only four per cent of the study population had an estimated radiation exposure greater than twenty millisieverts (mSv) from test participation, and seventy-nine per cent had an estimated exposure of less than one mSv.'[26]

The study said the estimated mean radiation exposure of the study population was 2.8 mSv 'only slightly greater than the background exposure received by every Australian every year'.[27] The study went out of its way to find excuses for the veterans' higher death rates through cancers; for example, higher lung and mouth cancers could be due to smoking. For some unknown reason the study concluded nuclear servicemen smoked much more than the general population. It said higher leukemia could be caused by benzene. Asbestos on ships could have caused higher cancers. The study said many of the nuclear participants went on to work in the construction industry where they would have been exposed to asbestos and other cancer causes.

The report managed to argue away every finding that nuclear veterans had higher health problems than the general population.

Veterans' Affairs Minister Bruce Billson announced that despite no link being found to the nuclear tests, the government wished to make a 'positive response' and allow free treatment for all participants.[28] Asked by the media why the government hadn't simply given the survivors free medical treatment back in 1999 when the study started, Billson said it was necessary to have the research done.

'We wanted to know what the facts are,' Billson said.[29] Curiously, the Australian finding was remarkably similar to a British government study in 1993, which found that although nuclear veterans were at higher risk for cancers, they had no 'excess' illnesses.[30]

Alan Batchelor, a retired major who had been a young lieutenant at Maralinga, was a consultant to the study, supplying them with many documents and case studies of afflicted veterans.

'It was a deliberate whitewash,' Batchelor said.[31] 'They failed to look at genetic complications. It only covered ionising radiation and didn't include other causes of cancer. They compared servicemen who had been fit and healthy youngsters against a general population that includes a lot of overweight and sick people. It wasn't a proper comparison.'

Batchelor said the study made no reference to the men most likely to be affected – those who were ordered into the contaminated blast zone shortly after the explosions. It grouped all veterans together, including the cooks who stayed well away at the base. It also ignored test participants who had died before 1982. The study didn't take into account men who had inhaled contaminated dust as the dosimeters only recorded radiation in the open air.

'We got a white health card, which gives us free medical treatment, but only for cancer. We are still below the gold card that the fellows who served overseas get. We walked into ground contaminated by atomic bombs – now if that isn't hazardous service, I don't know what is.'

Veterans were frustrated and furious. The Atomic Ex-Servicemen's Association said the government study was a deliberate cover-up and amounted to criminal fraud. The veterans did their own research on deaths among their colleagues and found police security records that listed 11,600 nuclear participants. They found ten out of every eleven men listed were dead by 2008. Within ten years of the last test in 1957, a total 512 were dead. Death rates shot up after that and were highest twenty to thirty years after the tests, when the men were aged in their forties and fifties. Between 1965 and 1974 almost 2000 men died. Between 1975 and 1984 deaths jumped to 3069. During the next ten years 2250 veterans died. Between 1995 and 2004 deaths topped 2000. A further 800 died between 2005 and 2008.[32]

The government disputed the figures.

Proving deaths were caused by exposure was made more difficult by the curious tendency for crucial medical reports to disappear. Hospital records for Emu Field, Maralinga and the RAAF base at Amberley have all mysteriously gone missing. The log of HMAS *Koala*, whose crew was exposed while recovering parts of the blown up HMS *Plym*, is missing. So are the ship's report of proceedings and film badge records. Dosimeter records for engineers and mechanics ordered into the blast zones shortly after detonation are missing. Records of names of personnel who had to carry out hazardous operations have disappeared. Many individuals who flew into radioactive clouds or entered ground zero found themselves left off lists showing who was there.

•

Australian and British servicemen weren't the only ones used as guinea pigs by the British. New Zealand servicemen were also exposed during nuclear tests in Australia and at Christmas Atoll. New Zealand nuclear veterans – mostly ex-navy – decided to take matters into their own hands. The leader of the group, Roy Sefton, was a seventeen-year-old sailor on HMNZS *Pukaki* in 1957 when the crew watched the British hydrogen-bomb test at Christmas Atoll. Like tens of thousands of other military men involved in nuclear tests, Sefton was ordered to turn his back on the blast and cover his eyes with his hands. 'All of a sudden there's this massive flash. I had my eyes closed and goggles, dark goggles, hands over them and there before me lay the skeleton, the bones of my hands.'[33] Sefton and his shipmates were in the area for months eating local seafood, drinking and washing in tropical water. A few years later Sefton developed aches and pains. By the time he was thirty he found it difficult to walk and everything he touched caused pain. Doctors didn't know what it was. Other veterans noticed many shipmates of the *Pukaki* and her sister ship at the tests, HMNZS *Rotoiti*, had died in their twenties.

What they didn't know was that before the start of the Australian bomb trials, the naval commander at the 1952 Monte Bello test, Royal Navy Vice Admiral Brooking, received a top secret memo from his superiors. It said, 'some degree of risk must be run by some people if we are to achieve the full purpose of the trial'.[34] The memo discussed the sort of dose of radiation exposure that would be 'acceptable', which would be decided by the UK Medical Research Council. The memo warned the council would 'play for safety to such an extent that we might be unable to achieve the scientific purpose of the trial'. In other words, the purpose of the test was to see how much radiation men could be exposed to before they collapsed or could no longer function. When the British Prime Minister Anthony Eden was told of this possible genetic time bomb, he said: 'A pity, but we can't help it.'[35]

Sefton and other nuclear veterans pressed the New Zealand government for answers. A study by Professor Neil Pearce of Massey University in Wellington found there was an increase in death rates among nuclear veterans – but only a slight one.[36] The veterans weren't convinced, and in 2000 took the extraordinary step of commissioning their own research. Dr Al Rowland of Massey University used a brand-new technique and equipment originally developed for Chernobyl victims. He looked at fifty veterans and fifty control subjects from the general population matched for age, health, smoking and drinking habits. Rowland found nuclear veterans had three times the number of 'translocations' – the shifting of genes inside the chromosome.[37] The more translocations, the higher the risk of getting cancer. The study released in 2007 scientifically proved that being present at the nuclear tests did increase the chance of getting cancer. It was to have a big effect on legal challenges to the UK government's refusal to acknowledge any harm was caused by using servicemen as guinea pigs.

•

In 1999 Sue Rabbitt Roff of the University of Dundee examined genetic traits among participants in the nuclear tests and their families – 1041 British, 238 New Zealanders and sixty-two Fijians.[38]

She found that of 5000 children and grandchildren born to the veterans, thirty-nine per cent were born with serious medical conditions. By contrast, the national incidence figure in Britain is around 2.5 per cent. There were twenty-six cases of spina bifida – five times the usual rate in the UK. Half of those offspring with health problems had the same dermatological, musculoskeletal and gastrointestinal conditions as many of the nuclear veterans. Among the 2261 children of 1041 British veterans more than 200 skeletal abnormalities were reported including more than thirty cases of short stature and eighteen spinal problems, mostly curvature and scoliosis. More than 100 skin conditions were reported – mostly eczema and dermatitis. More than fifty of the children suffer from arthritis before the age of thirty. Hip deformities were reported for nineteen children and fourteen had kneecap deformities. More than 100 of the veterans' children reported reproductive difficulties – twenty-four women had problems with their ovaries. This pattern was repeated in the grandchildren.

'UK scientists, military officers and politicians of the 1950s and 60s were aware that, as one document dated 1947 from the Medical Research Council puts it, "even the smallest doses of radiation produce a genetic effect, there being no threshold dose below which no genetic effect is unduced",' Roff wrote.[39]

In another study she found the average lifespan for nuclear veterans was 53.8 years and that sixty-eight per cent of the deaths were cancer-related.

A growing number of scientists believe that exposure to radiation can cause genetic damage, resulting in the development of new hereditary disorders. Children of nuclear veterans have suffered chronic musculoskeletal disorders; deformity of the hands, feet, bladder and genitals; heart malformation; hearing defects; spina bifida; and a host of other illnesses.

•

Tragically, Titterton had his own connection to possibile radiation exposure. In 1945, after a year of working on the Manhattan Project nuclear program, Titterton and his wife, Peggy, had their first child. Baby Jennifer was born with spina bifida. Despite operations in the US, she had limited control of her lower limbs for the rest of her life.

14
THE DIRTY CLEAN-UP

Military veterans and civilians involved in the nuclear tests and their families weren't the only ones left sick and deformed once the tests finally ended – the land itself was still highly contaminated. Fallout had spread across the continent. Even at Maralinga, where the land was supposed to have been cleaned up, there were still deadly cocktails of radioactive and toxic material left beneath a few inches of desert sand. Britain treated Australia like a nuclear dump. For decades, Australian politicians and nuclear authorities knew it, but turned a blind eye.

The first attempt by the British to clean up the site came four years after the minor trials ended in 1963. They called it Operation Brumby – a slick PR name evoking wild horses galloping in clean, crisp mountain snows. In reality, it was a light once-over attempt to cover up the toxic radioactive poisons Britain had left behind.

The British were allowed to get away with this because the Australian government did nothing to ensure Maralinga was properly decontaminated after the nuclear tests: the attention of the government was elsewhere at the time. After a record sixteen years as prime minister, Menzies retired in January 1966. His successor Harold Holt had to face an election ten months later, which he won in a landslide. Holt was to disappear while swimming in the sea on 17 December 1967. The Vietnam War was raging and Maralinga was largely forgotten.

The British government had offered to clean the site by turning over the topsoil and burying radioactive equipment such as vehicles, buildings and debris in pits with concrete lids. The British said this clean-up would 'constitute a full and final settlement of all obligations whatsoever of the British government arising out of its use of Maralinga and Emu including liability . . .'[1]

With no reaction from Canberra to the British clean-up proposal, it was left to the Australian safety committee under Titterton to accept this totally inadequate clean-up deal.

For four months in 1967, British army engineers used a tractor to scrape the soil to a depth of just ten centimetres over 180 hectares of the most heavily contaminated part of the site. Huge pits to bury contaminated soil, equipment and vehicles were dug then covered with concrete lids and ten centimetres of dirt. The aim was to make the site as featureless as possible so the casual visitor couldn't tell where the blast sites had been. There were no wire fences, no radiation danger signs. Only the two biggest burial pits had a wire fence put up around them. Clearly the Royal Engineers had no idea of the ability of Aussie rabbits to dig under fences to make the burial pits their home, nor the strong desert winds that would quickly blow away the loose dirt covering.

Brumby was a horrific assignment for those involved. The British air force men doing the work weren't told of the dangers as they dug deep trenches, bulldozed radioactive equipment and turned over the soil in a naïve attempt to hide the plutonium contamination. In 2010, Sam 'Frank' McGee, a flight lieutenant in charge of thirty-five airmen at Operation Brumby, set out to try to reunite the 'missing men of Maralinga'. He found only seven survivors. The others had all been ten to twenty years younger than him, but they had died of cancers, probably caused by their exposure to radioactivity in the 1967 clean-up.

'We were never told the materials we dealt with could be radioactive,' McGee said.[2] The men had no protective gear and worked in shorts and light shirts. McGee had accepted the task as it sounded like a challenge and the chance to go to Australia all expenses paid was attractive.

'At no time were the words "atomic" or "nuclear" mentioned, and I personally had no knowledge of what the UK had been doing in Australia.'

McGee said he'd had to sign the Official Secrets Act, which kept him silent for thirty years. It was only when he contracted cancer that he thought the government couldn't do anything more to hurt him and chose to speak out.

'Those people whose orders we were obeying didn't tell us anything. To find out that I had unwittingly exposed them [his men] to something that might have messed up the rest of the lives . . . I feel terrible.'

McGee died in 2011. His family had to pay $10,000 in medical bills as his service at Maralinga wasn't recognised as hazardous by the UK Ministry of Defence and he was refused compensation.

As noted earlier, the minor trials in 1963 were the dirtiest. The British were testing firing mechanisms to ensure a nuclear explosion would not be triggered by the accidental detonation of any of the explosive charges around the plutonium core. The minor trials resulted in plutonium being scattered around the blast site. Around twenty-two kilograms of deadly plutonium with a half-life of 24,000 years were splattered across the Maralinga scrubland. British nuclear scientist Noah Pearce prepared a top secret report on the Brumby clean-up, detailing how the plutonium and other toxic materials were buried and covered over. It was to remain top secret in London and Canberra for the next eleven years until the report was leaked to the press. Press exposure of the dangerous radioactive waste left behind caused huge embarrassment to the Fraser government. The British weren't coy about what they'd done. They'd told the Australian government of Harold Holt all about it in the report by British scientist Noah Pearce after Brumby was over. Successive governments of Holt, John Gorton, William McMahon, Gough Whitlam and Malcolm Fraser left the report to gather dust. It only came to light after veterans revealed the burial pits and the report was leaked to the media.

In 1984, just as the Royal Commission was starting up and the Maralinga lands were to be handed back to the traditional Aboriginal owners, the Labor government of Bob Hawke sent the Australian Radiation Laboratory to check the sites for contamination. What the ARL scientists found was far worse than the 1967 Pearce report had led them to believe. Instead of a land free of contamination, they found it riddled with deadly atomic residue. Plutonium and uranium permeated the desert sand and dust.

The safety committee had assured Prime Minister Holt the Brumby clean-up had been a success and the area was 'radiologically safe'.[3] It reported the area should now be permanently open to unrestricted access, except for a few small areas where there would be no hazard for 'short-term occupancy'. The committee said that didn't really matter as 'it is unlikely that there would be need or desire for permanent occupancy of any of these areas in the foreseeable future'.

Once again, it didn't cross their minds that Aboriginals still saw this land as their traditional country and would use it as they had for millennia for hunting, ceremonies and as an essential ingredient to their tribal culture.

In September 1968 Britain signed an agreement with the Australian government, now led by Liberal John Gorton, that formally ended Britain's responsibilities for Maralinga. It released Britain from 'all liabilities and responsibilities' for any claims which might be brought against the UK over its nuclear tests in Australia.[4]

The British officials who drew it up must have been laughing and toasting themselves with champagne all the way home.

Seventeen years later, the Royal Commission recommended the site be cleaned up properly. In 1986 the Hawke government appointed the Maralinga Rehabilitation Technical Advisory Committee to oversee reduction of contamination at Maralinga. The committee set the target of clean-up to an international standard of five mSv – the equivalent of five lung X-rays a year.

Next came the inevitable battle with the British government to get them to find some serious money to do a proper clean-up. Britain could insist they held all the legal cards – Menzies had signed off on an agreement that Britain had fulfilled all obligations towards cleaning up Maralinga in Operation Brumby. Documents released in 2014 showed the Hawke cabinet was warned that a complete rehabilitation of the land may not be possible and may be more expensive than the British government would be willing to contemplate. Resources and Energy Minister Gareth Evans told cabinet it could cost more than $500 million (in 2014 dollars). Evans said the remoteness of Maralinga meant it 'may be reasonable to set aside, even at this early stage, the option of absolutely unrestricted habitation'.[5]

Evans said the Thatcher government in Britain would continue to minimise its obligation to clean up the sites and it would be best to adopt a non-confrontational approach with the UK government to persuade them to pay half the clean-up costs if they were kept to $50 million or so.

'The British have also stated their concern that if personal compensation awards are opened up, precedents will be set for compensation of their own nuclear veterans.'

Evans urged the government to 'restrain' the issue of compensation to nuclear veterans to assist negotiations with the British over clean-up costs. A similar trade-off was suggested for Aboriginal grievances. Evans said if services, such as water and roads in the area, were paid for it would help Aboriginals to agree on a 'reasonable' clean-up program that dealt with the main hazards. The Hawke cabinet agreed.

Once again the Australian government secretly moved to deny compensation to nuclear veterans and Aboriginal people for the disgraceful way they had been treated during the atomic tests. Despite Labor publicly taking the moral high road in setting up the Royal Commission, behind closed doors it came down to money. They feared Britain might not help pay for the mess they had left unless the awkward matter of compensating people treated like guinea pigs was removed from the table.

Aboriginal Affairs Minister Clyde Holding did his best and refused to shy away from the Royal Commission's recommendation that Aboriginal people be compensated for dispossession of their lands for the tests.

'We have no option but to accept the principle of compensation for dispossession,' Holding told cabinet.[6] 'The actions of previous Australian governments in shepherding Aboriginal people from their traditional lands for the purpose of conducting atomic tests were both immoral and appallingly executed. The resultant disruption to Aboriginal life has been catastrophic; Yalata, where many resettled, is testimony to that. If we deny compensation we shall stand condemned as surely as those who committed the outrage of dispossession in the first place.'

Holding persuaded the government to immediately give half a million dollars as a down payment on a compensation sum that would be decided later.

The South Australian government and the Maralinga Tjarutja traditional owners were consulted, and an agreement reached for a clean-up. The Maralinga Tjarutja people would be given $13.5 million to re-establish its links with the traditional lands and provide better housing, water, schooling and other community services. The government would meet the cost of the clean-up.

The British eventually agreed to provide £20 million ($45 million) to help with the clean-up.

But the Hawke government reneged on its 1986 promise to fully rehabilitate Maralinga. From the start the clean-up was downgraded to a partial rehabilitation. Even this reduced clean-up program ran into problems and had to be further compromised.

At the contaminated grounds the engineering firm hired for the job scraped contaminated soil up to a depth of twenty centimetres and put it in sixteen-metre-deep trenches that had been excavated out of rock. The trenches were filled to within three metres of the surface then capped with a five-metre-deep layer of uncontaminated topsoil. There was no groundwater to wash it away and the contaminated soil couldn't escape through the rock. Plants on the surface would stop the top layer from eroding.

Safety precautions were far more stringent than during the atomic bomb tests. Every vehicle had a sealed cabin to stop contaminated dust getting in. Workers were checked several times during the day to make sure dust hadn't penetrated the protective gear. A raised walkway kept boots off potentially contaminated soil. Strict controls were kept on access to the 'hot zone', limiting the time workers could be exposed.

It took twelve months to clear the most heavily contaminated site at the 1958 Taranaki blast site. After the first twenty centimetres of soil was removed, highly sensitive detectors searched for traces of plutonium. When radiation still exceeded safety standards they removed another twenty centimetres of soil. Then it was checked again.

In 1967 the worst of the contaminated material had been left in twenty-one pits. The concrete covers had proved totally inadequate. Rabbits had made the pits their home, burrowing under the concrete slabs and flicking contaminated soil to the four winds. A large amount of plutonium-contaminated debris was covered by only a few centimetres of soil.

Huge furnaces were built to burn the contaminated debris at 2000 degrees Celsius. This would seal radioactive material inside glass-like vitrified rock. It would take about forty burns to treat all the contaminated debris in the pits. But during the thirteenth burn there was an explosion inside the furnace that severely damaged the equipment and flung molten material fifty metres from the pit. The burning process was abandoned and the remainder of the pit debris was buried in a shallow trench. It was covered by the solidified vitrified material and then two metres of relatively clean soil. It's not clear what was buried in these new pits.

The Howard government denied the swift reburial had anything to do with cutting costs. The clean-up expenses had blown out to more than $100 million and the Australian government was still having to pour millions of dollars into the operation, with millions more to come.

Nuclear engineer Alan Parkinson had been appointed by the Labor government to the Maralinga clean-up committee. The new Howard government sacked him when he complained about cost-cutting and the re-burial of contaminated material from the pits.

'The project was a compromise from the beginning and was never intended to be a total clean-up,' Parkinson said.[7] 'There are still hundreds of square kilometres of land contaminated with plutonium. The plutonium-contaminated debris is buried in a bare hole in the ground in limestone and dolomite which exhibits many cracks and fissures with only two metres of cover.'

Parkinson said the firm hired to do the clean-up lacked experience and government public servants appointed to oversee the project had no nuclear expertise. 'What was done at Maralinga was a cheap and nasty solution that wouldn't be adopted on white-fella land,' Parkinson said.

When the clean-up ended in March 2000, the Howard government declared the process had been a success and the land rehabilitated. 'We can shut the book on it,' said Senator Nick Minchin, the minister responsible.[8] Minchin declared the area was now safe to be returned to the Aboriginal traditional owners. The Howard government said the clean-up allowed unrestricted access to ninety per cent of the 3200 square kilometre Maralinga site.

Parkinson insists the operation stopped short of fulfilling a promise to clean up the legacy of the atomic tests. 'The government did not do what they agreed to do and they did it just to save money,' Parkinson told the ABC. He also published a book on the clean-up in 2007.[9]

Parkinson said that, after spending $108 million, less than two per cent of the land deemed contaminated had been properly cleaned. 'Almost eighty-five per cent of the original 24,000 grams of plutonium remains on the surface,' Parkinson said.[10]

Regardless of the reports that Maralinga still had contaminated land and there had been an inadequate burial of radioactive waste, bit by bit parts of the enormous stretch of land that had once been in the prohibited zone were handed back to the Aboriginal people.

In 1985 the South Australian government passed legislation handing back native title to the Maralinga Tjarutja traditional owners – a southern Pitjantjatjara people. In 1995 the Tjarutja people resettled on land outside the test sites and called it Oak Valley Community, 130 kilometres north-west of Maralinga.

While the entire area was now deemed safe for people to pass through, some areas will forever remain unsuitable for permanent human occupation. Aboriginals can safely hunt and eat kangaroos on the land, but the original blast sites will never be acceptable places for establishing a camp.

In August 2004 the South Australian government officially returned 21,000 square kilometres of land west of Maralinga at the border with Western Australia to the traditional owners. Then bearing the awkward name 'Unnamed Conservation

Park', it was to be open to visitors and jointly managed with the Maralinga Tjarutja traditional owners. They gave it a new name – Mamumgari. The park area was well outside the fallout area from the Maralinga tests, but fifty years earlier Aboriginals had been forced to leave this part of their traditional land as it was deemed part of the prohibited zone. Many were forced to live 1000 kilometres away in Yalata, the supervised settlement that became synonymous with terrible treatment of Aboriginals.

In 2009, Maralinga village was also returned to Aboriginal hands. It was the last section – about 3100 square kilometres – of the once vast test site and prohibited zone to be handed back to the traditional owners. Alice Cox, now aged eighty, was a young mother of two when the first atom bombs exploded at Emu Field. She was at a settlement hundreds of kilometres away at the time but immediately felt something was wrong with the land and warned her children not to eat fruit from a nearby quandong tree. At the ceremony to mark the handover she told a reporter she was pleased to have her land back.[11] The area included the huts and buildings left by the clean-up team. Aboriginal owners planned to open the area to tourists and set up a museum to explain to visitors what happened at this place, once home to 2000 people working on exploding atomic bombs.

Maralinga Tjarutja chairman Keith Peters said the final handback 'closed twenty-five years of healing'.[12] 'Now it falls to us to look after this land where Anungu and white people's heritage will forever walk together. We will look after this land the Anungu way and manage and care for it safely.'

•

Nothing stays buried forever. Canberra officials have received confidential survey reports that the burial pits of the 1990s are already subsiding and eroding. The *Sydney Morning Herald* reported in 2011 that files from the Department of Resources, Energy and Tourism obtained under Freedom of Information show erosion at the Taranaki burial trench needed significant remediation.[13] Other burial pits have been subject to subsidence and erosion, exposing asbestos-contaminated debris. No radioactive material had leaked out, but remedial work had to be done. The Maralinga Tjarutja tribal elders had requested further clean-ups including the 'Kuli' site east of the airstrip where a lot of contaminated material was buried.

Maralinga isn't the only toxic legacy of the atomic tests that continues today. Radioactive waste 'hotspots' continue to emerge long after the clean-up was 'finalised'.

In South Australia tests in 2001 found Caesium-137 in water at a bore hole at the Defence Science and Technology Organisation facility at Salisbury, north of Adelaide. The facility is next to the RAAF base Edinburgh where radioactive material was brought from Maralinga. Caesium-137 is a highly carcinogenic compound that can cause birth defects. Even low levels of exposure are regarded as dangerous. It is thought the contamination came from washing down the planes used to monitor the nuclear clouds. Radioactive parts of the planes and personal gear, such as gasmasks and clothing, were also buried in concrete-covered pits less than twenty metres from a public road. The contamination was found when the government planned to sell off part of the Defence land for industrial and residential sites. The inquiry was held in 1993 but not publicly released until the Adelaide *Advertiser* got hold of it in 2001.[14]

•

In 1984 Labor's Resources Minister, Senator Peter Walsh, confirmed that one of the Lincoln bombers used to test atomic clouds at Emu Field in 1953 was buried in a tip at the Amberley RAAF base near Brisbane. Walsh told parliament the Defence Department had changed its tune over the years about the buried bomber. In 1980 a veteran wrote to the then Resources Minister, Liberal Senator John Carrick, about buried radioactive material at Amberley. Carrick passed the question to Defence. Defence wrote back to Carrick but didn't mention anything about the heavily contaminated buried bomber. Four years later, when Walsh pressed Defence on the matter, Defence officials suddenly discovered there was indeed a radioactive Lincoln bomber buried at Amberley. Walsh said Defence advice was either inadequate or 'at worst misleading'.[15] He was being kind. It smacked of another cover-up. With a royal commission coming up, Defence officials probably thought it would be best for them if the truth came out then rather than be dragged out by the commission. So why cover up the burial of a contaminated bomber for decades? The answer is simple. If the bomber was so badly contaminated it had to be secretly buried, then what about the RAAF men who flew it and those ordered to try to clean it?

•

Merv Ashton was a leading aircraftman at Amberley working in the decontamination centre. He told the Royal Commission he was one of the first to work in the specially constructed decontamination building and the last one there when it closed down. Ashton said radioactive material from the planes was dumped by planes out over the ocean – once out of Brisbane and once out of Townsville. It was done at the crack of dawn so no one would notice. Nobody wore protective clothing and no radiation dose recordings were taken. When the drums floated they were fired on by the tailgunner to make them sink.

Those were the only shots fired by Australians during the entire nuclear weapons saga.

15

THE FIGHT GOES ON

However imperfect the $13.5 million land hand-back deal the Australian government struck with Maralinga's Aboriginal traditional owners, at least it went some way towards compensation and recognition that a terrible wrong had been done to Aboriginal people during the atomic tests.

It was part of the £20 million payment from the British government in December 1993 that was accepted by the Australian Keating government as 'full and final settlement of all claims arising out of the nuclear testing program'.[1]

In 2002 the Howard government appointed eminent barrister John Clarke QC to review veterans' entitlements. The Clarke report concluded service at the nuclear tests must be regarded as hazardous, and that individuals were put at risk of contracting disease from their exposure.[2] As a result, legislation was passed in 2006 recognising one cancer – malignant neoplasia – as an illness arising out of the nuclear tests. However the Clarke report did not recognise a string of radiation-related health problems such as other cancers, infertility or psychological injuries. Health claims were limited to those who were in defined exposure zones and excluded vast groups affected by radiation exposure outside those limited zones.

In 2010 the Rudd government amended the Veterans' Entitlement Act to allow nuclear veterans to receive the same benefits as military veterans who had operational or hazardous service. It was, at last, a recognition that the service done at the British nuclear tests was 'hazardous'.

But veterans and the civilian workers who were used as virtual guinea pigs in the nuclear tests still received no financial compensation or military recognition. Defence rejected nuclear veterans' appeals for a military medal to recognise their hazardous service. In the end they made their own.

The veterans didn't get a cent from the £20 million. The British payment went to the Aboriginal settlement or was supposedly spent on the clean-up.

Successive governments of both Australia and Britain did everything they could to make sure the thousands of servicemen and their families received absolutely nothing.

During the first decade after the tests ended, veterans had little contact with each other. Many of the military people deployed or 'volunteered' to the tests were in the military for up to ten more years, and it was impossible for them to talk to anyone about their concerns. The standard answer from the Defence Department was the same then as it is today – there were no personnel affected by radiation at the tests because there was no such exposure.

There was very little in the media in the 1960s and 70s saying veterans' health could have been affected by their presence at the atomic tests. For most, health problems didn't begin until about ten years after their exposure to the tests. They feared discussing anything about the tests could have them locked up. They'd had that drummed into them when they signed the Official Secrets Act.

A handful of individuals did seek compensation in the 1970s as their health worsened. Those who tried to get some sort of compensation continued to be met with a blanket refusal to acknowledge any health problems could have been caused by exposure to radioactive material during the tests by the government of the day or Defence bureaucrats. Sometimes, even when the link was obvious to all and officials could no longer keep up the pretence, the reaction was nothing short of vindictive.

Ric Johnstone, who fixed vehicles in the hot zone at Maralinga, ran into serious health problems within a year of his 1956 posting. He had bouts of nausea and diarrhea and in 1958 was discharged from the RAAF as medically unfit. His two children were born with genetically linked deformities. He had strong anxiety attacks, was given anti-psychotic drugs and shock therapy in a psychiatric clinic. On release he had agoraphobia and for years feared stepping outside his house. In 1968, he asked his doctor whether being close to exploding atom bombs could have anything to do with his health problems. His doctor told him not to be ridiculous – there were no atom bombs exploded in Australia. He promptly diagnosed Johnstone with schizophrenia.[3]

Four years later the doctor contacted Johnstone and apologised profusely. He'd discovered atom bombs had indeed exploded in Australia. The doctor helped Johnstone apply for a military pension, and in 1973 he received what is believed to be the very first compensation to a nuclear veteran associated with service with atom bomb tests. The Commonwealth Employees' Compensation Board awarded Johnstone $220 a fortnight – far below what was needed to support himself and his two children. He was below the poverty line, so the Social Services Department topped him up with a pension of $110 a fortnight.

The compensation wasn't a recognition that Johnstone's health problems were caused by his time at Maralinga. The board ruled Johnstone had a pre-existing condition aggravated by his military service. They ignored the fact Johnstone was perfectly healthy before he was sent to Maralinga.

Other veterans were facing another problem if they sought compensation for ill health caused by their time at Maralinga.

In Australia in the 1970s the statute of limitations for seeking compensation stated no action could be taken more than six years after the event. A legal question also arose over whether military personnel could sue the government for something that happened to them while they were in the military.

In 1980, in a legal first, the government granted Johnstone legal aid to pursue his compensation case against the Defence department. In 1988 a jury awarded him a significant amount in damages. It was a landmark case, but Johnstone remained the only nuclear veteran to have won a claim for negligence against the Commonwealth for injuries suffered during the tests.

The award did not silence Johnstone. He spoke out publicly time and again for veterans. A group of veterans joined him in 1972 to set up the Australian Nuclear Veterans' Association. The ANVA pressured the Hawke government into setting up the Royal Commission.

In the 1970s a handful of nuclear veterans or members of the families afflicted with health problems pursued compensation. They were fighting as individuals, often in the dark about the larger picture of the problems besetting survivors. One by one the applications were refused. The most common reason given for rejection was simple and one that successive governments used for decades – it was impossible to medically prove that a specific health problem was caused by exposure to radiation at one particular period while they were working at the tests.

Labor MP Tom Uren kept fighting in parliament for the veterans – asking a series of questions of the Fraser government about one case after another. Uren brought to light the air force men suffering from leukemia after flying into radioactive clouds, and the ground staff ordered to clean the radioactive planes. Newspapers, particularly the Adelaide *Advertiser*, published articles as veterans started telling their stories openly.

Some cases were tragic, but nothing seemed to melt the officials' hearts. Take the case of Margaret Prior.

High above the Monte Bello Islands region on 16 May 1956, her husband Colin was the pilot on an RAAF Neptune aircraft assigned to monitor the ocean to make sure no unauthorised ships ventured near the atomic test area. The plane shouldn't have been anywhere near the mushroom cloud. But the wind changed direction, and suddenly the plane was engulfed in the radioactive cloud.

Colin Prior later contracted chronic dermatitis. He continued a creditable career, serving briefly in the Vietnam War and rising to the rank of Air Commodore, before retiring in 1986. In 2001 he could no longer take the pain of his skin disease and took his own life.

The Howard government refused Margaret Prior the $840 fortnightly war widow pension because of the suicide.[4] She appealed, arguing the suicide was brought on by the pain of dermatitis that was caused by his exposure to radiation at Monte Bello.

After a ten-year fight the Veterans' Appeals Division of the Administrative Appeals Tribunal overturned the government's objections and awarded her a war widow's pension. The tribunal made a groundbreaking ruling that the skin disease and Colin Prior's subsequent depression could have been caused by exposure to radiation he received when flying through the radioactive cloud. It was a belated small victory.

•

Nuclear veterans in Australia and Britain formed associations believing there was strength in numbers. They compared notes and found the same stories of health problems not only among themselves, but also among their offspring. From the late 1980s the Brisbane-based Atomic Ex-Servicemen's Association published a booklet titled *Atomic Fallout*, with veterans' stories and news of the fight for compensation. The coming of the internet in the mid 1990s accelerated the campaign as veterans could now compare stories and information, as well as examine scientific reports and evidence from official inquiries.

The same was happening in Britain. Not only were there 22,000 Britons who had served at the atomic tests in Australia, thousands more had been at the far more powerful hydrogen bomb tests at Christmas Atoll in the Pacific.

In 2004 a handful of claims for compensation from British nuclear veterans were launched as a group litigation order – effectively ten lead cases to test in court. If they got through, thousands more were queued up behind them.

The cases quickly ran into the statute of limitations in the UK, which is just three years. In 2007 the veterans came back arguing they weren't aware of the possible link of their health problems to their exposure at the tests until Al Rowland's 2007 study in New Zealand found an abnormal incidence of chromosomal changes in blood samples of fifty New Zealand navy nuclear veterans. Rowland concluded nuclear veterans had a higher risk of cancer. It didn't prove that a nuclear veteran's health problems were caused by their exposure at a certain nuclear test, but it did establish that being at a nuclear test gave you a higher risk of developing cancer.

In London's High Court the UK Ministry of Defence continued to deny what happened at the tests could cause a health problem, and argued that the veterans knew this three years before they pursued their claims. Government lawyers were confident. They'd won every case so far. They were about to get a big surprise.

In 2009 Justice David Foskett ruled against the UK government, saying the veterans' claims had been issued within the limitation period because the veterans had only discovered in 2007 through the Rowland study that their health problems could have been caused by the tests. It was a technical legal victory, but for the first time the legal doors had been forced open for veterans to pursue a $400 million class action against the UK government. Justice Foskett decided the ten test cases could proceed. The seventy UK veterans watching cheered and toasted each other in pubs around the court. The decision made headlines in Britain and Australia.

'There have been a lot of lies,' former Royal Engineer James Dunne told reporters outside the courthouse.[5] 'We didn't know about radiation, that was science fiction to us then. We did our duty.' Dunne had been diagnosed with cancer in the nose, anaemic blood and zero sperm count. 'I was one of the lucky ones,' he said.

Alan Illett, seventy-three, RAF ground crew for the Christmas Atoll hydrogen blast, said it had been a long struggle. 'It's good to have a victory now but spare a thought for the poor souls who didn't make it here.'[6] Former Sapper Donald James said: 'We've won the battle but not the war. It's been a long struggle and to get this far we're very happy.'[7]

There was still a long way to go in the struggle for justice and compensation, but the ruling was the first bit of good news the veterans had ever had. It flashed around the world to thousands of nuclear veterans watching in Australia.

Ric Johnstone and Alan Batchelor, representing the Australian Nuclear Veterans' Association, had engaged prominent Sydney lawyer Tom Goudkamp and his team at the law firm Stacks/Goudkamp to fight for compensation in the British courts on behalf of Australian veterans.

'There was nothing we could do in the Australian courts as the statute of limitations had long passed here,' Goudkamp said.[8] 'We would try to see if Australian veterans could join the British veterans in pursuing the UK Ministry of Defence because they were in command of the bomb tests.

'It was always going to be a long shot, but we thought a terrible injustice had been done to these servicemen and we had to try.'

Like the British lawyers, the Australian lawyers were not charging veterans for their work. The extensive research and legal costs were being borne by the law firms themselves. They spent years gathering statements from around 300 Australian veterans in the hope they could take their cases to the UK Court.

The UK government, however, had bottomless pockets and was prepared to spend millions to stop the veterans winning a single case in the courts. They hired top flight barristers and reams of lawyers. They feared that if just one case got through it would open the floodgates to thousands of claims for compensation. The UK Ministry of Defence took the Foskett decision up to the Court of Appeal. The senior Law Lords were more sympathetic to Whitehall. The government won the appeal, knocking down nine of the ten cases and dashing the veterans' hopes.

Neil Sampson of the London law firm Rosenblatt representing the UK veterans said the appeals decision was a huge setback.

'The government did all it could to stop the veterans. The veterans had started off with a different law firm on legal aid in 2004, but in 2005 the government withdrew legal aid funding,' Sampson said.[9]

The veterans desperately looked around for another firm to take on their case, but it would have to be on a no-win no-fee basis.

'They'd been knocked back by many other law firms but we looked at it and decided it was an interesting case and these people needed someone to represent their interests. We had no idea how difficult it would be and the difficulties the government would throw up.'

Sampson took the case all the way to the UK Supreme Court, the highest court in the United Kingdom. Sampson and his team of one QC, four barristers and three junior barristers stood before a panel of seven Law Lords and one Lady. Opposing them for the government was a far larger team of two QCs and fifteen barristers.

'The resources they put against us were enormous. The government devoted a major resource to defending this case.

What we saw in court was just the tip of the iceberg – working behind the scenes were countless Ministry of Defence officials and civil servants.'

Sampson thought the veterans' case cost his law firm up to £6 million, but the government spent at least £15 million defending the cases. It paid off. They won. Just.

Four Lords ruled for the government, three dissented. The majority ruled that the veterans had very little chance of winning their case, and that despite the Rowland study establishing a statistical higher likelihood of contracting cancer, it wasn't evidence that the tests caused an individual's cancer.[10]

Sampson was mystified why the government was so determined to fight the nuclear veterans to the bitter end. At some point they would be spending more on lawyers defending the case than it would cost to grant compensation to the veterans.

'The political benefit government could have achieved by settling this vastly outweighs the cost to defending it. We are talking peanuts in terms of how much the court cases cost them.'

Sampson said the Supreme Court decision was not the end. He has 1002 veterans ready to pursue their cases in court and around 100 who contracted their disease less than seven years ago – meaning they are not outside the limitation time.

'The trouble is that if a veteran goes to court and loses they usually have to pay the winning side's legal costs. We've had insurance to cover this so far, but we can't get that insurance to go ahead with any more cases. Insurers aren't philanthropic and want a reasonable chance of success.'

Sampson and his legal team have launched an appeal to the European Court of Human Rights.

'We are saying the way the UK government has run the case has exhausted the financial resources of the veterans, so they can't proceed in their fight for justice and that's a breach of their human rights.'

In the meantime, Sampson is trying another tactic by going through the UK Pension Appeal Tribunal, where if you get a disease or a health problem contracted during military service you could be covered with an extra pension. 'We've won one case for a conscript, who don't normally get military pensions, and he got it for service at the tests. We've got another fifteen test cases before the tribunal.'

Through these processes Sampson has managed to get his hands on 250,000 pages of documents that weren't released to the Royal Commission. He believes there is a similar amount still locked in dusty vaults at the Ministry of Defence.

'Each of those files could hold one or two pages, or hundreds of pages. We don't know. There is a wealth of information that has not been disclosed. Scientists working at nuclear tests had a once-in-a-lifetime opportunity to measure radiation and many other things, but what has been disclosed so far gives the impression very little was measured.'

Sampson finds that hard to believe, and believes the 'good stuff' is still hidden away.

'They must have more information they haven't disclosed. The whole purpose was to find out about nuclear war – what radiation there would have been a mile from ground zero, all sorts of readings at certain distances. They would want to know where the radiation goes. But apparently nothing was recorded.

'They won't even show us an index of files which they have not disclosed. Judges have been highly critical of the government approach to disclosure, but the government continue to resist releasing documents.'

Sampson said there are files dubbed the Blue Books, which record exposure to radiation by personnel at the tests. They record the name and exposure on one particular day on the badges the test workers wore. They are not cumulative. They don't record inhaled or ingested material.

'We want the government to make them public. There are about nine volumes. They are still classified and can't be disclosed beyond lawyers involved in the case. They are pretty useless to determine the effect of exposure on the individual, but there is no reason the public shouldn't have that information.'

Sampson has two theories why the government is so determined to keep these thousands of documents secret after more than sixty years, and why it is still determined to fight the veterans to the bitter end.

'It could be that never admitting fault is so deeply ingrained in civil service mentality that it exceeds all reason and logic. Another possibility is that they fear an adverse spinoff for the nuclear power industry. I think the second is more likely.

'All the other nuclear powers have paid compensation to their nuclear veterans – the Americans, Russians, Chinese, Canadians, Indians, even the French. Only the UK government still refuses to acknowledge the men they sent to test their atomic bombs were exposed to radioactivity and steadfastly rejects paying any sort of compensation. But for the veterans it's not about the money. It never was. They simply want the government to admit what was done to them. These people are patriotic, certainly not radicals or revolutionaries. Most support their country having nuclear weapons.

'They just want to be able to say, "I have got cancer and I got it as a consequence of serving my Queen and Country".'

But the fight is producing some small victories. In 2008, British Defence chiefs finally admitted in papers filed to the High Court in London that 159 men died as a result of exposure at the tests. That's 159 out of 20,000 British servicemen. Two of them were RAF pilots irradiated flying through atomic mushroom clouds.[11]

•

In Australia the Sydney legal team at Stacks/Goudkamp wasn't ready to throw in the towel. Young lawyers Michael Giles,

Ruth Hudson and Joshua Dale spent years interviewing nuclear veterans around the country, preparing briefs in case they could pursue the case in the British courts. When the Law Lords finally knocked back nine out of ten UK cases it seemed all over. But Dale saw a chance for one last throw of the dice. It was a long shot, a very long shot, but his boss Tom Goudkamp encouraged him to try. Dale had read the Universal Declaration of Human Rights signed in 1948 by Australia and forty-seven other nations at the United Nations. It was a groundbreaking international agreement on what constituted human rights coming out of the horrors of the Holocaust and war crimes committed during the Second World War.

'Australia was key to the drafting of the declaration and pressed for it to be a binding document,' Dale said.[12] 'Australia was defeated in that, but it showed it was the intention of the Australian government for the declaration to be binding on Australia.'

In 2013 Dale took the veterans' case to the Australian Human Rights Commission, arguing the veterans weren't told the true nature of the nuclear tests and the consequences for their health had been covered up for decades. Dale said their rights had been breached in three articles of the Universal Declaration of Human Rights:

- Article 3: The right to life, liberty and security of person.
- Article 5: The right not to be subjected to torture or to cruel, inhuman or degrading treatment or punishment.
- Article 25: The right to a standard of living adequate for the health and well-being of himself and of his family, including food, clothing, housing and medical care and necessary social services, and the right to security in the event of unemployment, sickness, disability, widowhood, old age or other lack of livelihood in circumstances beyond his control.

The AHRC has no power to force the government to make restitution, but Dale hoped if the commission came back with a finding that the veterans' human rights had been breached it would put pressure on the government to finally do the right thing and award them compensation.

But the last hopes of the Australian veterans were dashed ten months later in December 2013 when the president of the AHRC Gillian Triggs decided what happened to the veterans at the nuclear tests lay outside the jurisdiction of the commission.

Dale was extremely disappointed, telling the media this was the end of the road for legal avenues nuclear veterans could pursue in Australia.[13] Unless there is a breakthrough in Britain, it is all over.

'A generation of our diggers have been lost to horrific radiation-related cancers and illnesses. Out of the 15,000 servicemen sent to Maralinga, Emu Field and the Monte Bello Islands, just 2000 remain living, fighting and still suffering,' Dale said.[14] 'To think of the prospect that any human being, let alone our diggers, would be knowingly exposed to the effects of radiation after seeing the consequences of atomic weapons just seven years earlier in Japan is unforgivable. Past, successive and the current government have failed these men. They have not acknowledged their wrongs, have broken policy promises and engaged in blatant and ongoing hypocrisy.'

•

Some individual politicians continue to fight for nuclear veterans. In 2006 Labor's shadow veterans' affairs spokesman, Alan Griffin, told parliament that servicemen were 'used as guinea pigs' in the tests and deliberately exposed to radiation.[15] South Australian independent Senator Nick Xenophon and West Australian Greens Senator Scott Ludlam have campaigned for the veterans and their families to receive ongoing financial and medical assistance. In 2013, Ludlam appealed to the British government to make an Act of Grace payment for Australian nuclear veterans. UK Minister for Defence Personnel, Welfare and Veterans, Mark Francois, replied that as the veterans could not prove in court their health problems were caused by exposure at the tests, they would not receive Act of Grace payments from the UK government. Among the large Australian political parties, support has been strong and full of promises – until they get into government, then it fades away.

In Britain, however, one Conservative MP hasn't been a fair weather friend. John Baron is a former army captain in the Royal Fusiliers who served in Northern Ireland, a former banker and a conservative MP from Essex. It's a pedigree that should rocket him to the top of the Tory table. But he's a maverick. Baron resigned from the frontbench in 2003 in protest at his party's support for the Iraq War. In 2011 he was the only Tory among fifteen British MPs who voted against British participation in the attack on Libya.

'War should always be a last resort. There is such a thing as a just war, but Iraq was a complete fool's errand,' Baron said.[16]

Baron is pushing the UK parliament to set up a £25 million benevolent fund for British nuclear veterans and their families to assist with health needs.

'Many nuclear veterans suffer from bad health, but they are more worried about their descendants suffering genetic problems they pass on from their exposure at the nuclear tests. We owe these veterans a debt of gratitude. They helped defend their country by assisting us to get nuclear weapons at time when the Cold War was raging.

'We all accept that when we are in uniform for our country we could face danger and risk our lives. But what happened to them was different and unique. We asked them to do something beyond the call of duty and governments were negligent in how they were treated.'

Baron said other veterans don't have to worry about any genetic damage they might pass on to their descendants. The fund would be run by trustees and provide assistance where needed to nuclear veterans, their families and descendants.

'It's a way to express our gratitude for their extraordinary service and give them some peace of mind that their descendants will be cared for.'

16

BACK TO THE FUTURE – THE OUTBACK AS NUCLEAR WASTE DUMP

After decades trying to clean up radioactive contamination left by the British nuclear bombs, a band of powerful figures are determined to turn the outback into a nuclear waste dump.

Just weeks after Tony Abbott got into government in 2013 he ordered public servants to draw up a plan to establish a nuclear waste dump in central Australia.[1] Abbott told planners in the Department of Industry he wanted a dossier he could take to cabinet outlining the business case for a nuclear waste dump to be built on Aboriginal land at Muckaty Station in the centre of the Northern Territory. The target was to have it ready by 2019. Consultants and contractors who had been anxiously waiting for just this opportunity were roped in by the officials.

A nuclear dump in central Australia had been mooted since the 1990s when British company Pangea Resources lobbied for a deep underground nuclear waste dump to be dug in the outback. Pangea argued central Australia was ideal to take the world's high-level radioactive waste because it was flat, isolated and geologically stable. It secured some high-profile supporters – former Labor Prime Minister Bob Hawke, Labor industry heavyweight Martin Ferguson, former Labor foreign minister

Gareth Evans and former Liberal foreign minister Alexander Downer.

Billions of dollars are at stake. Nuclear power nations around the world would be willing to pay a fortune to get rid of their high-level nuclear waste. There are a few underground nuclear waste repositories dug deep in salt and granite stratas around the world, but there is still a huge demand: there are an estimated 290,000 tonnes of spent nuclear fuel around the world, and it grows by 14,000 tonnes every year.

In the 1990s the prospect of having an international nuclear dump in the middle of the country that would be lethal for a million years didn't go down too well with the rest of Australia. Polls found eighty-five per cent of Australians were against Australia being used as the world's nuclear waste dump. There were anti-nuclear protests and pressure grew on the South Australian and Western Australian governments to pass legislation barring such a dump on their land.

By 1998 the Howard government was forced to concede the Pangea idea would go nowhere and the company backed away. It changed its name to ARIUS – the Association for Regional and International Underground Storage – and pursued more subtle tactics. Hawke continued to spruik an international waste dump in the outback, declaring in 2005 it would be an 'act of economic sanity and environmental responsibility to accept the world's nuclear waste'.[2] Tony Abbott was Health Minister at the time and described Hawke's suggestion as 'visionary'.[3] The Howard government wasn't giving up. The Liberals made an international nuclear dump in Australia party policy. The prospect of being paid millions of dollars to store the world's nuclear waste overrode any concerns about the welfare of the country and its people. It started to take form. Howard signed Australia up to the US-led Global Nuclear Energy Partnership (renamed in 2010 the International Framework for Nuclear Energy Cooperation) under which nuclear fuel 'supplier' nations like Australia take back high-level nuclear waste from 'user' nations that operate nuclear reactors.

Australia also has its own nuclear waste that needs to be safely disposed of. Most of it is currently stored in 10,000 drums at Woomera. Harmful intermediate-level waste is also stored at Sydney's Lucas Heights nuclear reactor. It needs to be isolated from humans for thousands of years. Hundreds of small low-level storage sites exist around the country, some in hospital basements or even in shipping containers. Most of the radioactive material will be dangerous for the next 400 years, and needs safe storage.

The Howard government was pushing for a national nuclear dump to be built near Woomera, but local Aboriginals protested. The South Australian Labor government passed laws banning such a national dump in the state. Not giving up, Howard looked north. In 2005 he passed the Commonwealth Radioactive Waste Management Act giving the federal government draconian powers to override environment and heritage laws as well as the Aboriginal Land Rights Act to build a nuclear waste dump anywhere it liked in the Northern Territory.

In 2007 the Howard government struck a deal with the Aboriginal Northern Land Council to build a national nuclear waste dump for low-level waste at Muckaty, an isolated Aboriginal pastoral property 120 kilometres north of Tennant Creek. The plan is for a thirty-metre-deep pit, until a more permanent deep underground vault is built. International safety standards say intermediate waste should be buried at least 300 metres underground.

Money secured the deal with the Aboriginal council. The dump would deliver $11 million to the council and local owners, another $10 million to the Northern Territory government, plus $2 million a year once the dump was operational. But some Aboriginal traditional owners connected to Muckaty complained they were not consulted, and took action in the Federal Court, forcing the council to abandon its plans.

Labor kept the push for an outback nuclear waste dump going. In 2012 the Gillard government passed legislation that would override State and Aboriginal objections to building such a dump. If Muckaty can't go ahead, the Abbott government could look elsewhere in the Territory or to Western Australia, which already has a low-level nuclear waste storage facility for Western Australian waste at Mount Walton, 125 kilometres north-west of Kalgoorlie.

In May 2014 Hawke was back arguing the economic benefits of Australia becoming the world's nuclear dump. 'If Australia has – as we do – the safest remote locations for storing the world's nuclear waste, we have a responsibility to make those sites available for this purpose,' he told business leaders in Perth.[4]

Wherever a dump is planned, there will be considerable local opposition. Federal officials already have concept designs for a $150 million nuclear waste dump from Spain's radioactive waste management agency, ENRESA. It would require transporting nuclear waste across oceans to an Australian port. The waste sealed in big containers would then be loaded on to trains or trucks and moved more than 1000 kilometres to the centre of the continent. A tunnel or trench would have to be dug 500 metres deep or more leading to a massive vault that would take thousands upon thousands of sealed drums. The underground vault would have to be sealed so securely that none of the radioactive poison could leak out for the next quarter of a million years.

That is an impossible length of time to be able to predict what will happen. If Neanderthals had nuclear waste we'd still be looking after it. Civilisation itself began only 12,000 years ago. If such a site had to be marked to warn people to stay away for tens of thousands of years it couldn't be written in English or simply labelled with the radiation sign; both would probably be long forgotten. The only marker that could possibly survive that long would be an Egyptian-style stone pyramid or something like Stonehenge.

A lot can go wrong in that time. In March 2014 the only long-term nuclear waste repository in the US, at Carlsbad in New Mexico, had to close down when a radioactive leak was detected and thirteen workers received a radioactive dose.

Supporters of a nuclear waste dump at Muckaty Station argue that central Australia is geologically stable.

It is in fact a high earthquake area. In 2013 a magnitude 4.3 earthquake rocked Tennant Creek. Geoscience Australia says the area is surprisingly active, with two or three quakes above magnitude 3 every year.[5] In 1988 Tennant Creek had three powerful quakes in one day, measuring 6.3, 6.4 and 6.7. The earth rose up two metres in one long fault scarp, causing damage and severe warping of a major natural gas pipeline. Senior seismologist Dr Jonathan Bathgate said the area is identified as a high seismic hazard.[6]

In 2014 a magnitude 4.7 earthquake rocked Western Australia's goldfields region. The epicentre was thirty kilometres west of Kalgoorlie at a depth of fifteen kilometres, 100 kilometres from the Mount Walton nuclear waste storage facility. It was felt more than 100 kilometres away. Ken Smith of the Grand Hotel was in bed when it hit, and declared it 'shook the shit out of me'.[7] A magnitude 5 hit the gold mining town in 2010. The biggest quake in Australia in fifteen years hit Ernabella in South Australia's far north in 2012. The 6.7 magnitude quake was felt in Alice Springs, 317 kilometres away.

Geoscience Australia seismologist David Jepsen said Australia has about 200 earthquakes a year measuring 3.0 or more and, on average, one a year higher than 5.5. Every five years there's a quake measuring 6 or more. Australia's largest earthquake recorded was 7.3 in Meeberrie, central-west Western Australia, in 1941. The 1989 quake in Newcastle, New South Wales, that killed thirteen people was 5.6 magnitude. Dr Jepsen said central Australia's earthquakes were caused by the release of stress from the earth's crust built up as the Indian–Australian tectonic plate moves north-east. The eastern part of the plate is moving slightly faster over Indonesia than the western part where India's advance northward has slowed down as it pushes up the Himalayan Mountains. This squeezes central Australia sideways by about 0.1 millimetres every year.[8]

Justifying a world nuclear waste dump in central Australia by arguing the area is geologically stable is clearly a nonsense. Strong earthquakes in central Australia are inevitable and likely to get worse in the thousands of years ahead.

It's also vital never to underestimate mankind's ability to stuff up. For decades of the Cold War the world was a mere fumble away from pressing the button on thousands of nuclear weapons that could destroy the human race.

Many events show just how close to the truth the 1964 movie *Dr. Strangelove* really was. Most of these events didn't come to light until decades later.

In 1961 two 4000 kiloton hydrogen bombs were accidentally dropped over North Carolina by the US Air Force. One bomb acted as though it was about to detonate, its parachute opening and its trigger mechanism engaged. Only one voltage switch prevented a cataclysm that would have spread fallout over Washington, Baltimore, Philadelphia and even New York City.[9]

In 1966 four hydrogen bombs fell over a small town in Spain after a B-52 US Air Force bomber broke up in midair. Documents released under Freedom of Information in 2013 showed the parachute properly opened on one bomb, two others broke up on crashing and one was found in the sea four months later.[10]

At least four US Air Force bombers crashed in the US while containing nuclear bombs. US official records showed thirteen nuclear bombs had been accidentally launched, set on fire, exploded or leaked radioactivity. At least 700 'significant' accidents and incidents involving 1250 nuclear weapons were recorded between 1950 and 1968.[11]

In 1961 the Soviet nuclear submarine K-19 had a meltdown killing several crew members including those who went in to halt the meltdown.[12]

Despite all the drama about secret launch codes being kept in a briefcase close to the US President by a military officer at all times, it was revealed in 2013 that the men in the launch silos had had the same launch codes for more than twenty years. To dial up Armageddon, all they had to do was put in the eight digits 00000000. The code to start a Third World War was kept deliberately simple in case command centres had been destroyed in a nuclear war. Former missile launch officer Dr Bruce Blair said Strategic Air Command 'remained far less concerned about unauthorized launches than about the potential of these safeguards to interfere with the implementation of wartime launch orders'.[13]

In 1959 the US planned to hit the moon with an atom bomb as a show of strength to the Soviets. The top secret Project A119 was a reaction to the Soviet success with Sputnik. It was abandoned when young astronomer Carl Sagan calculated fallout would spread around the moon.[14]

British public servants have prepared a speech for the Queen to read to her subjects if nuclear missiles start hitting England's green and pleasant land.[15]

The world came very close to a nuclear war during the 1962 Cuban missile crisis when a US Air Force U2 spyplane was shot down over Cuba and a Soviet submarine nearly launched a nuclear torpedo in response to being depth charged by the US Navy. Only the courage and common sense of the submarine's second in command, Vasili Arkhipov, in refusing to authorise the launch saved the world.

Human error caused the worst nuclear power plant disaster at Chernobyl, Ukraine, in 1986. During a test when normal safety procedures were set aside, workers allowed water to escape from the reactor to the point at which coolant pumps could not stop a meltdown.

Australian mining magnate Lang Hancock and his daughter Gina Rinehart proposed exploding nuclear bombs to create a new harbour in north-west Australia to ship out minerals. Hancock also weighed up using nuclear bombs to blow up his mountains of iron ore – far cheaper than sticks of dynamite. He had a strong supporter in Sir Ernest Titterton.[16]

Despite the nuclear madness, in 2014 the world seems determined to wind the clock back to the days when superpowers glared at each other over their nuclear weapons. There are an estimated 17,300 nuclear warheads on the planet – Russia with 8500, USA 7700, France 300, China 250, UK 225, Pakistan 120, India 110, Israel eighty and North Korea up to ten.[17] Of these, around 4300 are considered operational. There is some good news in that this is much less than the 70,000 nuclear warheads that existed in 1986. Despite reductions in numbers, nuclear states continue to modernise their nuclear weapons and are committed to retaining them into the future.

The Abbott government certainly doesn't want disarmament. Shortly after Abbott was elected in 2013, Australian diplomats at the United Nations were ordered to secretly undermine a New Zealand–led push for further nuclear disarmament. Australia refused a request from the conservative government of New Zealand to endorse a 125-nation joint statement at the UN highlighting the humanitarian consequences of any use of nuclear weapons. Australia objected to a sentence declaring it is in the interests of humanity that nuclear weapons never be used again 'under any circumstances'. Files released to the *Sydney Morning Herald* under Freedom of Information said Australian officials worked 'energetically' against the move because 'we rely on US nuclear forces to deter nuclear attack on Australia'.[18]

•

Many horrific scientific experiments on humans were done under cover of the Cold War. Most didn't come to light until decades later. The covert testing of Australian baby bones for Strontium-90 to see the effects of the British tests in Australia was but one of them. Others include:

- Hundreds of pregnant women in Scotland were secretly injected with radioactive isotopes right up until the 1970s.
- A similar experiment was done by Vanderbilt University in Tennessee in the late 1940s, injecting 800 pregnant women with radioactive iron. Their children died of cancers at a young age.
- Asian women in Britain were fed chapattis laced with radioactive substances in 1969 then tested to see how much radiation they had absorbed.
- During the Manhattan Project to develop the atom bomb, eighteen US cancer patients were injected with plutonium to see what happened.
- In Massachusetts in 1952, kids at a school for the disadvantaged were given special treats such as baseball games and breakfast – laced with radioactive calcium and pills.
- In 1958 Californian researchers exposed subjects' skin to radioactive phosphorus to test burn damage.
- In 1966 food covered in radioactive fallout was fed to volunteer students to see if they could survive nuclear war.
- In 1974 Oregon prison inmates had their testes radiated to see what happened.[19]

John Brownlow, who uncovered many of these shocking experiments for his 1996 documentary *Deadly Experiments*, was shocked at the reaction from scientists when confronted with the evidence: 'They don't actually see anything wrong with it . . . they couldn't understand what all the fuss was about.'[20]

•

The only memorial for the nuclear veterans of Australia is a small plaque on a green park bench in Adelaide's Peace Park. These veterans had a death rate higher than many units that served in the First and Second World Wars. The difference is the deaths caused by their service came many years after the nuclear tests were over, and that the horrific legacy of their service will last through many generations of their descendants.

The plaque from the South Australian government says simply: 'Dedicated to the traditional owners, service personnel and civilians who were affected by the British atomic bomb tests at Monte Bello, Emu Field and Maralinga'.

Opening the little memorial in 2006, South Australian Premier Mike Rann talked of the feelings of sadness and anger towards the wrongs that were done to these people. He had been involved as Minister for Aboriginal Affairs helping Aboriginal traditional owners travel to London to demand compensation for what was done to their land and people.

'When we think today about the naïve and cavalier way in which these tests were planned, promoted and conducted, and when we read about how the effects of the tests were ignored, covered up and denied, I think all of us are amazed and appalled.'[21]

Rann told the story of twenty-year-old soldier Peter Webb, sent to Maralinga in 1956. Webb described the searing heat of the bomb blast on his back and then walking into the crater where the ground had been turned to glass by the heat. Within ten years he developed skin cancers and had a melanoma removed from between his shoulder blades that was thirty centimetres long and was 'like the roots of a tree'.

Rann said the atomic tests 'left a permanent scar on people, on our land, on our nation's history'.

But at Australia's main military museum and memorial in

Canberra, the Australian War Memorial, the nuclear tests and the Cold War barely rate a mention. A handful of small red wall hangings outside the Korean War exhibit tell of Australia's clandestine engagement against communist forces in Malaysia, and a secret war against Indonesian forces in Borneo.

The British atomic tests are reduced to just three paragraphs under a photo of the first atomic test at Monte Bello.

'With the testing of British atomic bombs in Australia, the Cold War arrived within Australia's borders,' it says.

'Atomic tests were held between 1952 and 1957; on the Monte Bello Islands off Western Australia and at Maralinga and Emu Plains [sic] in South Australia.

'Although atomic testing was originally considered a success because it advanced British nuclear technology, some later questioned Australia's involvement.'

And that's it. It's a massive understatement. No mention of the subsequent revelations of lies, cover-ups and the depth of betrayal of our own people. No mention of the death toll among the 16,000 Australians sent to be guinea pigs for the British. No mention of the terrible toll on the health and wellbeing of the nuclear veterans or their families.

The thousands of military men who died through serving their country at the British tests don't get their name on the Wall of Remembrance. There is no glory in the cancers and genetic defects they contracted through their service.

Yet those who took Australia and its people into this act of betrayal continue to be revered and idolised. The Queen gave Robert Menzies a knighthood and appointed him successor to Churchill in holding the somewhat ridiculously antiquated titles Lord Warden of the Cinque Ports and Constable of Dover Castle. Menzies loved dressing up in the robes and fluffy hat that came with the pompous post. In 2014 his esteem among conservatives is growing even higher. Prime Minister Tony Abbott has a drawing of Sir Robert Menzies proudly displayed in his office – the Queen only makes the foyer. There is a Menzies Foundation, a Menzies Institute, a Menzies College and a refurbished Menzies Hotel in Sydney. Several universities have Menzies buildings.

Menzies' betrayal of his country by enthusiastically accepting the British atomic tests has been scrubbed from history. Most young people don't know atomic bombs were exploded in our outback. It's not taught in schools. It's like it never happened. Menzies himself didn't even mention the atomic tests in his two volumes of memoirs – that's how much thought he gave them. He put Australian citizens and Australian servicemen into harm's way, then abandoned them.

Those intimately involved in the lies and cover-ups of the truth, such as Titterton, also went on to receive honours, knighthoods and wealth.

The Royal Commission let them off lightly. What they did was criminal, and the evidence was there to charge at least Titterton with criminal negligence and fraud.

EPILOGUE

Today, Maralinga still has its secrets.

In the early morning and late afternoon there is an extraordinary sight at one of the old atomic bomb test sites. As the low lying sun strikes the ground at just the right angle, the flat red earth suddenly appears to come alive. It's like a switch is flicked, setting off shiny, sparkling lights for hundreds of metres all around.

This land around the Breakaway bomb site was never cleaned up. When the atom bomb exploded in a 100-foot-high tower with the force of ten kilotons, the red earth below was literally melted by the extreme heat. The blast transformed the sand instantly into glass, which still lies all over the ground. The globules of olive green glass vary from the size of ten-cent pieces to larger chunks the size of a fifty-cent coin. Most are riddled with holes, bubbles in the boiling sand that remained as it cooled.

The caretaker of Maralinga, Robin Matthews, picks up a handful of the larger green chunks near the concrete plinth marker for the Breakaway atomic test, exploded at 5 am on 22 October 1956.

'They're completely safe,' he says, jiggling them up and down. 'They didn't clean up this area because they found no sign of radiation. I've waved a Geiger counter over this green glass and it didn't register anything. The ground here is completely dead. It's been almost sixty years but still nothing grows for at least a kilometre around the blast site.'[1]

Dead it may be, but visitors are not allowed to souvenir any of the green glass globules and the rules for visiting Maralinga are strict.

Visitors must first obtain a permit from the Aboriginal traditional owners, the Tjarutja Lands Council in Ceduna, and then contact Matthews to see if he has time to escort them around. No visitor – even the scientists who come to test for radioactivity and leakage from the hundreds of burial pits – can enter the old testing area without being escorted by the caretaker.

Matthews has plans to open up the Maralinga test site to tourism, but he has the power to bar anybody he doesn't want on the site. When I tried to take whistleblower Avon Hudson with me on a visit to Maralinga in 2014, Matthews refused to allow Hudson onto the site. Hudson believes Matthews is downplaying the radiation risk to tourists. Matthews says Hudson is a troublemaker who didn't obey the rules when he was last there.

Matthews has two bosses – the Aboriginal traditional owners and the Commonwealth, which is responsible for safety, contamination and radiation matters at the site.

More than a decade after the Howard government declared Maralinga was clear of contamination, after a $106 million clean-up operation that took six years, two large sections of the test area are barred to visitors because they are still radioactive.

The Kuli site, twenty-one kilometres from the remnants of the old Maralinga village, is classified as dangerous with a sign warning of hazardous material in the soil. Kuli was used to conduct 262 minor trials, mostly involving burning uranium to see what happened. The tests spread 7.4 tonnes of uranium into the surrounding environment.

Matthews also doesn't take visitors to the Tadje site as Geiger counter readings at that bomb site pick up what he calls a 'faint tingle'. Visitors can see Taranaki and several other sites but no one can stay there too long, certainly not camp overnight. Matthews believes some day there will have to be yet another clean-up to finally do the job properly.

Every twelve months, scientists test the 292 burial pits around the site to see if there is any leakage of toxic or hazardous material. They also test rabbits, kangaroos and dingos, if they can get them. Matthews and his Aboriginal wife are required to give blood tests every twelve months to see if they have been contaminated.

'So far they've found nothing, and I've been working here since 1972,' he laughs. His biggest danger has been finding unexploded artillery shells. 'We collect things we find around the site and if the scientists say they are clear we put them in a little museum at Maralinga village. One day I found what I thought was a smoke rocket used during the tests to detect shock waves. Well, when the military experts came and looked at it they said it was an unexploded anti-tank shell shot by the Yanks at the Centurion tanks that were lying around after the tests. They blew it up, thank goodness.'

Maralinga village, where visitors stay, is thirty-seven kilometres away from the bomb sites. Just six buildings are left of the original village, and it is an eerie place to visit. Two barrack buildings still stand, but the place that was most popular during the tests – the swimming pool – has been filled in with debris from the dismantled buildings. Visitors bunk down in transportable huts or dongas left after the last clean-up, and Matthews hosts a great barbecue outside his home, the former Maralinga hospital.

Twenty kilometres down the road to the north is the former settlement of Roadside, a small camp where forward area workers stayed during the tests. The settlement has been completely razed, with just the concrete foundations of the old huts left.

The footage of the military men facing away from the blasts and then turning around to see the rising mushroom cloud was filmed here – about seventeen kilometres from the blast sites.

The biggest burial pits are around the Taranaki bomb site, the last atmospheric blast on 9 October 1957. The bomb itself didn't leave the worst of the contamination – that was left by the subsequent minor tests at the same site, which included burning plutonium.

The British erected concrete plinths marking each atomic bomb blast site after their inadequate Operation Brumby clean-up in 1967. They read: 'Warning. Radiation Hazard. Radiation levels for a few hundred metres around this point may be above those considered safe for permanent occupation.'

It's a masterful piece of British understatement. Even after the Brumby clean-up the ground was still so badly contaminated the British had to come back twice to do the job properly.

The ground was so contaminated around the Taranaki site the final clean-up operation involved scooping up two square kilometres of contaminated soil and burying it in huge 15-metre-deep pits. Plutonium was burned and the remains encased in glass containers and buried inside more leak-proof containers deep underground. Huge shields marked with the radiation sign declaring, 'Warning. Buried radioactive materials' surround the mounds of dirt and rock that cover the burial pits. Uncontaminated soil was brought in to cover the area but efforts to grow vegetation on the soil have been difficult. It is still largely bare earth, but scrub is starting to grow on the fringes.

Underneath the plinth for the Marcoo explosion is a 45-metre-deep crater that was filled in with contaminated tanks, planes, vehicles, clothing and equipment during the 1967 clean-up. Sixty years later still nothing grows on the little hillock.

Documents obtained under Freedom of Information by the *Sydney Morning Herald* say the burial pits have required significant remediation and some have been subject to subsidence and erosion exposing asbestos-contaminated debris.[2]

The documents show the government declined requests from the Tjarutja people to clean up uranium contamination at the Kuli site closest to the village as they deemed it did not constitute a radiological hazard.

The documents also revealed Commonwealth officials were more concerned the yellow uranium fragments visible on the ground 'could create an image issue' than they were that Aboriginal children might play with the toxic material.

Even though Maralinga's Tjarutja traditional owners were handed back what they were assured was radiation- and toxic-free land in 2009, they still don't venture into the area.

'When the land was formally returned to them in 2009, they had one big meeting at Maralinga airport where a medical team flew in to see them,' says Matthews. But since then the Aboriginal people built a new settlement at Oak Valley well outside the test area. Signs are erected at Maralinga in the local Aboriginal language warning not to camp anywhere in the area. Matthews hasn't ever seen them enter the test site.

It's understandable.

Maralinga and the land around it was once a place the Aboriginals knew intimately. They followed ancient Dreamtime tracks leading to water holes as they hunted and journeyed towards sacred sites. The water holes at places like Ooldea next to the Indian Pacific Railway have long since dried up, sucked dry by bores and demands of the steam trains. The land that once sustained them was killed by atomic bombs.

Now Maralinga has only bitter memories for the Aboriginals. It is a bad place, traditional land that was ripped from them, where terrible things happened, their people killed by mysterious black mists and radiation. The ancient red land is now a gravesite, land killed by the white man and the destructive science he brought.

Alice Cox, an Aboriginal elder, remembered Maralinga as a place of fear, a place of evil. 'Soldiers everywhere. Guns. We all cry, cry, cryin'. Men women and children, all afraid.'[3]

Yami Lester, who as a boy went blind after the black mist passed over him, said his family and people thought the radioactive cloud was 'Mamu' coming to get them, evil living-dead spirits taking the guise of grotesquely shaped humans with long sharp teeth to suck out your soul.

But when the real Mamu came they were dressed in white laboratory coats and the grey suits of politicians.

APPENDIX 1
NUCLEAR TESTS

British atomic weapons tests in Australia

(1 kiloton equals 1000 tons of TNT)

Monte Bello Islands – Operation Hurricane

1952, 3 October, 8 am, 25 kiloton, in hull of HMS *Plym*

Emu Field – Operation Totem

Totem One	1953, 15 October, 7 am, 10 kt, tower
Totem Two	1953, 27 October, 7 am, 8 kt, tower

Monte Bello Islands – Operation Mosaic

Mosaic G1	1956, 16 May, 11.15 am, 15 kt, tower
Mosaic G2	1956, 19 June, 10.14 am, 60 kt, tower

Maralinga – Operation Buffalo

One Tree	1956, 27 September, 5 pm, 15 kt, tower
Marcoo	1956, 4 October, 4.30 pm, 1.5 kt, ground burst
Kite	1956, 11 October, 2.27 pm, 3 kt, aircraft drop
Breakaway	1956, 22 October, 5 am, 10 kt, tower

Maralinga – Operation Antler

Tadje	1957, 14 September, 2.35 pm, 1 kt, tower
Biak	1957, 25 September, 10 am, 6 kt, tower
Taranaki	1957, 9 October, 4.15 pm, 26.6 kt, balloon-suspended

The minor trials

Year	Location	Trial	Material	Quantity (kg)
1953	Emu Field	Kittens	Beryllium	0.036
1955	Naya 3	Tims	Uranium	138
1955	Naya	Kittens	Uranium	5
1955–57	Naya	Kittens	Beryllium	0.75
1955–57	Kittens area	Kittens	Uranium	120
1956–60	Kuli TM4	Tims	Uranium	6605
1956–58	Naya 1	Rats	Uranium	151
1957	Naya	Tims	Beryllium	1.6
1957	Naya 3	Kittens	Uranium	23.4
1957	Wewak	Vixen A	Uranium	67.8
1957	Dobo	Rats	Uranium	28
1957	Taranaki	Vixen B	Uranium	25
1959	Wewak VK33	Vixen A	Plutonium	0.008
1959	Wewak VK29	Vixen A	Beryllium	0.14
1959	Wewak VK28	Vixen A	Beryllium	0.25
1959	Wewak VK27	Vixen A	Beryllium	0.27
1959	Wewak VK30	Vixen A	Beryllium	0.1
1959–60	Kuli TM11	Tims	Beryllium	26.2
1959–60	Kuli TM11	Tims	Uranium	67
1960	Naya TM100	Tims	Plutonium	0.6
1960–62	Naya 2	Kittens	Uranium	32
1960–61	Kuli TM16	Tims	Beryllium	39
1960–63	Kuli TM16	Tims	Uranium	731
1961	Kuli TM50	Tims	Uranium	90
1961	Naya TM101	Tims	Plutonium	0.6
1961	Wewak VK60A	Vixen A	Plutonium	0.294
1961	Wewak VK60C	Vixen A	Plutonium	0.277
1961	Wewak 60A	Vixen A	Beryllium	1.72
1961	Wewak 60B	Vixen A	Beryllium	1.72
1961–63	Taranaki	Vixen B	Beryllium	17.6

(uranium includes U-235 and U-238)

Total number of British tests (excluding minor trials)

Australia 12
Malden Island (Pacific) 3
Christmas Atoll (Pacific) 6
Nevada USA 23 (all underground)

The nuclear club – number of tests

USA 2 (dropped on humans in war)
USA 1054 (331 atmospheric tests)
USSR 715 (219 atmospheric tests)
France 210 (181 at Mururoa Atoll, the last in 1996)
Britain 45 (12 in Australia)
China 45
India 3
Pakistan 2
North Korea 3

Key Nuclear Facts

- The most powerful hydrogen bomb of fifty megatons (50,000 kilotons) was exploded by the Soviet Union in 1961. In 1962 the Soviets exploded four bombs between nineteen and twenty-four megatons.
- The most powerful US bomb of fifteen megatons (15,000 kilotons) was exploded in 1954 at Bikini Atoll.
- In 1957–58 Britain exploded nine hydrogen bombs in the Pacific, the biggest reaching three megatons (3000 kilotons).
- The biggest year for atomic explosions was 1962 with 178.
- The longest period with no nuclear explosion was between 1999 and 2006 when North Korea joined the nuclear club.
- A total 2053 nuclear bombs have been exploded since Hiroshima. Radiation was spread by the 528 bombs exploded in the atmosphere. The last nuclear weapon test was an underground explosion in North Korea in 2013.

APPENDIX 2
NUCLEAR TIMELINE

1933	Leo Szilard patents concept of atomic bomb.
1938/39	German scientists discover nuclear fission, Nazis begin nuclear energy project.
1939	US President Roosevelt orders secret research to develop nuclear weapon.
1942	Stalin orders research into nuclear weapons.
1942	US established Manhattan Project to produce atomic bomb.
1943	British join Manhattan Project.
1945	16 July, First nuclear test explosion in New Mexico. 6 August, Atomic bomb dropped on Hiroshima killing 80,000 people immediately, radiation killing another 100,000 within six months. 9 August, Atomic bomb dropped on Nagasaki killing 70,000 people, another 200,000 within a year. 2 September, Japan surrenders.
1948–49	Soviets block overland access to West Berlin leading to airlift of food and fuel. Soviets install puppet communist regimes across eastern Europe.
1948	Australia joins Britain battling communist insurgents in Malaya.

1949	Mao Tse Tung wins civil war and China goes communist. Soviet Union declares its part of occupied East Germany to be separate communist nation.
1949	Soviet Union explodes its first atomic bomb to surprise of US, which believed Soviets not able to build bomb until 1953. Cold War intensifies with race to build first hydrogen bomb. Western Europe and US form NATO mutual defence pact.
1949	Robert Menzies elected for second time and stays Australian prime minister for next sixteen years.
1950	Klaus Fuchs, senior British nuclear scientist, confesses he's been a Soviet spy for past six years. US no longer trusts UK security. This suspicion confirmed in 1951 when double agents Burgess and Maclean flee to Soviet Union. US bars UK from US nuclear program.
1950	North Korea, with Chinese backing, invades South Korea, starting Korean War. Australia joins United Nations force to repel invasion.
1950	US Senator Joseph McCarthy leads anti-communist hysteria in US.
1950	RAAF bombers join fight against communist insurgents in Malayan Emergency.
1951	Australia, New Zealand and US sign ANZUS mutual defence pact.
1952	Britain explodes its first atomic bomb at Monte Bello. That year the US explodes ten atomic bombs.
1953	Soviets explodes hydrogen bomb with power of 400 kilotons.
1953	UK explodes two atom bombs on Australian mainland at Emu Field.
1953	CIA overthrows Iran government and installs puppet regime under the Shah.

1953	Armistice ends fighting in Korean War.
1954	US explodes thermonuclear bomb at Bikini Atoll twice as large as expected.
1954	Vietnamese nationalists defeat French at Dien Bien Phu.
1954	Petrov affair, Labor Party splits, Menzies re-elected.
1955	Warsaw Pact formed to counter NATO.
1955	Australian troops sent to fight in Malayan Emergency.
1956	Suez crisis: UK, France and Israel attack Egypt to remove leader Nassar.
1956	Hungarian revolt crushed by Soviets.
1956	Britain explodes two nuclear bombs at Monte Bello and four at Maralinga.
1957	Britain explodes last three nuclear bombs at Maralinga, minor trials continue.
1957	Soviets launch Sputnik 1, world's first satellite, into space.
1958	116 atomic bombs exploded over the year: seventy-seven by US, thirty-four by USSR and five by UK.
1958	Soviet-backed revolt in Iraq topples UK-backed leaders.
1958	US and UK sign a mutual defence agreement after UK explodes its first hydrogen bomb at Christmas Atoll in the Pacific. UK moves atmospheric tests from Australia to joint experiments with US in Nevada.
1959	Cuban revolution.
1959	US launches first nuclear powered submarine with Polaris missile. No atom bombs exploded for first time in eight years.
1960	France explodes its first atom bomb in French Sahara.
1960	American U2 spyplane shot down over USSR.

1961	CIA-backed invasion of Cuba fails at Bay of Pigs.
1961	Soviets explode Tsar Bomba (at 50,000 kilotons the most powerful nuclear weapon ever detonated).
1961	Berlin Wall goes up.
1961–62	Mass rallies around world against nuclear tests.
1962	Cuban missile crisis brings world to brink of nuclear war.
1962	A record 178 nuclear bombs exploded: ninety-six by US, seventy-nine by USSR, two by UK and one by France.
1962	Australian military advisers join US advisers in South Vietnam
1963	President Kennedy assassinated.
1963	UK nuclear weapon testing in Australia ends.
1964	China explodes its first atomic bomb.
1964	US sends combat troops to Vietnam, heavy bombing of North Vietnam.
1965	Australia sends combat troops to Vietnam. In Indonesia 500,000 communists killed in retribution for attempted coup.
1966	Menzies retires and Harold Holt becomes prime minister of Australia.
1967	Holt disappears while diving. John Gorton sworn in as prime minister.
1968	Nuclear Non-Proliferation Treaty signed, limiting nuclear weapons to those nations who already have them.
1968	Soviets crush revolt in Czechoslovakia.
1969	Americans land on moon.
1971	US and Soviets sign Anti-Ballistic Missile Treaty and Strategic Arms Limitation Treaty (SALT 1).
1971	William McMahon replaces Gorton as Australia's prime minister.

1972	Labor's Gough Whitlam ends twenty-three years of conservative rule in Australia.
1972	Last Australian troops leave Vietnam.
1973	CIA backs coup in Chile.
1974	India detonates first atomic bomb.
1975	Whitlam sacked by governor-general; Malcolm Fraser wins election for Liberals.
1979	Nuclear accident at Three Mile Island plant in Pennsylvania.
1979	US and Soviets sign SALT 2.
1981	Israel bombs Iraqi nuclear plant near Baghdad.
1983	Labor wins election, Bob Hawke becomes Australian prime minister.
1984	Hawke sets up Royal Commission into British Nuclear Tests in Australia.
1986	Israel's secret nuclear weapons program revealed.
1986	Nuclear plant accident at Chernobyl in Ukraine.
1989	Cold War melts with fall of Berlin Wall.
1991	Soviet Union dissolves. Cold War officially over.
1998	Pakistan explodes its first atomic bomb.
2005	Eight years without a nuclear test.
2006	North Korea explodes its first nuclear bomb.
2011	Japan's Fukushima nuclear plant leaks after tsunami.

APPENDIX 3

CONCLUSIONS OF THE ROYAL COMMISSION

- Menzies alone lent Australia to the British for their nuclear tests without asking about possible hazards the tests might involve.
- The Australian government willingly accepted the British view that the terms of the agreement for the tests meant Australia could not be given information on technical aspects of the tests.
- Australia was forced to accept UK assurances of safety for the early Hurricane test without any critical examination by its own scientists.
- The Australian media could only report what the British government wanted on the Hurricane test.
- The decision to use the mainland for atomic tests was done without consultation with Australian scientists regarding whether it was safe.
- Federal Cabinet was not informed, neither the parliament nor the media, until preparation of the Emu Field site was well under way.
- Britain made no formal approach to the Australian government before the Totem tests at Emu for approval for a long-term

testing program, even though Britain's plans were well developed.

- The Totem explosions at Emu were twice as powerful as planned.
- There was a black out on information to the media about any possible hazard for the Australian population.
- The Australian government had no intention of testing public reaction before agreeing to a permanent testing ground at Maralinga. It was only announced after a formal commitment had been made.
- The Atomic Weapons Safety Committee was intended to provide the Australian government independent scientific advice on safety. The British vetted membership of the committee and did not comply with the requirement that there be no conflict of interest with respect to Titterton.
- The public was not informed of the true nature of the hazards of the nuclear tests.
- Titterton acted alone in recommending the go-ahead for the minor trials.
- The safety committee failed to carry out its tasks in a proper manner.
- Titterton was Britain's man and withheld information from the Australian government and the safety committee to help Britain continue its nuclear testing.
- Nuclear tests were conducted with a belief there was a safe level of exposure to radiation even though these standards were uncertain and challenged internationally by the time of the later tests.
- Genetic effects of exposure were not considered important.
- Safeguards against exposure at the tests were inadequate.
- It is 'probable' cancers that would not otherwise have occurred were caused by fallout across Australia.
- Nuclear veterans had an increased risk of cancer due to exposure in the tests.

- Monte Bello was not an appropriate place for atomic tests because of the prevailing weather.
- The safety of Aboriginals was not properly considered during the Monte Bello or Maralinga tests. Inadequate resources were allocated to ensuring Aboriginals were kept away from the danger zones and the native patrol officer had an impossible task.
- The welfare of air crews flying into the radioactive clouds and ground crews cleaning radioactive planes was not properly considered. Failure to provide protective equipment was negligent.
- The black mist stories have credibility and there is no reason to disbelieve Aboriginal accounts that it occurred and made some people sick.
- Several of the tests at Maralinga should not have been detonated as conditions at the time were not ideal. Fallout exceeded safe levels as far away as Coober Pedy. Maralinga village was contaminated when the wind changed at the third test. The people responsible for safety of Aboriginals demonstrated 'ignorance, incompetence and cynicism'. Aboriginals continued to move around the danger zone and the reporting of them was discouraged and ignored.
- Some Aboriginals lived in the prohibited zone for years and some perished when they were eventually told to leave the area.
- Titterton withheld knowledge of the Cobalt-60 contamination of the ground after the Tadje test, thereby contributing to an 'unnecessary radiation hazard'.
- The Vixen series of tests should never have been conducted at Maralinga because of the known long half-life of plutonium.
- The first clean-up called Operation Brumby was inadequate and left the area worse than when they started.

- The British government must pay for the Maralinga site and Monte Bello to be properly cleaned up to the point Aboriginals could have access to the area without restriction.
- The Australian government must compensate Aboriginal people for the loss of their lands.
- A national register of servicemen, civilians and Aboriginals exposed to radiation at the tests should be compiled.

ENDNOTES

Prologue

1 'Arrangements for determination of strontium 90 fallout in Australia', UK National Archives DEFE 16/808
2 ibid.
3 Some of the dialogue in this chapter has been re-created by the author, based on facts and insights gleaned from the minutes of the meeting and associated documents.
4 'Arrangements for determination of strontium 90 fallout in Australia', op. cit.
5 ibid.

Chapter 1

1 David Day, *The Politics of War*, HarperCollins, 2003, p.134
2 National Museum of Australia profile Earle Page http://www.nma.gov.au/primeministers/earle_page
3 *Australian Dictionary of Biography*, Ward, Edward John (Eddie), Vol. 16. Melbourne University Press, 2002
4 Australian War Memorial, Menzies declaration of war broadcast
5 Graham Freudenberg, *Churchill and Australia*, Macmillan, Sydney, 2008, p.265
6 ibid., p.274
7 ibid., p.279
8 Report of the Royal Commission into British Nuclear Tests in Australia, 1985, p.10
9 'Defence must be on world basis', *The Age*, 21 September 1950

10 Report of the Royal Commission into British Nuclear Tests in Australia, 1985
11 ibid., p.12
12 ibid., p.13
13 ibid., p.14
14 ibid., p.15
15 Robert Milliken, *No Conceivable Injury*, Penguin, Australia, 1986, p.30
16 General Sir Frederick Morgan, UK controller of atomic energy, 1951 memo to Penney. Cited in the official history of UK atomic weapons, *Independence and Deterrence: Britain and Atomic Energy 1945–1952*, volume 2, Margaret Gowing, Macmillan, London, 1974, p.474
17 Stewart Cockburn and David Ellyard, *Oliphant: The Life and Times of Sir Mark Oliphant*, Axiom Books, Adelaide, 1981, p.122
18 Transcript, Titterton to Royal Commission, 14 May 1985, p.7922

Chapter 2

1 'Monte Bello Island for UK Atomic Weapon Test', *Queensland Times*, 15 May 1952, p.1
2 'Operation Spoofer was security hoax', *The West Australian*, 17 November 1952, p.2
3 'Atomic Fleet sails from Fremantle', *The West Australian*, 23 April 1952, p.1
4 'Stage nearly set for tests at Monte Bello Islands', *Canberra Times*, 29 September 1952, p.1
5 Author interview with Kelvin Gough, May 2013
6 'HMS *Plym* – Her Final Days', World Naval Ships Forum, http://www.worldnavalships.com/forums/showthread.php?t=3082
7 Transcript, Henry Carter to Royal Commission p.5134
8 ibid., p.5137
9 'The terrifying weapon in action', *Courier-Mail*, 23 September 1953, p.2
10 'Observers' account of explosion', *Canberra Times*, 4 October 1952
11 ibid.
12 'A flash, then a red glow', *Sydney Morning Herald*, 4 October 1952, p.1
13 'The breakfast cups shook', *Sydney Morning Herald*, 4 October 1952
14 Author interview with Kelvin Gough, May 2013
15 Author interview with John Quinn, September 2013
16 Noel Jensen-Holme, 'HMAS *Murchison* sickness from radioactivity at Hiroshima', *Atomic Fallout*, Journal of the Atomic Ex-Servicemen's Association, Vol. 5, No. 2, June/July 2013
17 'Atomic History', Editorial, *The West Australian*, 4 October 1952, p.2
18 Editorial, *Sydney Morning Herald*, 4 October 1952
19 'Penney reveals blast's secrets', *The Mail* (Adelaide), 8 November 1952, p.1

20 Ernest Titterton, 'Some Good Guesses on Future of Atomic Energy' *The West Australian*, 4 October 1952, p.2
21 Transcript, Thomas Wilson to Royal Commission, p.4106
22 Transcript, Maurice Westwood to Royal Commission, p.38
23 Written statement, Sheila Taudevin to Royal Commission, 19 October 1984
24 Author interview with Lewis Rice, June 2013
25 Author interview with Howard Bird, June 2013
26 Author interview with Carl Godwin, June 2013
27 Milliken, op. cit., p.48
28 Letter marked confidential, dated 20 September 1951 from Rear Admiral AD Torlesse, Trials Planning Section of the Admiralty, to William Penney's deputy Mr Brooking. Cited in J.L. Symonds, *A History of British Atomic Tests in Australia*, Department of Resources and Energy, Canberra, 1985, p.36

Chapter 3

1 Cited in Milliken, op. cit., p.74
2 Beale in answer to question from Eddie Ward, Hansard, House of Representatives, 14 October 1953
3 Author interview with Edward Cheney, June 2013
4 Author interview with Lance Edwards, June 2013
5 Written statement, Roy Cosgrove to Royal Commission, no. RC107
6 Royal Commission Report, p.130
7 ibid.
8 Milliken, op. cit., p.150
9 UK National Archives File no. FCO 1/2
10 Transcript, Bruce Stein to Royal Commission, p.487
11 Colin James, 'After 46 years the truth about the flight into a death cloud', Adelaide *Advertiser*, 30 June 2001
12 Royal Commission Report p.132
13 Written statement, Frank Bingham to Royal Commission, number RC167
14 Radiation is measured in a sometimes bewildering variety of methods. The first measurement was the curie. Named after Madame Marie Curie, it is the count per second of radioactive emissions. One curie is that amount of a radioactive material that emits 37 billion radioactive particles per second.

Translating that emission into a measurement of a dose of radiation received by a person is far from precise. All life on earth is exposed to and impacted by natural sources of ionising radiation such as alpha, beta and neutron particles or rays such as gamma and X-rays. Most of the measurements of the effects of radiation on humans began with the atomic bombs on Hiroshima and Nagasaki, and was expanded on by tests of atomic and nuclear bombs around the world.

The Rad measures energy absorbed by living tissue exposed to radioactivity. In Europe the unit for 100 Rads is called a Gray.

The Rem combines the amount or radiation exposure – a Rad – with its estimated impact on health. One thousand millirems make up a Rem. In Europe 100 Rems is called a Sievert. However, it is not a precise measurement and different people will react in different ways to a Rem. It depends on the duration of exposure, the level and intensity of radiation and the type of radioactivity and the physiology of the person exposed.

The US Environmental Protection Agency said in 2014 the average American is exposed to about 620 millirems a year, half of it from natural background sources, half from medical diagnostics. Many scientists say there is no such thing as a 'safe' level of exposure, but governments around the world have set 'permissible' levels of exposure for nuclear workers and the public. The usual 'permissible' level beyond natural background radiation is 100 millirems a year. A medical X-ray delivers around 10 millirems.

Source: Nuclear Information and Resource Service, Washington DC, and US Environmental Protection Agency

15 Author interview with Merv Bale, September 2013
16 Author interview with Michael Hubert, June 2013

Chapter 4

1 Transcript, Yami Lester to Royal Commission, pp.7111–7140
2 Transcript, Kanytji and Pingkayi and other Aboriginals speaking through interpreters when the Royal Commission heard evidence at Wallatinna Homestead, 21 April 1985, pp.7175–7216
3 Transcript, Lalli Lennon to Royal Commission, pp.7141–7160
4 Transcript, Almerta Lander to Royal Commission, pp.7094–7109
5 Prime Minister Robert Menzies in Question Time, Hansard, House of Representatives, 21 October 1953
6 'A "Black Mist" that brought death', Adelaide *Advertiser*, 3 May 1980, p.1
7 Senator Jim Cavanagh, Hansard, Senate, 15 May 1980
8 Senator John Carrick, Hansard, Senate, 15 May 1980
9 Titterton speaking on ABC Radio, *PM* program, 14 May 1980
10 Royal Commission exhibit no. RC469
11 'High Explosives Research Report No. A32', British Ministry of Supply 1953 document obtained by Royal Commission 1984, exhibit no. RC247
12 Royal Commission exhibit no. RC523
13 Transcript, Derek Vallis to Royal Commission, p. 5729.

14 Royal Commission Report, p.596
15 ibid., p.597
16 Milliken, op. cit., p.163
17 Len Beadell, *Blast the Bush*, Rigby, Adelaide, 1967, p.173.
18 ibid.
19 Milliken, op. cit., p.165
20 The Aboriginal Stonehenge survived the atomic blasts at nearby Emu Field and still stands today, protected by signs saying visitors must keep out unless they have permission from tribal elders. Maralinga site caretaker Robin Matthews, however, says he sometimes find tracks of unauthorised four-wheel drives at the site.

Chapter 5

1 Nic Outterside, 'Memos show government complicity', *Scotland Herald*, 20 March 1995
2 Royal Commission exhibit no. RC800
3 Milliken, op. cit., p.191
4 ibid, p.192
5 Author interview with Doug Brooks, May 2013, plus Brooks' unpublished memoirs
6 Author interview with Bob Dennis. June 2013
7 Author interview with Bill Hunter, March 2013
8 Author interview with David Brennan, June 2013
9 Transcript, James Hole to Royal Commission, pp.5147–5259
10 Transcript, Titterton to Royal Commission, p.7621
11 'Atomic rain in Qld', Adelaide *Advertiser*, 22 June 1956, p.1
12 Transcript, Bernard Perkins to Royal Commission, p.4167
13 Royal Commission Report, p.253
14 Transcript, Titterton to Royal Commission, p.7622
15 Transcript, Stewart Stubbs to Royal Commission, p.7586
16 Royal Commission Report, p.256
17 ibid., p.257
18 Memorandum of Arrangements between the UK and Australian governments – Atomic Weapons Proving Ground Maralinga, signed in Canberra 7 March 1956. Summary in Royal Commission Report, p.278

Chapter 6

1 Author interview with Ric Johnstone, January 2010
2 Terry Smyth, 'After the Fallout', *The Sun-Herald*, 7 February 2010
3 Author interview with John Hutton, May 2013
4 Author interview with Bruce Baker, April 2013
5 UK War Office plan for field trials during Buffalo tests, UK National Archives no. DEFE 16/552

6 Author interview with Bill Hunter, March 2013
7 Author interview with Glynn Key, September 2013
8 Author interview with Neal Longden, June 2013
9 Author interview with Anthony Spruzen, May 2013
10 Author interview with Alan Dennis, May 2013
11 Transcript, Ken Meredith to Royal Commission, pp.77–90
12 UK National Archives, no. DEFE 16/696
13 Royal Commission Report, p.338
14 ibid., p.339
15 Transcript, Peter Lowe to Royal Commission, pp.4190–4206
16 'Atomic blast ends wait at Maralinga', *Canberra Times*, 28 September 1956, p.1
17 Milliken, op. cit., p.211
18 ibid.
19 Transcript, Richard Durance to Royal Commission, p.2384
20 UK National Archives, no. DEFE 16/695
21 Milliken, op. cit., p.185
22 ibid., p.180
23 UK National Archives, no. 16/695

Chapter 7

1 Gallup Opinion poll, 1 June 1957
2 Opinion poll published 10 February 1957 in *The Sun-Herald*
3 Scott Kaufman, *Project Plowshare*, Cornell University Press, 2013, p.189
4 UK National Archives, Cable from UK High Commission, Canberra, to Whitehall, 10 January 1957
5 Milliken, op. cit., p.188
6 Transcript, Penney to Royal Commission, p.7033
7 UK National Archives, no. FCO 1/2
8 Author interview with Alan Batchelor, March 2013
9 Author interview with Brian McCloskey, October 2013
10 Roger Cross and Avon Hudson, *Beyond Belief*, Wakefield Press, Adelaide, 2005. p.75
11 ibid., p.75
12 ibid., p.78
13 Author interview with Stewart Harrison, September 2013
14 UK National Archives, file no. DEFE 16/81
15 ibid.
16 Author interview with Fred Stallard, January 2014
17 Author interview with John Hutton, April 2013
18 Author interview with David Farnell, October 2013
19 Royal Commission Report, p.352
20 ibid., p.294

21 ibid., p.256
22 ibid., p.257

Chapter 8

1 Author interview with John Hutton, April 2013
2 Transcript, Frank Smith to Royal Commission, p.8568
3 Transcript, Richard Durance to Royal Commission, p.2384
4 Transcript, Edie Milpuddie to Royal Commission, p.7267
5 Royal Commission Report, p.320
6 Cable to T.W. Aston, Commonwealth Relations Office, Downing Street, London, from G.A.C. Witheridge, UK Ministry of Supply, containing telegram sent from UK Ministry 'people in Australia', dated 16 May 1957, located in UK National Archives
7 Transcript, Frank Smith to Royal Commission, p.8593
8 Cabinet papers from 1952, released in 1982
9 Royal Commission Report, p.301
10 ibid., p.304
11 ibid., p.307
12 West Australian Parliamentary Select Committee report of conditions at Laverton and Warburton Ranges, December 1956, Australian National Archives, A452 1957/245
13 Statement by Australian Minister for Supply, Mr Beale, issued on 18 January 1957, copy held in UK National Archives
14 Transcript, Alan Flannery to Royal Commission, p.2686
15 Transcript, Terry Toon to Royal Commission, p.363
16 Transcript, Gordon Wilson to Royal Commission, p.4106 and Wilson statement RC203
17 Gordon Wilson interview with Imperial War Museum, www.iwm.org.uk/collections/item/object/80012458
18 ibid.
19 Widow of Bill Grigsby, quoted in UK House of Commons by MP David Alton on 25 July 1983, UK Hansard, p.956
20 'Four Aborigines died in Maralinga atomic test witness says', *Canberra Times*, 28 April 1984
21 Transcript, Patrick Connolly to Royal Commission, pp.7441–7460
22 Transcript, William Henderson to Royal Commission, p.8562

Chapter 9

1 'When Hollywood Came to Melbourne', Philip Davey, Australian Centre of the Moving Image, http://www.acmi.net.au/on_the_beach_essay.htm.
2 Neil Jillett, 'We were all wrong Ava', *The Age*, 14 January 1982
3 UK National Archives, no. DEFE 16/81

4 Milliken, op. cit., p.249
5 Royal Commission, no. RC 523
6 ibid.
7 Milliken, op. cit., p.248
8 Secret UK Defence Ministry internal memo no. 738, UK National Archives, dated 27 August 1958
9 Author interview with Geoff Gates May 2013
10 'RAF veteran says government covered up scale of nuclear tests', *The Independent*, 14 November 2011
11 Author interview with Avon Hudson, May 2013
12 Royal Commission no. RC525

Chapter 10

1 Cross and Hudson, op. cit., p.91
2 Transcript, Doug Rickard to Royal Commission, p.3137a
3 Cross and Hudson, op. cit., p.101
4 ibid.
5 Transcript, Harry Turner to Royal Commission, p.2864
6 Transcript, Ernest Titterton to Royal Commission, p.7940
7 ibid., p.7942
8 Transcript, Doug Rickard to Royal Commission, p.3122
9 Roger Cross, *Fallout*, Wakefield Press, ebook, Adelaide, 2001
10 *Silent Storm*, documentary, Peter Butt, 2006
11 Howard Beale, *This Inch of Time: memoirs of politics and diplomacy*, Melbourne University Press, 1977
12 *Silent Storm*, op. cit.
13 ibid.
14 ibid.
15 ibid.
16 ibid.
17 Royal Commission document no. RC523
18 ibid.
19 *Stock and Land*, 3 September 1958
20 Cross, op. cit.
21 Clyde Cameron, Hansard, House of Representatives, 15 May 1957
22 Author interview with Avon Hudson, May 2013
23 'Nuclear waste dump in SA: ex-RAAF man', Adelaide *Advertiser*, 3 December 1976
24 ibid.
25 Author interview with Avon Hudson, May 2013
26 Tom Uren, Hansard, House of Representatives, 11 October 1978
27 Author interview with Avon Hudson, May 2013
28 'Killen warns on plutonium pile', *Australian Financial Review*, 5 October 1978

29 'Govt boosts A-waste guard', *Australian Financial Review*, 6 October 1978
30 Milliken, op. cit., p.267

Chapter 11

1 Joan Smith, *Clouds of Deceit*, Faber & Faber, London, 1985. p.111
2 Transcript, Commissioner James McClelland to Royal Commission, 3 January 1985. p.4090
3 Transcript, Lord Penney to Royal Commission, p.4294.
4 'Did Nuclear Radiation Kill Sir William Penney?' *Daily Mirror*, 1 March, 2009
5 Transcript, Robin Auld to Royal Commission, pp.8984–8990
6 Transcript, Peter McClellan and Robin Auld to Royal Commission, p.9024
7 Milliken, op. cit., p.336
8 Transcript, Robin Auld summation to Royal Commission, p.10,274
9 Transcript, Ernest Titterton to Royal Commission, p.7643
10 ibid., p.7717
11 Royal Commission Report, p.526
12 Transcript, Ernest Titterton to Royal Commission, p.7716
13 Royal Commission Report, p.526
14 ibid.
15 ibid., p.272
16 ibid., p.102
17 ibid., p.438

Chapter 12

1 UK Hansard, 16 July 1956, p.928.
2 UK National Archives, no. DEFE 16/863
3 Joseph Herbert, 'Government sought dead bodies in 1950s to study fallout effects', Associated Press, 21 June 1995 http://www.apnewsarchive.com/1995/Government-Sought-Dead-Bodies-in-1950s-to-Study-Fallout-Effects/id-4bea6c0cf828fb2e59a1cbc1f53ae028
4 Letter from J.R. Moroney, 2 December 1957, noted in Australian Radiation Protection and Nuclear Safety Agency (ARPANSA) 2001 report, 'Australian strontium 90 testing program 1957-1978'. The report can be found in full at: http://www.nuclearfiles.org/menu/key-issues/nuclear-weapons/issues/testing/PDFs/sr90pubrep[1].pdf
5 *Silent Storm*, op. cit.
6 UK National Archives, no. DEFE/724
7 Note by John Moroney, 19 September 1968, cited in ARPANSA report

8 Letter from J.R. Moroney, 20 August 1969 cited in ARPANSA report
9 ARPANSA report p.11
10 A good account of the growing scientific awareness in the 1960s of the dangers to health in global fallout is found in *Secret Fallout* by Ernest Sternglass, McGraw-Hill Book Company, New York, 1972. It is online at http://www.ratical.org/radiation/SecretFallout/SF.html#TOC
11 Kennedy's 26 July 1963 televised address to the nation in full from John F. Kennedy Presidential Library and Museum: http://www.jfklibrary.org/Asset-Viewer/ZNOo49DpRUa-kMetjWmSyg.aspx
12 Memo from Titterton to Prime Minister Menzies, 23 March 1959
13 Transcript, Ernest Titterton to Royal Commission, p.7927
14 *Deadly Experiments*, BBC documentary, 6 July 1995
15 ARPANSA report, op. cit.
16 Michael Perry, 'Australian babies' used in nuclear tests', Reuters, 4 September 2001
17 'Secret atomic child files opened', Adelaide *Advertiser*, 5 September 2001
18 Susie O'Brien, Colin James and Rebecca Holmes, 'Corridor of shame', Adelaide *Advertiser*, 27 June 2001
19 ibid.
20 'Ethical and practical issues concerning ashed bones from the Commonwealth of Australia's Strontium 90 program 1957-1978', advice of the Australian Health Ethics Committee to the Minister for Health, Senator Kay Patterson, March 2002, p.6
21 *Silent Storm*, op. cit.
22 Colin James, 'Answers for 300 mothers', Adelaide *Advertiser*, 5 May 2003
23 Michael Perry, 'Australian babies' bones used in nuclear tests', Reuters, 7 June 2001
24 Rhianna King, 'Lost baby leaves lasting fears', *The West Australian*, 9 June 2013

Chapter 13

1 Author interview with Jeff Liddiatt, August 2013
2 Author interview with Colin James, February 2014
3 'Mums, babies had picnics during tests', Adelaide *Advertiser*, 8 May 2003
4 Colin James and Paul Starick, 'What killed Woomera babies', Adelaide *Advertiser*, 7 May 2003
5 'Mums, babies had picnics during tests', Adelaide *Advertiser*, 8 May 2003

6 ibid.
7 Senate Foreign Affairs, Defence and Trade Legislation Committee, Hansard, October 2010, Answers to questions on notice from Department of Defence. File W18, British nuclear testing and nuclear veterans, answers (d) to (f), p.36
8 Commonwealth Record Series D2185 register of births 1951–1983, created by Woomera Hospital, South Australia. National Archives of Australia
9 Bryan Littley, '100 South Australians join class action against Britain for Maralinga-related deaths', Adelaide *Advertiser*, 1 March 2010
10 'Blair "bone cancer risk" after Maralinga', Australian Associated Press, 31 August 2004
11 ibid.
12 *Backs to the Blast*, documentary by Harry Bardwell, 1981
13 Tom Uren, Hansard, House of Representatives, 20 March 1980
14 Liam Bartlett, 'Nuclear time bomb', Channel 9, *60 Minutes*, producer Howard Sacre, 22 April 2011
15 ibid.
16 ibid.
17 Colin James, 'Our nuclear family', Adelaide *Advertiser*, 3 May 2003.
18 Redfern Inquiry into human tissue analysis in UK nuclear facilities, 2010, chapter 3, p.11
19 ibid., p.554
20 'RAF airman who stood and watched H-bomb tests in his shorts fears he has passed rare radiation-linked brain conditions to his grandson', *Daily Mail*, 26 January 2014
21 Author interview with Jeff Liddiatt, August 2013
22 Alan Rimmer, 'Curse of the A-Bomb – 50 years of Lies', UK *Sunday Mirror*, 3 November 2002
23 Rob Edwards, 'Nuclear fallout killed thousands in US', *New Scientist*, 1 March 2002
24 *Today Tonight*, Channel 7, 21 February 2013
25 Australian Participants in British Nuclear Tests in Australia, Dosimetry and Mortality and Cancer Incidence Study, May 2006
26 op, cit., main findings summary, Vol. 2, page vi.
27 ibid.
28 'Free cancer treatment for nuke test veterans', Australian Associated Press, 28 June 2006
29 ibid.
30 Nuclear Weapons Test Participants Study of UK personnel present at UK nuclear tests in Australia and South Pacific. Second analysis done in 1993. A later study in 2003 found no difference in mortality rates between nuclear veterans and the general population. The study is in *Occupational and Environmental Medicine Journal* 2003, volume 60,

pages 165–172 can be viewed at http://www.ncbi.nlm.nih.gov/pmc/articles/PMC1740497/pdf/v060p00165.pdf
31 Author interview with Alan Batchelor, March 2013
32 *Atomic Fallout*, June/July 2008, p.3
33 Dr Jonica Newby, 'New Zealand Nuclear Veterans', *Catalyst*, ABC TV, 8 November 2007
34 Admiralty letter from Rear Admiral Torlesse to Vice Admiral Brooking, 20 September 1951
35 'Secret papers reveal A-Test deceit', *The Scotland Herald*, 20 March 1995. It cites Eden's memo dated 16 November 1955 which was presented in court in 1995 by UK nuclear veterans trying to get compensation.
36 ABC TV *Catalyst* report, op. cit.
37 ibid.
38 S.R. Roff, 'Mortality and morbidity of members of the British Nuclear Tests Veterans Association and the New Zealand Nuclear Tests Veterans Association and their families', University of Dundee Centre for Medical Education, http://www.ncbi.nlm.nih.gov/pubmed/10467894
39 Sue Rabbitt Roff, 'The dark side of the nuclear family', *New Statesman*, 15 January 1999.

Chapter 14

1 Royal Commission exhibit no. RC800
2 Bryan Littley, 'Maralinga's few survivors pay last respects to leader', Adelaide *Advertiser*, 22 December 2011
3 Royal Commission Report, p.539
4 ibid., p.540
5 Paul Chadwick, 'Why cabinet sought only a partial clean-up of British nuclear test site', theguardian.com., 1 January 2014
6 Damien Murphy, 'Cabinet Papers 1986–87: The struggle for indigenous land rights', *Sydney Morning Herald*, 28 December 2013
7 Alan Parkinson, 'Maralinga: The clean-up of a nuclear test site', *Medicine and Global Survival*, February 2002, Vol. 7, No. 2
8 'Maralinga finally cleaned up', ABC TV *7.30 Report*, 1 March 2000; 'The Man from Maralinga', reporter Mike Sexton, ABC TV *Stateline* South Australia, 2 November 2007
9 Alan Parkinson, *Maralinga: Australia's Nuclear Waste Cover-Up*, HarperCollins, 2007
10 *Ockham's Razor*, ABC Radio, 2 September 2007
11 Pia Akerman, 'A new vision for Maralinga Village', *The Australian*, 19 December 2009
12 Bryan Littlely, 'Healing of the spirit', Adelaide *Advertiser*, 19 December 2009

13 Philip Dorling, 'Ten years after the all-clear, Maralinga is still toxic', *The Sydney Morning Herald*, 12 November 2011
14 Colin James, 'Water fouled by nuclear waste', Adelaide *Advertiser*, 20 July 2001
15 Senator Peter Walsh, Hansard, Senate, 8 October 1984, p.1362

Chapter 15

1 Senator Kim Carr, Minister for Industry, Science and Research, 25 March 2003, Hansard, House of Representatives, p.10089
2 Report of the Review of Veterans' Entitlements (Clarke Report), January 2003
3 Author interview with Ric Johnstone, January 2010
4 Administrative Appeals Tribunal decision, 24 September 2013, http://www.austlii.edu.au/au/cases/cth/aat/2013/684.html
5 Charles Miranda, 'Brits lied to troops – Nuke test "guinea pigs"', *Daily Telegraph*, 23 January 2009
6 Charles Miranda, '$400m for A-Bomb blasts' guinea pigs', Adelaide *Advertiser*, 13 June 2009
7 ibid.
8 Author interview with Tom Goudkamp, February 2014
9 Author interview with Neil Sampson, London, August 2013
10 UK Supreme Court, 14 March 2012, summary Ministry of Defence v AB and others
11 'British Defence chiefs admit deadly radiation risks', *The Australian*, 4 August 2008
12 Author interview with Joshua Dale, February 2014
13 Paul Farrell, 'Maralinga nuclear test case rejected by Human Rights Commission', *The Guardian*, 10 December 2013
14 Author interview with Joshua Dale, February 2014
15 Alan Griffin in parliament debate on Australian Participants in British Nuclear Tests (Treatment) Bill 2006, 11 October 2006, Hansard, House of Representatives, p.194
16 Author interview with John Barron, London, August 2013

Chapter 16

1 Sean Parnell, 'Nuclear dump back on NT table', *The Australian*, 7 October 2013
2 ARIUS newsletter Number 11, October 2005
3 ibid.
4 'Dump nuclear waste in NT: Hawke', *Northern Territory News*, 21 May 2014
5 Geoscience Australia – earthquakes list for Australia: http://www.ga.gov.au/earthquakes/staticPageController.do?page=list

6 Geoscience Australia press statement, 'Tennant Creek shakes again', 19 July 2013. http://www.ga.gov.au/news-events/news/latest-news/tennant-creek-shakes-again
7 'Earthquake rocks WA's goldfields', AAP, 26 February 2014
8 'Jolts across desert as earthquake strikes central Australia', AAP, 24 March 2012
9 Ed Pilkington, 'US nearly detonated atomic bomb over North Carolina', *The Guardian*, 21 September 2013
10 Eric Schlosser, *Command and Control*, Penguin, 2013, p.314
11 'US nearly detonated atomic bomb over North Carolina', op. cit.
12 http://www.nationalgeographic.com/k19/index.html
13 'Dial 00000000 for Armageddon', *Daily Mail*, 29 November 2013
14 'US planned to nuke the moon', *Sydney Morning Herald*, 29 November 2012
15 '"Bleak" Queen's speech in event of World War Three revealed', *The Telegraph*, UK, 27 January 2014
16 Adele Ferguson, *Gina Rinehart*, Macmillan, Sydney, 2012, pp.29–31.
17 'Status of world nuclear forces 2014', Federation of American Scientists. http://www.fas.org/programs/ssp/nukes/nuclearweapons/nukestatus.html
18 Philip Dorling, 'Government pushed against NZ on nukes', *Sydney Morning Herald*, 10 March 2014
19 Jordan Goodman (ed.), *Useful Bodies*, Johns Hopkins University Press, Baltimore, 2003
20 Barry Oliver, 'Exposure to radiation's deadly past', *The Australian*, 2 July 1996
21 Transcript of Rann's speech in *Atomic Fallout*, journal of the Atomic Ex-Servicemen's Association, Vol. 4, No. 1, June/July 2006, pp.4–7

Epilogue

1 Author interview with Robin Matthews, March 2014
2 Philip Dorling, 'Ten years after the all-clear Maralinga is still toxic', *Sydney Morning Herald*, 12 November 2011
3 John Keane, 'Maralinga's afterlife', *The Age*, 11 May 2003

BIBLIOGRAPHY

Books

Barnaby, Frank, *How to Build a Nuclear Bomb: And Other Weapons of Mass Destruction*, Granta, London, 2003.

Beadell, Len, *Blast the Bush*, Rigby, Adelaide, 1967.

Beale, Howard, *This Inch of Time: Memoirs of Politics and Diplomacy*, Melbourne University Press, 1977.

Chomsky, Noam and Polk, Laray, *Nuclear War and Environmental Catastrophe*, Seven Stories Press, New York, 2013.

Cockburn, Stewart and Ellyard, David, *Oliphant: The Life and Times of Sir Mark Oliphant*, Axiom Books, Adelaide, 1981.

Cross, Roger, *Fallout*, Wakefield Press, Adelaide, 2001

Cross, Roger and Hudson, Avon, *Beyond Belief: The British Bomb Tests: Australian Veterans Speak Out*, Wakefield Press, Adelaide, 2005.

Day, David, *The Politics of War*, HarperCollins Publishers Australia, Sydney, 2003.

Department of Veterans' Affairs, *Preliminary Nominal Roll of Australian Participants in the British Atomic Tests in Australia*, Canberra, 2001.

Ferguson, Adele, *Gina Rinehart*, Macmillan Australia, Sydney, 2012.

Freudenberg, Graham, *Churchill and Australia*, Macmillan Australia, Sydney, 2008.

Gaddis, John Lewis, *The Cold War: A New History*, Penguin Books, New York, 2005.

Goodman, Jordan, McElligott, Anthony and Marks, Lara (editors), *Useful Bodies: Humans in the Service of Medical Science in the Twentieth Century*, Johns Hopkins University Press, Baltimore, 2003.

Gowing, Margaret, *Independence and Deterrence: Britain and Atomic Energy 1945–1952, Volumes 1 and 2*, Palgrave, Macmillan, London, 1974.
Hoffman, David, *The Dead Hand: The Untold Stories of the Cold War Arms Race and its Dangerous Legacy*, Anchor Books, 2010.
Holdstock, Douglas and Barnaby, Frank (editors), *The British Nuclear Weapons Programme 1952–2002*, Frank Cass Publishers, London, 2003.
Kaufman, Scott, *Project Plowshare: The Peaceful Use of Nuclear Explosives in Cold War America*, Cornell University Press, Ithaca, 2013
Menzies, Robert, *Afternoon Light: Some Memories of Men and Events*, Cassell, Melbourne 1967.
Menzies, Robert, *The Measure of the Years*, Cassell, Melbourne, 1970.
Milliken, Robert, *No Conceivable Injury: The Story of Britain and Australia's Atomic Cover-up*, Penguin Books, Melbourne, 1986
Parkinson, Alan, *Maralinga: Australia's Nuclear Waste Cover-Up*, HarperCollins Publishers Australia, Sydney, 2007.
Rimmer, Alan, *Between Heaven and Hell*, ebook, lulu.com, 2012
Schlosser, Eric, *Command and Control: Nuclear Weapons, the Damascus Accident and the Illusion of Safety*, Penguin Books, London, 2013
Smith, Joan, *Clouds of Deceit: The Deadly Legacy of Britain's Bomb Tests*, Faber & Faber, London, 1985.
Smith P.D., *Doomsday Men: The Real Dr. Strangelove and the Dream of the Superweapon*, Penguin Books, London, 2007
Sternglass, Ernest, *Secret Fallout: Low level radiation from Hiroshima to Three Mile Island*, McGraw Hill Book Company, New York, 1972.
Symonds, J.L., *A History of British Atomic Tests in Australia*, Department of Resources and Energy, Canberra, 1985.
Tame, Adrian and Robotham, F.P.J., *Maralinga: British A-Bomb, Australia's Legacy*, Fontana, Melbourne, 1982.

Newspapers and journals

The Advertiser
The Age
Atomic Fallout (Journal of the Atomic Ex-Servicemen's Association)
The Australian
Australian Financial Review
Associated Press
Australian Associated Press
Canberra Times
Courier-Mail
Daily Mail (UK)
Daily Mirror (Australia)

Daily Mirror (UK)
Daily Telegraph (Australia)
Daily Telegraph (UK)
The Guardian (UK)
The Independent (UK)
The Mail (Adelaide)
New Scientist
New Statesman
Queensland Times
Reuters
The Scotland Herald
Stock and Land
Sunday Mirror (UK)
Sun-Herald
Sydney Morning Herald
West Australian

Documentaries, television and radio news broadcasts

Australian Atomic Confessions, documentary by Katherine Aigner (producer), 2005.
Backs to the Blast, documentary by Harry Bardwell, 1981.
Catalyst, ABC TV, 8 November 2007.
Deadly Experiments, BBC documentary 1995.
'Nuclear Time Bomb', *60 Minutes*, Channel 9, producer Howard Sacre, 22 April 2011.
'New Zealand nuclear veterans', *Catalyst*, ABC TV, Dr Jonica Newby, 8 November 2007.
'Maralinga – Australia's nuclear waste cover-up', *Ockham's Razor*, ABC Radio, 2 September 2007.
PM ABC Radio 14 May 1980.
'Nuclear Time Bomb', *60 Minutes*, Channel 9, 22 April 2011.
Silent Storm, documentary by Peter Butt, 2003.
'The Man from Maralinga', *Stateline South Australia*, ABC TV, 2 November 2007.
Today Tonight, Channel 7, 21 February 2013.

Private archives and memoirs

Brooks, Douglas, *Countdown to Contamination.*
Davey, Philip, *When Hollywood came to Melbourne.*
Jensen-Holm, Noel, *HMAS* Murchison *sickness from radioactivity at Hiroshima.*

Reports, inquiries, studies

Australian Ionising Radiation Advisory Council report 9, 1983.

'Australian Participants in British Nuclear Tests in Australia', Dosimetry and Mortality and Cancer Incidence Study, May 2006.

Australian Radiation Protection and Nuclear Safety Agency Report: Australian Strontium 90 Testing Program 1957–1978, 2001.

Geoscience Australia – earthquakes in Australia.

'Maralinga, the clean up of a nuclear test site', Alan Parkinson, *Medicine and Global Survival*, February 2002.

National Health & Medical Research Council: Ethical and Practical Issues Concerning Ashed Bones from the Commonwealth of Australia's Strontium 90 Program 1957–1978

New Zealand Nuclear Test Veterans Study – A Cytogenetic Study, Massey University, 2007.

Nuclear Handbook for Instructors and Staff Officers, UK Ministry of Defence, 1957.

Redfern Inquiry into human tissue analysis in UK nuclear facilities, 2010.

Royal Commission into British Nuclear Tests in Australia: Volume 1 and 2. 1985. Conclusions and Recommendations.

University of Dundee Centre for Medical Education.

Wayward Governance, Chapter 16, A Toxic Legacy – British Nuclear Testing in Australia, Australian Institute of Criminology, 1989.

Author interviews

Nuclear veterans:

Bruce Baker, Merv Bale, Alan Batchelor, Howard Bird, David Brennan, Doug Brooks, Ray Cameron, Edward Cheney, Percival Daley, Alan Dennis, Robert Dennis, Lance Edwards, David Farnell, Vincent Frawley, Geoff Gates, Carl Godwin, Kelvin Gough, Stewart Harrison, Neville Howard, Michael Hubert, Avon Hudson, Bill Hunter, John Hutton, Ric Johnstone, Glynn Key, Ben Lette, Jeff Liddiatt, Neal Longden, Brian McCloskey, John Quinn, Lewis Rice, Brian Ross, Tony Spruzen, Fred Stallard, Terry Toon.

Others: John Baron, Joshua Dale, Tom Goudkamp, Colin James, Robin Matthews, Neil Sampson.

AUTHOR'S NOTE FOR THE NEW EDITION

Since publication of the first edition of *Maralinga* I have received hundreds of letters and emails through my website from nuclear veterans, families of nuclear veterans, scientists, government officials, students, teachers, historians, researchers and even some who were involved in the secret service.

Most wanted to express their shock and dismay at what they had read in the book about the deceit of the great conservative hero Sir Robert Menzies, the cover-up by successive Liberal and Labor governments regarding the nuclear tests at Monte Bello and Maralinga, and the lasting legacy of the radioactive fallout across Australia. Several veterans' families affected by ill health formed groups to help each other. Contact me through my website www.frankwalker.com.au and I can put you in touch with them.

Many said *Maralinga* ought to be on the school syllabus so that young Australians could know what was done to their country by their own government.

The Maralinga site is becoming better known as people visit the remote location after a campaign to attract more tourists. The old Maralinga village has been modernised to take campervans. Tourist buses are making the trek from Adelaide. Awareness of what happened at the remote spot is growing. There may even be a *Maralinga* movie.

Hundreds of people involved in the nuclear tests contacted me with new information about what they had seen and experienced. Sixty years after the tests, some of those who came forward were still concerned about the Official Secrets Act and didn't want their names used, but still wanted the truth to come out.

Several sources told me ASIO had run the entire baby-bone testing program detailed in Chapter 12. According to these sources, it was ASIO that contacted the pathologists and told them that the bones of dead babies and infants were needed for testing as a matter of 'national security'. It was ASIO that arranged for the bones to be collected and transported to secure locations where they were catalogued, recorded and crushed to powder, then sent to the United Kingdom for testing to determine how much Strontium-90 they contained. This explains why pathologists cooperated for 21 long years with the body-snatching program and kept their mouths shut.

Wendy Young was a trainee nurse at Royal Adelaide Hospital in the early 1960s and was encouraged to watch post mortems. She wrote to me about what haunts her still: 'I was horrified to witness the removal of the dead toddler's left femur, a piece of wood inserted and the wound roughly closed with what looked like thick, coarse brown string . . . it wasn't catgut. I thought it was very insensitive and disrespectful, carried out as if it was of no real consequence. The wound ran the length from hip to knee. When I asked the reason for the removal, the pathologist curtly replied, "It's for scientific purposes" . . . no other comment. That horrific, undignified, and secretive image has stayed with me always. I do know that parental permission was not sought. I recall thinking that the resulting wound could not possibly be missed, unless the little body was swathed in thick clothing or blankets.'

From October 1970 to March 1971, young university student Peter Bullen had a holiday job at the Defence Department laboratories in Melbourne. The person in charge of the unit where Bullen was working was Jack (John) Moroney, the scientist heading the clandestine baby-bone sampling program and deputy to Sir Ernest Titterton.

'I was employed as a manual "computer" collating and calculating the values and effects of the strontium and iodine entering our diet and the soil courtesy of the remnants of the English – and later the French – atmospheric testing,' Bullen told me.

'The permanent staff in the Maribyrnong lab ashed the bone samples revealed in your book, along with sampling tens of thousands of litres of fresh milk gathered weekly from all over Australia; as well as personally digging soil samples.

'My last task was to assist in the preparation of a detailed "effects" report for the then Prime Minister John Gorton. It ran to around 150 pages or so. Security was so tight that armed guards were placed at the copying machine and counted each piece of blank paper in and out; and all done after hours when the rest of the staff had left for the day.

'On completion of the report, and being well aware of the numbers, I was concerned for the health of the portion of our population consuming fresh milk on farms, and therefore [having] "fresh" radioactive iodine in their children's diet. The facts suggested an excess of some 20,000 thyroid cancers that the public were not to know about.

'I was told by Jack Moroney that the PM did not allow the report to go public as he did not want to upset our trade with France [France was conducting controversial nuclear tests in the Pacific at the time]; and that as our work was in a top secret military-run lab, that was the end of the matter.'

Bullen said he was sworn to secrecy under threat of jail, but felt compelled to reveal what he knew after reading *Maralinga*.

Internal cabinet documents released in 2015 reveal that both sides of politics were prepared to suppress the truth about the lasting impact of the nuclear tests.

Cabinet papers from 1990 and 1991, when Bob Hawke was Prime Minister, reveal the Labor government chose to fight against Aboriginal claims for compensation from the UK government as it might harm efforts to get the British to pay for a clean-up of the test sites.

Australia was seeking $70 million from the UK government to help cover the $93 million cost of rehabilitating the sites. Primary Industries Minister Simon Crean told cabinet that the UK had refused to accept responsibility for compensating Aboriginal people affected by the tests.

'Insistence on payment by the UK of Aboriginal compensation would seriously detract from Australia's efforts to seek rehabilitation funds from the British,' Mr Crean told cabinet.

The Hawke cabinet decided to oppose Aboriginal claims for compensation and to plead the statute of limitations if any Aboriginal – and they singled out Yami Lester for special mention – initiated a common law action against Canberra.

In the end, Britain paid just $44 million towards the clean-up, which included enabling the Maralinga Tjarutja people to return to all but 120 square kilometres of their traditional lands. The clean-up cost $103 million. The British got a good deal.

Despite publication of *Maralinga* causing a great deal of public anger and calls for justice, governments in both Australia and the UK remained steadfast in blocking claims for personal compensation.

One widow of a nuclear veteran had a small victory that may open the door for other families battling the terrible legacy of the tests. RAAF serviceman Alonzo Blakeney had to cart material from contaminated nuclear test sites at Maralinga for British scientists. He was in normal desert clothing while the British wore full protective clothes. He died of heart disease in 2012. Mrs Blakeney applied to the Repatriation Commission for a war widow's pension. It was rejected on the grounds his death could have been caused by smoking.

The Administrative Appeals Tribunal overturned that decision saying Blakeney only started smoking heavily after his time at Maralinga and that might have been due to stress from his exposure at contaminated sites. Blakeney's death was determined to be caused by his time in the RAAF and Mrs Blakeney was entitled to a war widow's pension.

There was more success in the UK where, after a long campaign, Conservative MP John Baron managed to ensure nuclear veterans would be included in a special £25 million compensation fund set up in the 2015 budget to assist struggling military veterans. Baron wants the fund to include families of nuclear veterans suffering from hereditary health problems.

Also in 2015, Fiji paid $2 million to the 24 surviving Fijian nuclear veterans who were exposed to the British tests at Christmas Island (now called Kiritimati) and families afflicted with health problems. Fiji acted after the UK refused to pay any compensation.

'We are righting a wrong, we are closing an unfortunate chapter in our history,' said Prime Minister Frank Bainimarama.

There was no such recognition from the Australian government. On the contrary, the government launched a program to find Australia's first nuclear waste dump, nominating six locations around the country as possible dump sites – three in South Australia, historic Hill End in New South Wales, one in Queensland and one in the Northern Territory. Bob Hawke said once again that Australia would make a fortune taking nuclear waste from the entire world.

Locals are fighting against being forced to live next to a radioactive waste facility. Facing that kind of opposition, it may be that politicians' eyes once again turn towards Maralinga, this time to turn it into the world's nuclear waste dump.

Frank Walker
Sydney, 2016

ACKNOWLEDGEMENTS

This book could not have been possible without the help and cooperation of nuclear veterans who told their stories, many of them wondering why they are still alive when they have watched so many of their mates and colleagues die in pain and agony over the years. They are frustrated and angry at the continued refusal by officials and governments to acknowledge they were used as guinea pigs during the nuclear tests. I admire their spirit for refusing to give up their fight against the bureaucratic brick wall. Many said all they really want is recognition of what was done to them. Many feel guilty and angry that their children, grandchildren and further generations could inherit genes damaged by their exposure at the nuclear tests.

Many veterans collated valuable data over the years, and I thank those who were willing to share information with me to help produce this book – in particular, Avon Hudson, Alan Batchelor, Ric Johnstone (since deceased), John Hutton, Brian McCloskey, Geoff Gates, Doug Brooks, Kelvin Gough and Glynn Key. I am grateful to Terry Toon and the team of veterans who produce the journal *Atomic Fallout* – it is a mine of information.

I thank the people who have gone before me to investigate and document the truth of what happened. Robert Milliken did an incredible job with his 1986 book *No Conceivable Injury*, detailing the history and outrage of the atomic tests up to the release of the Royal Commission's report.

The investigative work done by the Royal Commission and their questioning of witnesses and officials is invaluable to researchers. I thank the Australian archives people for putting transcripts and evidence online. I also thank the people at the UK National Archives in London for their help in my search there for documents.

Documentary maker Peter Butt generously shared research he did for his excellent 2004 film, *Silent Storm.*

I pay tribute to the work done by journalists, writers and scientists before me who uncovered chunks of the truth about the nuclear tests. In particular, the determined work done by reporters and editors at the Adelaide *Advertiser* over many years to reveal what really happened in the north of their state. The scoops of *The Advertiser* journalists such as Colin James, David English, Peter de Ionno, Robert Ball, Susie O'Brien, Bryan Littley and Rebecca Holmes make fascinating reading. My former boss at the *National Times*, Brian Toohey, cracked major breakthrough stories on government cover-ups. Whether I write books about the Vietnam War or nuclear tests, I always find Brian was there thirty years earlier. The *60 Minutes* crew and many journalists at the ABC brought the harrowing stories behind the nuclear tests to life and made people watching TV at home sit up and demand answers. Many other journalists worked on uncovering the truth of the nuclear tests over the decades, and I hope I have managed to credit them for their work.

I thank friends and colleagues who helped me in a personal way – such as a bed or couch – as I travelled Australia and overseas interviewing veterans and others for this book. In London, David Arkless and Connie Czymoch were generous and gracious hosts. I thank Maggie Hall and Gary in northern England for their hospitality. In Brisbane, Bronwyn Watson was kind enough to listen to my ramblings. In South Australia, Avon Hudson sat with me until the early hours going through his masses of files and clippings. At Maralinga, Robin Matthews, the caretaker, was an excellent host and guide. I hope his plans for Maralinga come to fruition.

Thanks to my ex-journo brother Peter who went through the manuscript and fellow writers Terry Smyth and Matthew Benns for their support.

I first came into contact with the plight of the nuclear veterans while assisting the Sydney law firm Stacks/Goudkamp with the media for the campaign to get compensation for the veterans. Media pressure on politicians to finally do the right thing was key to the campaign, and the fight goes on. My thanks to Tom Goudkamp, Michael Giles, Ruth Hudson and Joshua Dale for their help in explaining the legal side of the struggle. In London, Neil Sampson of the firm Rosenblatt generously came in from holidays to recount the long legal battle on behalf of the British nuclear veterans. The lawyers were working for free because they believed an injustice had been done to the veterans. It was when I discovered most young people I talked to didn't know atom bombs had been exploded in Australia that I decided to write this book.

I thank my publisher Vanessa Radnidge at Hachette Australia, without whom there wouldn't be a book, and editor Deonie Fiford and proof reader Kylie Mason, without whom the book would resemble the leftovers of a nuclear blast.

Finally, a thank-you to my family for their help and support. My daughter Hannah gave sage advice as she completed her Masters degree in English and my wife Esther Blank was, as always, an enormous help even as she battled to write her own book about Australia for a German publisher. Luckily our deadlines coincided. And of course my four-legged friend under the table who kept my feet warm before dragging me out for walks in the fresh air.

I welcome comments and questions from readers and I can be reached by email through my website: www.frankwalker.com.au

INDEX

Also by Frank Walker

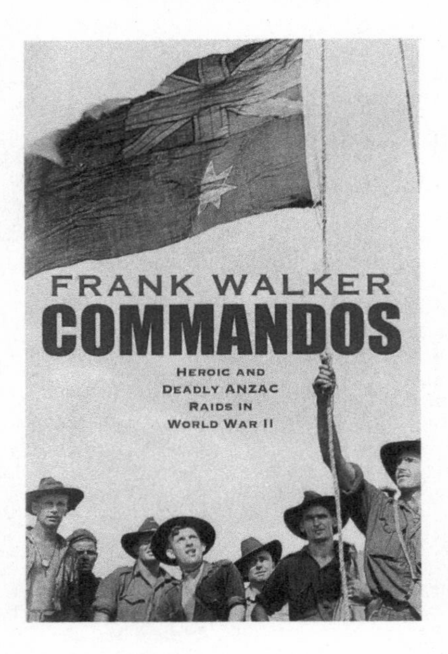

Lightning raids on Rommel's forces in the deserts of North Africa. Paddling canoes 4,000 kilometres to attack Japanese ships in Singapore. Flying bombers at tree-top level deep into Nazi Germany. Fighting in the jungles of South-East Asia. Rescuing sultans and a future US president from under the noses of the Japanese. Silently steering midget submarines under a German battleship in the fjords of Norway. ANZAC soldiers, sailors and airmen were there, carrying out the most dangerous missions of World War II.

The Aussie and Kiwi special forces showed incredible bravery in the face of overwhelming odds. Determined to complete their missions, often alone and behind enemy lines, they demonstrated resourcefulness, spirit and a humanity that inspired others to follow them.

Commandos brings to life the amazing exploits and extraordinary stories of this select band of ANZAC heroes.

Frank Walker has been a journalist for 40 years. He has worked on the *Sun-Herald*, the *Sydney Morning Herald*, for News International in New York, Deutsche Welle radio in Germany and the investigative weekly *The National Times*. He's reported from the war in Afghanistan, terrorist attacks in Indonesia, a military coup in Fiji, and the tsunami in Thailand. He's been a foreign correspondent in the United States and Europe. Based in Sydney, he also writes for the German newsagency DPA.

Frank has written two bestselling investigative non-fiction books on the Vietnam War published by Hachette Australia – *The Tiger Man of Vietnam* and *Ghost Platoon*. *Maralinga* is his third book. His fourth book, *Commandos*, examines the extraordinary exploits of Australian and New Zealand special forces in World War II.

For more information on Frank, you can visit his website: www.frankwalker.com.au